THE OFFICIAL F

A Guide Book of
PEACE DOLLARS
History • Rarity • Grading • Values • Varieties
3RD EDITION

Roger W. Burdette

with
Barry Lovvorn

A Guide Book of

PEACE DOLLARS

3RD EDITION

© 2016 by Whitman Publishing, LLC
3101 Clairmont Road, Suite G, Atlanta, GA 30329

ISBN: 0794844138

Printed in China

Disclaimer: Expert opinion should be sought in any significant numismatic purchase. This book is presented as a guide only. No warranty or representation of any kind is made concerning the completeness of the information presented. The author is a professional numismatist who regularly buys, trades, and sometimes holds certain of the items discussed in this book.

Caveat: The price estimates given are subject to variation and differences of opinion. Before making decisions to buy or sell, consult the latest information. Past performance of the rare-coin market or any coin or series within that market is not necessarily an indication of future performance, as the future is unknown. Such factors as changing demand, popularity, grading interpretations, strength of the overall coin market, and economic conditions will continue to be influences.

Advertisements within this book: Whitman Publishing, LLC, does not endorse, warrant, or guarantee any of the products or services of its advertisers. All warranties and guarantees are the sole responsibility of the advertiser.

If you enjoy *A Guide Book of Peace Dollars*, you'll also enjoy these books (in Whitman's Bowers Series of numismatic references): *A Guide Book of Morgan Silver Dollars; A Guide Book of Double Eagle Gold Coins; A Guide Book of United States Type Coins; A Guide Book of Modern United States Proof Coin Sets; A Guide Book of Shield and Liberty Head Nickels; A Guide Book of Flying Eagle and Indian Head Cents; A Guide Book of Washington and State Quarters; A Guide Book of Buffalo and Jefferson Nickels; A Guide Book of Lincoln Cents; A Guide Book of United States Commemorative Coins; A Guide Book of United States Tokens and Medals; A Guide Book of Gold Dollars; A Guide Book of the Official Red Book of United States Coins; A Guide Book of Franklin and Kennedy Half Dollars; A Guide Book of Civil War Tokens; A Guide Book of Hard Times Tokens; A Guide Book of Mercury Dimes, Standing Liberty Quarters, and Liberty Walking Half Dollars; A Guide Book of Half Cents and Large Cents; A Guide Book of Barber Silver Coins; A Guide Book of Liberty Seated Silver Coins,* and *A Guide Book of Modern U.S. Dollars.*

For a complete catalog of numismatic reference books, supplies, and storage products, visit Whitman Publishing online at Whitman.com.

If you enjoy *A Guide Book of Peace Dollars*, join the American Numismatic Association. Visit Whitman.com/ANA for membership information.

Contents

Foreword

by Steve Roach

The Peace dollar is often unfairly overshadowed by its predecessor, the Morgan dollar. The sensitive Peace dollar offers a different, and perhaps a more accessible, collecting experience than the sturdy Morgan dollar. The series is short, with just 24 issues produced between 1921 and 1935 (though no Peace dollars were struck between 1929 and 1933). There are no real rarities among these 24 dollars that compose the series in circulated grades. The 1921 Peace dollar, with its high relief, is undoubtedly one of the most attractive 20th-century coins.

That Anthony de Francisci's Liberty is based on his young bride Maria Teresa Cafarelli, whom he married in 1920, adds a touch of sentiment and warmth to an issue which has been accused of being a bit too sleek and slick.

The Peace dollar can be viewed as a triumph from a young artist struggling to make his mark. After unsuccessfully applying for a fellowship in sculpture at the American Academy in Rome, De Francisci told friends he would try again for the fellowship, writing on Feb. 28, 1915, "It is due to that irresistible impulse of a youthful ambition that I am ready for a second effort to win that coveted prize in Rome." In a March 1, 1915, letter recommending De Francisci for a fellowship at the American Academy in Rome, Adolf A. Weinman wrote, "He has been with me as a pupil and assistant for several years, during which time he has always proven himself strictly reliable, very studious" adding that he had shown "a high degree of artistic ability." Nevertheless, De Francisci did not secure the fellowship.

Yet he would score a major victory a few years later, when his Peace dollar design was selected to grace a new dollar coin in 1921. His design was selected from an all-star group of artists who were invited to submit designs including Victor D. Brenner, John Flanagan, Hermon MacNeil, and Adolph Weinman. A dream of many numismatists would be to find images of all the designs that each of these artists submitted, and perhaps such an archive exists somewhere, waiting to be discovered. That these artists were closely connected makes such documentation plausible.

Perhaps De Francisci's youth and hunger were his biggest assets in the competition, where the artist had little more than two weeks to prepare designs based on a broad directive. The assignment: "It is the desire of the Director of the Mint that the dollar shall be decidedly American in spirit, and in some way represent Peace or Limitations of Armaments. It is to be called the Peace Dollar."

The Peace dollar represents just a tiny part of De Francisci's oeuvre, which includes dozens of medals; many public commissions; portrait plaques of the kind seen in office-building lobbies, public libraries, and the sort; and sculptures designed for home display.

Among the thousands of documents in the artist's files, now housed at the Smithsonian Institution's Archives of American Art in Washington, D.C., are dozens of press clippings the artist kept about his works where it is clear that the artist took particular pride in his Peace dollar and its depiction of his wife.

In reviewing the files, some elements of the artist's personality become clear. He was a hard worker, generally maintaining several teaching positions in addition to his sculptural works. His friends called him Tony, and he had a solid sense of humor. In an undated letter addressed to the General Manager of The Chase National Bank in New York, he wrote, "May I candidly suggest the following ideas so as to increase the intra-mural income of your great institution; the present service charges being rather inadequate." Among his tongue in cheek suggestions are a 3 cent fee "to enter building and incurring erosion of marble floors," and a five cent fee to use the rest benches in the hobby. He was opinionated, passionate about protecting artists' rights and ensuring fair compensation, and committed to his family.

Burdette's revised third edition of *A Guide Book of Peace Dollars* documents the continued discoveries in this series by unveiling a newly discovered die variety and showing a photo of the 1964 Peace dollar die. To help clarify the Proof issues of 1921 and 1922, the author has added a new table of pattern and experimental pieces and has updated the 1922 pattern and experimental piece information.

Despite Anthony De Francisci's many successes, it is the Peace dollar that preserves the artist's name in the minds of coin collectors. It is a series where discoveries remain, waiting for sharp-eyed collectors willing to invest time in studying this beautiful dollar.

Steve Roach
Coin World *Editor-at-Large*

Steve Roach is a lifelong coin collector and the former editor-in-chief of *Coin World*. He is a certified member of the International Society of Appraisers and sits on its board of directors. In 2015 he was appointed to a 4-year term on the Citizens Coinage Advisory Committee and previously served on the Michigan State Quarter Commission. A life member of the American Numismatic Association, Steve is an instructor at its annual Summer Seminar and frequently educates people on rare coins and appraisal methodology across the country.

1

BACKGROUND

The silver dollar was the only coinage representation of our national unit of value until the gold dollar was introduced in 1849. Since its initiation in 1794, the silver dollar has served only a minor role in commerce. Its real value lay in establishing a national presence before the rest of the world for the new country. The first decade saw relatively modest mintages, but coinage was suspended in 1803, as metal content exceeded face value of the coins. Reinstated in 1836 and regularly issued from 1840 through 1873, the large silver coins saw commercial use in the West and the South, but seldom circulated in the eastern United States. The Mint Act of 1873 removed the unused coin from production and many thought that was the end of silver dollars. However, passage of the Bland-Allison Silver Purchase Act in 1878 opened the door to production of silver dollars on a scale unmatched by any country.

From 1878 through 1904, the U.S. Mint Bureau produced approximately 570,272,610 standard silver dollars using a design by George T. Morgan. These coins were composed of 90 percent silver and 10 percent copper (.900 fine), weighed 26.73 grams (0.803 troy ounces),[1] and had a diameter of 38.1 mm (1.5 inches). Each coin contained 0.77344 troy ounces (25.7556 grams) of pure silver. A flat-relief version of the Morgan design was used to strike an additional 86.7 million silver dollars from February through December 1921.

In December 1921, medalist Anthony de Francisci (pronounced "deh fran-*chee*-shee") produced a new design. The new "Peace" dollar was struck from 1921 through 1928, 1934 through 1935, and in May 1965 (dated 1964). All of the 1964 mintage was melted and the coin never officially released for circulation. Total Peace dollar mintage was approximately 187 million coins.

THE BLAND-ALLISON SILVER PURCHASE ACT OF 1878

The Bland-Allison Silver Purchase Act (passed February 28, 1878) provided for the issuance of Silver Certificates and authorized the coinage of silver dollars as backing for paper currency. The federal government was required to purchase between two and four million dollars' worth of domestic silver each month and coin the metal into silver dollars. In effect, this subsidized production of silver by mines located in Western states.

George T. Morgan, who held the title of special engraver reporting directly to Mint director Henry Linderman in Washington, D.C., but working at the U.S. Mint in Philadelphia, designed the silver dollars issued under authority of the Bland-Allison Act. Patterns for the anticipated coinage were prepared by Morgan and mint engraver William Barber in 1877. Morgan's design was selected and put into production the next year. Minor modifications were made to the design during its use from 1878 to 1904 and 1921.

In 1890, the Bland-Allison Act was replaced by the Sherman Silver Purchase Act, which required government purchase of 187 tons (4,488,000 troy ounces) of silver per month. Although the Sherman Silver Purchase Act was repealed in 1893, it took until 1904 for the accumulated silver to be coined into dollars. Most of the coins (referred to as "Bland dollars") sat in Treasury, Mint, and bank vaults, unwanted in commerce, but unable to be melted because they were the legal backing for Silver Certificates.

THE PITTMAN SILVER PURCHASE ACT OF 1918

By 1918, the dominant precious metal used in trade between Europe, India, and China was silver. It was usually encountered in bar or ingot form rather than as coins. With Germany and the United Kingdom at war, the imperial German government wanted to destabilize British rule in India, and the United Kingdom needed to maintain the value of silver in order to encourage trade and support the war effort. Unfortunately, the U.K. lacked sufficient metal to maintain the target price of $1 per troy ounce. Extensive hoarding by the populace in India, and German propaganda saying that the U.K. did not have silver sufficient to redeem its paper currency, caused the British ambassador to turn to the United States for help. According to an Associated Press article published in June 1921, "Director Baker suggested that the standard silver dollars lying idle in the treasury could be used to meet the situation." Raymond T. Baker, a former political campaigner and committee assistant to Nevada senator Key Pittman, wrote the bill for the Pittman Silver Coinage Act (cosponsored by Senator Pittman), which passed on April 23, 1918, after only six days of debate.

The Pittman Act required the U.S. government to sell to the United Kingdom the refined silver from up to 350 million standard silver dollars (270,704,000 troy ounces). This was accomplished during 1918 and 1919 by melting 270,232,722 silver dollars: silver from 259,121,554 coins (200,414,975 troy ounces) was sold to England, while the silver from the remaining 11,111,168 coins (8,593,822 troy ounces) was intended for minting minor coins but was not used. (Authority for this use was rescinded on November 29, 1922, because the silver was not needed.[2]) This resulted in destruction of approximately 47 percent of all silver dollars minted between 1878 and 1904.[3] The United Kingdom paid $1 per troy ounce for the silver, plus 1-1/2 cents for melting, transportation, and recoinage, plus the market value of the copper in the alloy.

Because silver dollars in the United States were used as backing for Silver Certificates, an equal value of Silver Certificates (mostly $1 and $2 denominations) had to be destroyed. Another provision of the law required the government to purchase an equal amount of silver from domestic producers at a price not to exceed $1 per ounce. The law further directed that the new silver be used to mint replacement silver dollars for ones that had been melted. This allowed the government to reissue Silver Certificates, and also provided a subsidy for U.S. silver producers at the expense of British taxpayers. At $1 per troy ounce, each silver dollar contained only 77 cents' worth of silver. The government picked up the 1-1/2¢ handling fee from the British, plus a 23¢ profit on coinage, for a profit of more than 24¢ per new silver dollar. Many of the old silver dollars had been made with metal costing much less than a dollar. Thus, even more profit was gained when the old coins were sold to the British.

Beginning in 1920, the federal government purchased silver from domestic mines equal to the amount of silver that had been melted in

1918 and 1919. Huge quantities of refined silver flowed into the three mints. The market price was to reach a low of 59¢ per ounce during the summer of 1920, and the government was paying $1 per ounce delivered. Initially, this "Pittman silver," as it was commonly called, was used for subsidiary coin production. However, near the end of the year it became evident that economic demand for coins was declining, and a way had to be found to use the silver while minimizing storage costs. The silver was paid for by issuing government certificates (bonds) bearing interest at 2 percent per year. Eventually, this domestic silver produced 86,730,000 1921-dated Morgan dollars and 183,502,722 Peace dollars (from 1921 to 1928). This exactly matched the quantity melted in 1918 and 1919.

In late 1920 George T. Morgan, engraver of the U.S. Mint at Philadelphia, was directed to produce dies for the coinage of replacement silver dollars. No hubs or master dies for the 1878 to 1904 standard silver dollar design were available. These had been destroyed in May 1910 on orders from Mint director A. Piatt Andrew. Morgan, now 76 years old, reworked his original design for the new dollar coins. The flat-relief 1921 Morgan dollars were produced from February 20 to November 17 in Philadelphia, May 5 to December 31 in Denver, and April 21 to November 14 in San Francisco. They were struck in huge quantities, approaching a million coins each day. Most went directly from coinage press to storage vault.

Artists and coin collectors saw the resumption of silver dollar production as an opportunity to create a new design—possibly one commemorating peace after the conclusion of the Great War. The "Peace dollar," the last U.S. coin to be redesigned during the renaissance of coinage design begun in 1905, was the result of public and political interest. Like its predecessors, the coin did not enter into daily commerce except in the Western states and parts of the South where "hard money" was preferred. Large quantities sat in government vaults, and the Mint had little commercial reason to strike more after the Pittman coins were replaced.

THE WAR TO END ALL WARS

The Great War—what we now call World War I—was an event that affected nearly everyone in America. Recruiting posters and films urged men to join the Navy, Army, Marines, or possibly the Cavalry or high-tech Air Corps.

Top left to bottom right: Possibly the second-most-famous recruiting poster from World War I was Howard Chandler Christy's portrait of a beautiful young woman in a sailor's suit. The Army Air Service was the day's high-tech adventure for daring young men. The U.S. Marines emphasized patriotism and adventure, while the British sought men to protect the nation's families. *(Library of Congress)*

For the first time, motion pictures and newsreels brought home the full force of destruction and death. Improvements in military field medical care meant that many who might once have died of their wounds came home as invalids, with missing limbs, burned lungs, or profound psychological injury. To counter the public's dismay at the carnage, government propaganda glorified and romanticized service and military leaders.

The American home front made do with relatively minor inconveniences. There was no food rationing, although coal was in short supply and there was a major lumber workers' strike in 1917. The railroads were nationalized until

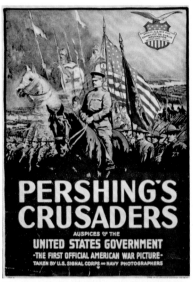

General Pershing rides at the head of a vast army as specters of 14th-century crusading knights escort him to victory. *(Library of Congress)*

1920 so that military mobilization could take precedence over civilian travel. Like all wars, it was expensive, and every nation had its appeals for war-loan donations.

Conservation was the emphasis at home with citizens encouraged to order coal and heating oil early (left), and to grow and preserve fruits and vegetables (right). Meat, wheat, and other foods needed for the soldiers were preferentially shipped to Europe. The first widespread use of evaporated milk allowed this perishable to be shipped to France. *(Library of Congress)*

Appeals for war funds were ubiquitous. Top left to bottom right: Joan of Arc told American women to save their country and buy war savings stamps. The Austrians encouraged children to give to the war effort. A French appeal was more pointed: "Gold fights for victory." Another asks the citizens of France not to hoard small change, but let it circulate for the good of commerce. *(Library of Congress)*

Posters, newspaper ads, and movie productions encouraged people to support charities such as the Red Cross and Salvation Army. Other nations also had their posters supporting themes of the Great War. In an unusual numismatic connection, former Mint director A. Piatt Andrew went to France in 1915 and helped reorganize the American Ambulance Field Service. The ambulances—mostly converted Ford Model T's—brought wounded French soldiers from the front lines to field hospitals where they could be treated. The service saved many lives and Andrew was awarded the French Legion of Honor.

Women played a significant role during the war. Approximately 25,000 served in military and civilian capacities at the European front as nurses, clerks, drivers, canteen operators, readers, and entertainers. On the home front, women took over for men in many military office functions and in equipment factories. Although less well known than their World War II "Rosie the Riveter" descendants, women war workers further opened the doors to political and social equality.

Both the American Field Service and the American Red Cross depended on volunteers to bring aid to wounded Allied soldiers. The AFS poster (left) depicts an ambulance, radiator overheating, making its way back to a hospital through the gloom of night over precarious terrain. The ambulance in the Red Cross poster is emerging heroically from the sun. *(Library of Congress)*

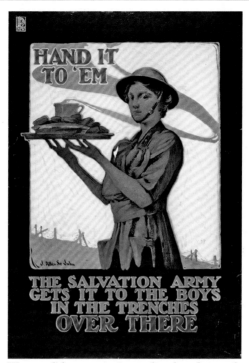

HAND IT TO 'EM

THE SALVATION ARMY
GETS IT TO THE BOYS
IN THE TRENCHES
OVER THERE

Women did not serve in combat, but thousands
helped as clerks, drivers, canteen workers, and
nurses. The next generation's war would see
women welding steel and testing tanks and
fighter aircraft. *(Library of Congress)*

America's involvement coincided with suspension of gold coinage in the United States from 1917 through 1919. During the war, the Treasury Department made a consistent effort to retain gold coins and Gold Certificates. The Treasury went so far as to discourage the public from requesting gold coins for Christmas and New Year's gifts,[4] suggesting the use of war savings certificate stamps and thrift stamps or new bank notes as alternatives.[5] Some newspaper stories carried an ominous undertone not included in official announcements:

> Use of gold coins as Christmas gifts has been almost entirely eliminated this year by a campaign of educating the public to the need of conserving the gold supply in bank vaults. Banks have persistently declined to give out gold on demand, explaining to customers that the tendency of persons to hoard gold pieces given as Christmas presents for weeks or months, has a serious effect in depleting the aggregate gold reserve.

On Christian S. Pearce, Cashier of the Treasury, has fallen the task of dissuading persons applying direct to the Treasury for gold money from their plans. Some apparently were men afraid of a war panic, intent on transforming their assets into gold for hoarding. Those presenting gold certificates were forced to give their names and addresses.

It is understood government agents have been asked to investigate them on the suspicion that the plan is to export the coins to enemy interests.[6]

During the war gold coin did not circulate extensively, and most was kept in Treasury and bank vaults. Corporations and individuals sequestered what they could either in coin or Gold Certificates. Wartime restrictions technically were lifted in 1919, but only in 1922 did the Treasury Department "inform Reserve Banks throughout the country that all objections to the release of gold have been lifted."[7] This was the same year a new series of Gold Certificates was released.

With the armistice on November 11, 1918, exhausted belligerents laid down their military apparatus. The world took a deep, collective breath free of gunpowder and poison gas. As demobilization began, so did negotiation of a peace treaty. Generally known as the Treaty of Versailles, it marked the end of one Great War and sowed the seeds of international depression and the next World War.

Artists, writers, and musicians sought to express the war and its aftermath in their work. Postwar music reflected the sense of confusion and loss of orderly structure brought by the war. Irregular rhythms, combined with atonal and polytonal sounds, were intended to incite listeners and force them out of their comfortable late-romantic-era complacency. Arnold Schoenberg, Aaron Copeland, and Alban Berg explored 12-tone music; George Gershwin experimented with an amalgamation of popular jazz with classical romanticism. French painters turned to the nihilistic Dadaism and finally Surrealism; German portraits explored the inner evil of their subjects, breaking them into

AMERICA'S TRIBUTE TO BRITAIN

A simple but forceful tribute to the United Kingdom summed up much of the American attitude. *(Library of Congress)*

primal elements. German army veteran Erich Remarque wrote his classic anti-war novel *Im Westen nichts Neues (All Quiet on the Western Front)* to express the brutal futility and pointlessness of the Great War.

American and European sculptors marked the war's end with statuary, memorials, and commemorative medals in the more traditional neoclassical style. All of the sculptors associated with American coinage created at least one medal or sculpture to honor war heroes. The Congress approved a victory medal and special medals to honor the City of Verdun and, much later, General Pershing.

James Earle Fraser, famous among numismatists for his Buffalo nickel and contributions to commemorative coinage, was commissioned to design the Victory medal awarded to American soldiers. Some of the victorious Allied nations issued companion medals of similar, but not identical, design.

The lengthy battle of Verdun, France, resulted in nearly 700,000 casualties among French and German forces, with the German attack ultimately being repulsed. A Congressional gold medal, created by John Flanagan (later to design the Washington quarter of 1932), was presented to the city as a token of America's respect.

Left to right: Official Victory medal for "The Great War for Civilization" and James Fraser's reverse of the Williams College War Service medal "For Humanity—1918." *(Archives of American Art, Smithsonian Institution, Peter A. Juley & Son collection)*

Verdun City Congressional gold medal by John Flanagan. See page 12 for de Francisci's version and his Peace of Versailles medal design. *(Archives of American Art)*

Robert Aitken, designer of several commemorative coins, fought in Europe and on his return designed evocative sculpture based on his experiences. Likewise, sculptor Cyrus Dallin, who created the 1920 Pilgrim half dollar, used his war-veteran son as a model for his depiction of a common soldier. Anthony de Francisci, a runner-up in the Verdun competition, also designed a series of medals of war heroes, including Generals Joffre and Pershing, King Albert of Belgium, President Woodrow Wilson, and British Prime Minister David Lloyd George.

Sculptor Robert Aitken's service in France brought firsthand perspective to his sculpture *Machine Gunner* (left) and the frieze for a war memorial. (*Archives of American Art*)

Verdun city medal by de Francisci (left) and the same sculptor's Peace of Versailles medal design. (*Archives of American Art*)

De Francisci also designed medals honoring war leaders. Pictured, from left to right, are General Joffre (France), General Pershing (U.S. 1947 Congressional gold medal), and King Albert (Belgium). (*Archives of American Art*)

Victor D. Brenner also created a Peace of Versailles medal, as did many other medalists. The massive outpouring of creative energy was based on the hope—nearly a certainty to most people of the time—that this kind of war could never be fought again, and it wasn't.

The next war would be much worse.

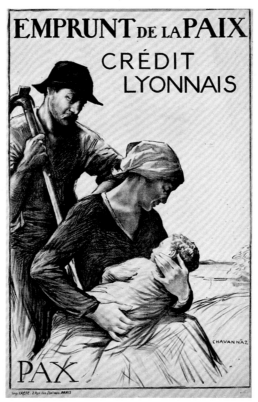

Although the war was over, in 1920 the French were still trying to raise money for a "Peace Loan" for relief and infrastructure repair. *(Library of Congress)*

ORIGIN OF THE PEACE DOLLAR

The Peace dollar has been something of a mystery coin since it was first announced to the public on December 20, 1921. Initial press releases told conflicting tales of its design and promoted the sculptor's use of his attractive wife as a model. Only the most superficial information was publicly released on how the coin came into existence. Huge quantities were produced before vanishing into musty vaults. Of the tribulations the Mint director and others faced from November 1921 through February 1922, only isolated fragments reached numismatists. After more than 85 years, new discoveries presented in the book *Renaissance of American Coinage 1916–1921* (Burdette, 2005) provided collectors with the complete, historically accurate story for the first time.

THE ANA BREAKS THE ICE

Following the end of the Great War there was widespread sentiment for issuance of a coin or other item of significance to commemorate the restoration of peace. We do not know who first publicly advocated the idea; however, among coin collectors, an article by Frank Duffield printed in the American Numismatic Association (ANA) journal, *The Numismatist*, in November 1918 should receive credit. Duffield suggested that a "victory coin" be issued, "in such quantities it will never become rare, and it should circulate at face value. The coinage of the usual type might well be suspended for a year to permit such a quantity being issued. Let such a Victory coin be issued." Apparently Duffield's idea circulated among numismatists, generating occasional suggestions such as the letter by M. Sorensen in the May 1919 *Numismatist:* "Why don't [*sic*] our government issue a Victory dollar—a silver dollar commemorating the downfall of the biggest arch-criminal the world has ever seen . . . ?"

It wasn't until August 1920, when coin dealer / promoter Farran Zerbe submitted a letter to the ANA convention, that a more thorough framework was given to the peace-commemorative idea. Zerbe proposed that a special coin of pleasing design be issued to commemorate peace following the Great War. It would be, "distributed at face value for all the people, to illustrate America's influence for peace and the moral force of democracy." He suggested that it was the ANA's responsibility to draw public and government attention to the peace commemorative. As for the design, Zerbe proposed a popular competition among the best sculptor-medalists of the nation. Further, he felt that the coin should be large enough for an artistic design and suggested that, although the half dollar was probably the best denomination for a commemorative, the silver dollar was the more practical choice, if recoinage of the melted Pittman Act coins was begun.

Convention members debated the subject and decided on the appointment of a committee "to cooperate with government officials to secure the issue of a Peace-Victory coin, and to aid in the selection of a design and size of the coin." The Peace-Victory Commemorative Committee consisted of Judson Brenner, chairman; J. M. Henderson, MD; Howland Wood, American Numismatic Society curator; Farran Zerbe, coin dealer / promoter; and Representative William A. Ashbrook, a member of Congress.

Representative Ashbrook was a coin collector, six-time member of the Mint's Assay Commission, and former chairman of the House Committee on Coinage, Weights, and Measures, and thus should have brought considerable clout to the ANA's efforts. However, when the Republican Party gained control of the House in 1918, Albert H. Vestal replaced him as committee chairman; Ashbrook was defeated for reelection in November 1920. Vestal and Ashbrook were friends, however, and Ashbrook was well regarded by committee members from both parties. He used his waning influence to persuade Vestal to call an informal committee meeting on December 14, 1920, for the purpose of hearing the ANA's suggestions for a peace commemorative. Of the ANA

Congressman William Ashbrook. *(Courtesy Ashbrook Center Archives, Ashland University, Ashland, Ohio)*

members appointed to the committee, only Brenner, Henderson, and Ashbrook attended the House Coinage Committee meeting.

The session got off to a rough start, but things improved as the House Committee warmed to the peace-commemorative idea. Brenner had this to say about the House Coinage Committee meeting:

> It was only after much persuasion that the House committee agreed on the silver dollar for the commemorative coin. Other coins were proposed by them, and they seemed reluctant to accept the dollar. But as our committee was acting on the suggestion made by Mr. Zerbe in his paper before the convention, that the silver dollar afforded greater opportunity for artistic effect, on account of its size, than any other coin, it felt that it would fall short of its duty if it did not insist to the limit on the selection of the dollar as the peace coin.

Brenner indicated that he and Henderson brought with them examples of all previous commemorative coins. The committee members seemed to enjoy looking at the pieces and Brenner pushed the idea that, unlike these coins that were sold for a profit, a meaningful peace commemorative should be available to all at face value.

Representative Ashbrook brought the ANA before the House Coinage Committee, and Brenner and Henderson's efforts convinced Vestal and the members to support the ANA's view. Attention now turned from what to do to how to accomplish the goal. The ANA's approach was strictly legislative—they concentrated on getting a

Judson Brenner, chairman of the ANA Peace-Victory Commemorative Committee. (*Courtesy American Numismatic Association Library*)

bill authorizing the coin passed by Congress. The Coinage Committee, however, doubted that it was possible to secure any favorable legislation until peace was formally declared by Congress (the United States never ratified the Versailles Treaty, and Congress didn't declare peace with Germany until summer 1921), and certainly not before the Harding administration took office on March 4, 1921.

The House committee and its chairman liked the peace-commemorative idea, had settled on the silver dollar as the preferred denomination, and suggested a bill could be introduced after the Harding administration took office. Brenner and Henderson headed back to Ohio feeling they had accomplished much of their task. Unknown to them, it appears that Charles Moore, chairman of the Commission of Fine Arts, who kept current on the activities of Congress, learned of the House Coinage Committee's meeting and decided to investigate. In February 1921, James Earle Fraser, sculptor-member of the Commission of Fine Arts, met with Raymond T. Baker, director of the Mint, to discuss the peace commemorative. Using notes obtained from the December 14, 1920, committee meeting (probably from Vestal), Fraser outlined key points of the ANA proposal to Baker.

Representative Albert Vestal, chairman of the House Coinage Committee. *(Library of Congress)*

In March the Harding administration took office. Vestal met with the new secretary of the Treasury, Andrew Mellon, and with Mint Director Baker. Both supported the concept of a peace commemorative, "providing no expense was attached to it or to the designing of the coin." Vestal promised Brenner he not only would write a bill authorizing the coin, but would sponsor and introduce it in the special session of Congress scheduled for April.

Brenner's ANA report continued:

> I heard nothing further from Mr. Vestal until the morning of the 11th of April when Congress would convene in special session. I telephoned him at 10:30 o'clock (Congress convened at noon), and was very much disappointed to learn that on account of his absence and illness at his home, he was unable to prepare the bill to be presented to Congress.
>
> He asked me to make a draft of a bill, send it to him, and he would put it into action at once. I immediately drew up the following.

Brenner prepared the draft as requested, but in doing so he made a major error. His bill included an appropriation of $10,000 to cover design and production expenses. He probably did not realize the proposed appropriation was contrary to desires of the secretary of the Treasury and director of the Mint, both of whom Vestal had already consulted.

In early May, Brenner telephoned Vestal again only to learn that the Treasury would not support an appropriation. To keep the possibility of a peace coin alive, Representative Vestal introduced Joint Resolution 111 (67th Congress, Session 1) on May 9, 1921, calling for the issuance of a new silver dollar marking the postwar peace.

> Resolved by the Senate and House of Representatives of the United States of America in Congress assembled: That as soon as practicable after the passage of this resolution, all standard silver dollars coined under the provisions of section 2 of the Act entitled *An Act to conserve the gold supply of the United States; to permit the settlement in silver of trade balances adverse to the United States; to provide silver for subsidiary coinage and for commercial use; to assist foreign Governments at war with the enemies of the United States; and for the above purposes to stabilize the price and encourage the production of silver,* approved April 23, 1918, shall be of an appropriate design commemorative of the termination of the war between the Imperial German Government and the Government and people of the United States.
>
> Such design shall be selected by the Director of the Mint with the approval of the Secretary of the Treasury. Each standard silver dollar of such design shall be known as the "peace dollar."

Vestal sent copies of the resolution to Secretary Mellon and Director Baker. He also asked Baker, "Will you please write me giving me the 'dope' we talked of, relative to the number of silver dollars to be coined, etc." Mellon replied that the Treasury would have no objection to the new coin, and Baker wrote outlining the requirements of the Pittman Act. Baker also stated:

> When the silver dollars were sold a charge sufficient to cover the cost of recoinage, together with the cost of copper for the alloy, was collected in addition to the price of $1.00 per ounce for silver. The recoinage of the standard silver dollar now going on is therefore being paid from charge collected to cover the cost of these operations, so that the Government is not put to additional expense to restore the silver dollars. The amount collected in addition to the price of the $1.00 for silver was placed in a trust fund and is available to pay for labor and material in the recoinage of the silver dollars.

On June 29 the House Coinage Committee issued a report supporting the peace coin. Vestal was so encouraged by the response from members of Congress that he decided to place the resolution on the "Unanimous Consent Calendar." This would speed passage of the resolution since the bill was automatically approved unless a member objected. As often happens when Congress becomes involved, though, things dragged on, and they adjourned without taking action on the resolution.

In the next session of Congress, Vestal made a final attempt at passage of the resolution by again requesting unanimous consent on August 1, but the motion failed when a lone member, former Speaker James R. Mann from Illinois, objected. The last meeting between Brenner, Henderson, and Vestal took place in Philadelphia around August 18, 1921, as Brenner and Henderson were heading to Boston for the ANA convention. The meeting left the ANA committee hanging on promises from Vestal that "there was no question but that the resolution would pass and we would see peace dollars plenty. On account of the tremendous amount of legislative matters to be disposed of at this special session, the resolution may not be reached until after Congress regularly convenes in December, next." If Representative Vestal knew about the plans being made by the Mint director and the Commission of Fine Arts, he did not tell Brenner.

The ANA committee had been very successful in bringing the peace commemorative to the attention of Congress and officials in Washington. However, their influence vanished with rejection of Brenner's draft bill, and in the face of more fully developed plans of the Commission of Fine Arts and the director of the Mint. Politics being what it is, there is the distinct possibility that Vestal, Moore, and Baker had been communicating privately since December. Each man controlled a key part of the process of getting a commemorative peace dollar into the hands of the American public. Vestal was chairman of the House Coinage Committee and could easily promote or obstruct legislation by off-the-record comments; Moore and the Commission of Fine Arts routinely handled design and selection for coins and medals and were well known to Congress and government officials; and Baker managed approval, production, and distribution of U.S. coins. All three were in Washington, D.C., much of the time and better positioned to converse, respond to inquiries, and formulate plans than the Ohio-based ANA committee. Additionally, Baker and Moore headed organizations that were part of the executive department of the government and were expected to be responsive to the administration's desires. The rejection of H.J. Res. 111 on August 1 was the "official" end of Congressional action on a peace commemorative.

COMMISSION OF FINE ARTS

Although Congress was quiescent, the Commission of Fine Arts had been listening. The old Morgan-design dollar had been produced for more than the legal minimum of 25 years, and the design was subject to replacement without specific legislative approval.

A decade earlier, in 1910, Congress had passed legislation creating the Commission of Fine Arts to oversee and advise the government on matters involving art and architecture in the District of Columbia, and executive departments of the U.S. government. The commission, operating with support from the Army Corps of Engineers and other agencies, routinely reviewed plans for public buildings, fountains, statues, medals, coins, and other public objects and provided suggestions to the designers and artists involved.

Although it did not officially "approve" designs, the commission's recommendation was seldom ignored; commission members often worked directly with the architects and artists to modify and perfect their designs.

The support of commission chairman Charles Moore was particularly important for any artist aspiring to work on a government-funded project. Included in the commission's authority was the implicit ability to arrange competitions for the design of government medals, insignia, and

Group photo of the Commission of Fine Arts taken between 1912 and 1915. Left to right: Cass Gilbert, Pierce Anderson, Edwin H. Blashfield, Frederick Law Olmsted, Arno B. Caemmerer (clerk, standing), Colonel William W. Harts (secretary), Daniel Chester French (chairman), Thomas Hastings, Charles Moore. No group photo was taken in 1921. *(Courtesy Commission of Fine Arts)*

coins, among other things. The commission conducted these competitions in cooperation with the appropriate executive department subject to available funding, and could choose the artists who would be invited to participate. Recommendations of the commission were forwarded to the relevant cabinet secretary for final approval.

Chairman Moore and Fraser met with Raymond T. Baker, director of the Mint, on May 26 to discuss the joint resolution. Baker stated that he wanted to have a peace dollar commemorating the end of the war and that the design should be distinctively American. During its June 9 meeting, the commission considered the procedure for designing the coin and felt that a competition similar to one they had sponsored for the Verdun medal the previous year would be the best method. The names of several sculptors were suggested, including John Flanagan, Adolph Weinman, Robert Aitken, Chester Beach, Anthony de Francisci, Henry Hering, Robert McKenzie, Hermon MacNeil, Paul Manship, Victor D. Brenner, and Harvey Wiley Corbett.

One of the impediments to a peace-commemorative coin was that the United States and Germany were still officially at war. The armistice of November 11, 1918, had stopped the fighting and most troops had already returned home, but the war technically continued. Congress took care of its responsibilities in ending the war by joint resolution on July 2: it declared that the war with Germany was over. This removed one of the obstacles to a peace dollar and pushed along the commission's plans. By the commission's July 26 meeting, the recommendation had been made to the Mint director that a closed competition be used. The obverse was to retain a portrait of Liberty and the commission would pay each sculptor $100 for their sketch models:

> At a meeting in New York City today the members of the Commission discussed the question of the silver dollar. It was decided, subject to your approval, to retain the head of Liberty for the obverse, and try to obtain a very fine head. Will you please state—
>
> 1. What according to the existing law must go on the reverse?
> 2. Whether you can change the design on the reverse?
> 3. Any suggestions you have as to the design.
>
> For the Verdun Medal we had a competition of eight of the best medallists [sic] of this country and the War Department paid each competitor $100.00. The winning competitor received $1,500.00 for his design and model. The same price is being paid to the man

who designed the Missouri Centennial Coin [Robert I. Aitken]. Will you please inform the Commission if a similar arrangement would be satisfactory to you?

On September 6, Baker returned from visiting the Western mints and his home state of Nevada and wrote to Moore, advising, "The bill authorizing the issue of the 'Peace Dollar' failed of enactment [on August 1] and I would suggest that nothing definite be undertaken in the way of preparing a design at the present." There was still lingering concern that Congressional action was necessary to authorize the Peace dollar and Baker didn't want to step on any political toes. The Mint was also under pressure to re-coin the Pittman silver and recall the bonds.

THE DESIGN COMPETITION

Apparently nothing more was done until Fraser spoke with Baker sometime around November 5. During the conversation, Fraser determined that the director now approved of a design competition and wanted the commission to handle things. The commission also sent a letter reviewing the competition plan and the costs associated with it. The reawakened enthusiasm of the Mint director was likely caused by the imminent declaration by President Harding that war with Germany was officially at an end. The presidential proclamation was issued on November 14, and a path cleared for adoption of the Peace dollar. The commission's plan was confirmed by Baker in a letter on November 17, in which he said, "I have to advise you that your proposal . . . is hereby approved." Baker also halted Philadelphia production of the old Morgan-design dollars in anticipation of soon having a new design.

Coincidentally, the commission also endorsed the idea of a medal to commemorate the Harding administration's goals for the Conference on the Limitation of Armament, then underway in Washington. Both the goals of the conference (prevention of a "naval arms race" between the United States, Japan, the United Kingdom, France, and Italy) and the concept of a lasting peace were popular with the public: this had been the "war to end all wars." The Conference on the Limitation of Armament, Washington, D.C. (November 12, 1921, to February 6, 1922), was a major foreign-policy effort of the new Harding administration. It is possible that the administration pushed the Peace dollar as part of U.S. support for the conference. The invitation to the design competition was dated November 23, and the specifications stated that the designs should "in some way represent Peace or Limitations of Armaments." Also, the coin was to be known as the "Peace dollar." Design, production, and highly publicized distribution of the new dollars occurred while the conference was in session. This could help explain the short schedule for competition and production. There was also an exchange of letters between Treasury Secretary Mellon and senator Henry Cabot Lodge in early January 1922 in which Mellon said: "This new design will be known as the Peace Dollar and is so named in honor of the Conference on Limitation of Armaments."

From our perspective in the 21st century, it may be difficult to imagine how deeply the war affected people in America and Europe. The mechanized, impartial death and destruction; the use of poison gas; the futile sacrifice of a generation of young men to trench warfare; the pestilence of influenza; the flickering, silent images of carnage on the cinema screen—these were all new, and they profoundly altered the public perception of war and peace. Commemorating a lasting peace, and the limitation of weapons of war, with a coin could be considered an appropriate expression of the nation's sentiments.

Whatever the administration's political motivation, the commission left no doubt about the aggressive schedule for its design competition. Fraser informally notified the participants by personal letter on November 19. Official invitations and specifications were dated November 23 and the artists had little time to prepare suitable designs—sketch models were due by December 12. Eight New York–area artists were invited to participate: Robert I. Aitkin, Chester Beach, Victor D. Brenner, Anthony de Francisci, John Flanagan, Henry Hering, Hermon A. MacNeil, and Adolph A. Weinman. All except Beach had previously designed regular-issue or commemorative U.S. coins and had experience working with the Mint. Robert Aitken had seen a notice about the Peace dollar in the October issue of *The Numismatist* and, as a former U.S. soldier who had fought in France, he wrote to Director Baker:

> It seems to me, as the only sculptor medalist who had a hand in the making of Peace, I have a slight claim upon the design of the "Peace Dollar."
>
> The Fine Art Commission would, I am sure, endorse my nomination for this important coin, if it is issued.
>
> What do you think my chances are?

New York City was the center of American sculpture during the post–World War I period. Most of the sculptors and medalists who are now well known to coin collectors lived in or near New York, and the companies that provided casting, photography, die cutting, and other services clustered in nearby urban and suburban areas. The fact that seven of the eight Peace dollar competitors lived in the city was nothing more than confirmation that sculpting talent was concentrated there.

DE FRANCISCI'S DESIGNS

The Peace dollar competition specification stated:

> On one side a Liberty head is to be used similar to that on the present coin, but made as beautiful and full of character as possible. The other side is left to the imagination of the artist, exercised within the limits of the coinage law . . . It is the desire of the director of the mint that the dollar shall be decidedly American in spirit, and in some way represent Peace or Limitation of Armaments. It is to be called the Peace Dollar.

Further,

> The object of the competition being to secure a silver dollar of the highest artistic excellence, the director of the mint reserves the right to make separate selections for the two sides of the coin.

The competitors set to work, each of them first making pencil sketches on paper, gradually refining the design with each revision and working in elements required by the competition. Of the eight competitors, none appear to have left a written account of his designs or the competition. Most had recently submitted designs for the Verdun medal and these ideas were likely in the artists' minds as they worked.

Although he did not win the 1920 Verdun City medal competition, de Francisci's work impressed Fraser and Moore enough to keep him on the "short list" of preferred sculptors. His only previous coin models had been made for the Maine Centennial half dollar in 1920. Often credited with the coin's design, de Francisci was actually required to work from drawings prepared by artist Harry Cochrane from Monmouth, Maine, and provided by the Maine Centennial Commission. Fraser had recommended him for sculpting the model because of his solid technique and ability to work quickly. Although the design is not very attractive, de Francisci's ability to create a detailed model from the roughly defined drawings of Cochrane indicates artistic initiative and maturity requisite for a sculptor of the highest caliber. "The design was basically suggested

Drawing

Obverse **Reverse**

Model

Obverse **Reverse**

Maine Centennial half dollar. Original drawings signed by Harry Cochrane are at top, with de Francisci's finished models below. (*Archives of American Art, Smithsonian Institution*)

by sketches submitted to me by the office [of the] Maine Governor." No changes were permitted and the resulting coin was a dull, uninspired token. "I do not consider it very favorably," was the sculptor's comment some years later.

Anthony de Francisci made multiple sketches for the Peace dollar competition. Several of the trial designs draw on prior work for the Peace of Versailles (1919) and the Verdun medals. The sculptor tried several different concepts before finally settling on two, Reverses 3 and 4, as prelude to the final reverse designs. No sketches of the obverse are known to exist.

Reverse 3

Reverse 4   Reverse 5

Three Peace dollar design sketches by de Francisci. The artist prepared more than 20 pencil sketches for the coin. *(Archives of American Art, Smithsonian Institution)*

After deciding on an obverse and two reverse designs, de Francisci made several rough plaster or clay relief models. With each iteration, the designs were refined and adjusted for balance and effect. The final steps were to make a plaster or clay sketch model of the best obverse and two best reverse designs, and have photos taken for submission to the commission.

All eight sculptors delivered their sketch models and coin-sized photos of the models to Fraser in New York City by the December 12 deadline as instructed. De Francisci chose to enter two different styles of reverse design: one with a placid, benign eagle holding an olive branch, and the other with an aggressive, bellicose eagle breaking a sword. The aggressive eagle clearly borrows from his mentor, Adolph Weinman, while the resting eagle is similar to those on de Francisci's Verdun City medal. The obverse is similar to the final version but has the date in

Obverse

Reverse 1   **Reverse 2**

Anthony de Francisci's silver dollar designs submitted to the Commission of Fine Arts in December 1921. *(NARA Collection)*

Roman numerals—MCMXXI—and different modeling of Liberty's chin and mouth.

Promptly at 10:00 a.m. on Tuesday, December 13, the commission members assembled in James Earle Fraser's New York studio to review the submissions. Daniel Chester French and Herbert Adams, former sculptor-members of the commission, assisted them. Fraser reported that 10 sets of models had been submitted: eight from the invited sculptors and one set each from George T. Morgan, engraver at the U.S. Mint in Philadelphia, and a Mr. Folio of New York City. Morgan had been ordered by director Baker to submit designs. These last two were not considered a part of the competition.

We do not know how the 24 anonymous models were displayed for judging—by sculptor, by coin side, in a large group or several small groups. We also do not know whether the commission members had any specific criteria they used to evaluate the entries other than the competition specifications, or how the unsuccessful designs were separated from the finalists.

Artist Harry Siddons Mowbray later wrote: "The models were carefully inspected by the members and considering the fact that the medallists had only three weeks for their work the results were considered remarkable." After much deliberation by the commission members and negotiation between Moore, Fraser, and Adams (who preferred a seated eagle design), the award was unanimously made to 34-year-old Anthony de Francisci.

The obverse portrait of Liberty was modeled on classical themes, after his 22-year-old wife, Teresa, and the reverse included an eagle standing on a mountaintop, viewing a new dawn of peace. The commission made the award to de Francisci with the understanding that he would prepare finished models under the direction of Fraser, and that the models would then be approved by the director of the Mint. The recommended designs were sent to Baker along with a cover letter on December 14. De Francisci, Fraser, and Baker met in Washington on the 15th to review the designs in person. This also gave Baker an opportunity to reinforce the very tight deadline the Mint had to complete its work. Baker approved the designs on condition that additional changes be made. It was at this point that use of the broken sword from the alternate model was incorporated into the final reverse design. After recommending removal of the periods before and after the date, de Francisci was invited to Washington on December 19 to present his designs to Treasury officials. (See the second pair of models on the opposite page.)

Throughout the process, de Francisci had only a few days to make revisions and submit completed models. Fraser returned the three sketch models to de Francisci. To help him with getting the Liberty head the way the commission wanted it, Fraser loaned him a small bust of "Victory" designed by Augustus Saint-Gaudens for part of the General Sherman monument in New York, "as an example of what we consider a beautiful type." This was similar to the portrait originally proposed by Saint-Gaudens in 1907 for the cent and later modified for use on the 1907 gold eagle. No major changes were proposed by the commission or Fraser, but there were important minor adjustments made to each design. The illustration shows the originally accepted (top) and revised (bottom) designs taken to Washington, D.C., on December 19 for approval.

Revised

Obverse | Reverse

Final

Obverse | Reverse

Revised Peace dollar designs (top) as approved by Secretary of the Treasury Mellon and President Harding. Final designs (bottom) as issued. Note the removal of the obverse text stops and the sword on reverse. *(NARA Collection)*

On the final obverse design, the portrait was made slightly smaller, and Liberty's mouth and chin were altered to make them less prominent. The date was changed to European-style numerals. Finally, the artist's monogram was added above the date. The reverse was altered by making the eagle broader at the shoulder and bringing its neck and head more erect, making the bird look stronger. Borrowing from the rejected reverse, the eagle now grasped a sword with the tip broken off, as well as holding a larger olive sprig. The intent was to signify destruction of the implement of war (the sword) and the initiation of peace (olive branch). To further reinforce the symbolism, the word PEACE was added at the base of the mountain, although there was no authority to add the word to the coin.[1] The commission evidently thought of the broken sword as a clear symbol of the end of hostilities and of arms limitations, and must have recommended its use on the revised design. It had been used on several art medal designs in this context without dissent. No one who approved it realized that a broken sword carried a different meaning for soldiers.

De Francisci worked on the final models through Saturday and completed them on Sunday, December 18. He made two sets of models and left one set with Fraser in New York. The second set and the sketch models he took to Washington for final approval the next day.

On Sunday, Anthony and Teresa de Francisci took the late sleeper train to Washington, D.C., arriving Monday morning, December 19, 1921. After a short taxi ride up Pennsylvania Avenue, they met commission chairman Charles Moore at the Treasury Building on 15th Street. The weather was fair and comfortable, the light snow of the previous week melted. In addition to the finished models, they had the sketch models to show Treasury officials the difference between preliminary and finished design models. Accompanied by Moore, de Francisci showed the plaster models to Baker, undersecretary of the Treasury Seymour P. Gilbert Jr., and secretary of the Treasury Andrew W. Mellon. Photos were taken of Baker and de Francisci for distribution to newspapers. Baker was careful to allow only the backs of the models to be photographed. Moore described the meeting in a letter to Fraser on December 20:

> Everybody beginning with the Director of the Mint and going up to the under Secretary and Secretary of the Treasury is pleased with the Peace Dollar, in fact they are quite enthusiastic over it.
>
> I met the delightful little midgets at the office of the Director of the Mint. They were beaming all over with fun and it was very good to see them. Unfortunately I was called away after a few words of greeting and congratulations.
>
> I reinforced what you had to say about following the coin through the Mint. Mr. Baker was very glad to have the support of the Commission in this particular, and he is really depending upon you and Mr. Francisci to get a perfect coin. He will back you up to the very last in the struggle to obtain the highest possible degree of excellence at the Mint, and he will be seriously disappointed if this result is not attained. I know the difficulties as to time, and of course the impossible cannot be accomplished excepting on such extraordinary occasions as this. I am particularly happy over the head which is exactly what I have been longing for and expecting some day to see realized. I feel that through your good offices the Commission has been able to make another real contribution to the coinage of the country.

Finally, everyone except Moore went to the White House to show the models to President Harding. The little group was escorted into the president's office between scheduled pre-luncheon appointments. The president made a few flattering remarks, quickly approved of the design, and everyone left. Secretary Mellon officially approved the designs on December 20 and the new Peace dollar seemed on its way to completion. As agreed, de Francisci telephoned Fraser to give him the results. Fraser had recommended that bronze casts be made from the plasters immediately after approval of the designs. He felt this would prevent damage or alteration of the design at the mint. Fraser had the casts made at a cost of $15 each.

By December 20, photos of Baker models, along with accompanying descriptions of the new design, appeared in the *Washington Evening Star* and other newspapers. Word of the commission's decision was not sent to the other competitors until January 11, 1922, but they knew the result through newspaper accounts.

De Francisci received congratulatory notes from Victor D. Brenner (designer of the Lincoln cent) and Hermon A. MacNeil (designer of the quarter). Brenner mentioned adding one of the coins to his collection.

Director of the Mint Raymond T. Baker (right) and Anthony de Francisci examining model of the new silver dollar. *(Library of Congress)*

Dear de Francisci

I admired your work often and I take pleasure in congratulating you upon winning the dollar coin competition. I am looking forward to one of the first issue for my collection.

With best wishes of the Season, believe me,

Sincerely yours,

V.D. Brenner

Evidently, the press release distributed when the photos of Baker and de Francisci were taken incompletely described the reverse as having, "a large figure of an eagle perched on a broken sword, and clutching an olive branch bearing the word 'peace.'" No photos of the designs were released because Treasury officials felt it was illegal for newspapers to publish pictures of a U.S. coin. Also, the pictures of de Francisci and

Baker were taken before the president had seen the models. Had the design photos been published and then the president objected, Baker would have been in a lot of trouble with his boss.

BRONZE CASTS

As Moore's letter suggests, the Peace dollar project was going extremely well. Not only had a good design been selected but everything was on schedule; everyone from the president on down was pleased with the design and the efficient manner in which the commission and Mint had worked together. The plaster models and bronze casts arrived at the Philadelphia Mint on December 21:

Detail of original obverse cast of Peace dollar. Note rough surface and guideline below motto.

> I beg to advise you that we received at 2:30 P.M. today the plaster casts of both sides and bronze castings of the obverse side of the models for the "Peace Dollar." The messenger who delivered these models stated to Mr. Morgan that Mr. Fraser said that the casting was poor, and suggested that we get an electrotype from the obverse as well as the reverse side and if better than the one made in New York, to use it. Mr. Morgan is of the opinion that Mr. Fraser meant the casting was a little rough but he thinks it is not so much so as to give us trouble in the reduction.
>
> The bronze casting of the reverse was a failure and we must now get our electrotype from the reverse plaster cast here. It would be impossible to get electrotypes of both sides and make our reductions in time to produce coins this year. Mr. Morgan is quite satisfied that he will be able to get a satisfactory reduction from the casting made in New York.
>
> Unless something unforeseen happens, and by using the New York casting, we ought to have dies for coinage on December 29th.
>
> Respectfully,
>
> *Freas Styer, Superintendent*

With Morgan's assurances that the mint could use the obverse cast, and delivery of a new cast the next day, production of the coin seemed assured. Yet this would be the last night of pleasant dreams for Moore, Fraser, Baker, de Francisci, and Morgan for several weeks. While they slept, an unknown newspaper editorial writer was interpreting the press release in a way no one had previously considered.

PRODUCING
PEACE DOLLARS

The *New York Herald*'s late edition of December 21 printed a brief but caustic editorial titled "The Broken Sword":

> A new silver dollar, intended to be symbolic of the era of peace, is about to be minted by the Government. This is a good idea, but many Americans must read with regret that the designer, in his effort to picture the idea behind the Washington arms conference, represents the American eagle as standing on a broken sword.
>
> If the artist had sheathed the blade or blunted it there could be no objection. Sheathing is symbolic of peace; the blunted sword implies mercy. But a broken sword carries with it only unpleasant associations.
>
> A sword is broken when its owner has disgraced himself. It is broken when a battle is lost and breaking is the alternative to surrendering. A sword is broken when the man who wears it can no longer render allegiance to his sovereign.
>
> But America has not broken its sword. It has not been cashiered or beaten; it has not lost allegiance to itself. The blade is bright and keen and wholly dependable.
>
> It is regrettable that the artist should have made such an error in symbolism. The sword is emblematic of Justice as well as of Strength. Let not the world be deceived by this new dollar. The American effort to limit armament and to prevent war or at least reduce its horror does not mean that our sword is broken.

The *Herald*'s comments hit a responsive chord with its readers. The Great War was still too immediate for the public to have patience with its artists. Symbols, which in other times or contexts might be more deeply understood, retained the stark, absolute meanings from wartime propaganda. The sword, which de Francisci used as a symbol of war on the Peace dollar and on his previous Versailles medal, could also be symbolic of national strength and power. Although only commission and administration officials had seen the reverse design, public perception through the editorial's interpretation of the sword's meaning had been cast. Letters objecting to the broken sword began to flow to the Treasury, the Mint, and the commission. The following letter from Edward F. Reimer, of Near East Relief, Inc., to the commission is typical, although possibly more articulate than many:

> Gentlemen:
>
> My attention has been directed to the fact that a design for the issuing of new coinage has been accepted and that one of the elements of this design is a broken sword.
>
> I do not know, of course, who may be responsible for the adoption of this design, but, as an American citizen, I write to register my protest against the adoption of any design embodying a broken sword as one of its constituent parts.
>
> Throughout all history the symbolism of the broken sword is clear and unmistakable. It has always stood for the hauling down of the colors, for defeat, for surrender, and many times for shame and dishonor.
>
> On the other hand, throughout all history the sheathed sword has symbolized peace after warfare, rest from conflict, and security. It is to be observed that in the symbolism of the sheathed sword, the sword in the scabbard is a *whole sword* and that, in a righteous cause, its keen edge is ready to defend life and honor.
>
> I write to you to express the hope that no issue of our coinage will contain a symbol concerning which there is so much question as there is concerning the adoption of a design embodying a broken sword. By all means let the sword be there, but *let it be a whole, sheathed sword*, never a broken sword!
>
> Very Sincerely,
>
> *Edward F. Reimer, National Secretary Organizational Relations*

The Harding Administration received many more letters, cards, and notes objecting to the broken sword, and few supporting the concept. In just 225 words, an anonymous editorial writer had wiped away months of planning and the unanimous judgment of some of the nation's finest artists. It was obvious that including a broken sword in the design was a political disaster and had to be changed. Acting Mint director Mary O'Reilly sent an anxious telegram to Director Baker, who was at the San Francisco Mint:

> Vigorous protests being received against use of broken sword on dollar design. Fraser and Moore suggest same be removed from model. Cast on reducing machine but change can be made in hub before dies are made and no time will be lost in preparing dies. Will you approve.

A follow-up telegram stated:

> If Mr. Baker is not at Mint please open telegram sent him today in your care, locate and read same to him over telephone.
>
> *M.M.O'R.*

Fraser, Moore, and O'Reilly acted quickly to correct the problem as evidenced by the following memorandum to the commission dated December 23:

> With reference to the numerous protests which were received against having a broken sword appear on the design of the Peace Dollar the matter was taken up immediately with the Director of the Mint, Mr. Fraser and Mr. Francisci, the sculptor, and satisfactorily adjusted. Miss O'Reilly, Acting Director of the Mint, advised that the matter was brought to the attention by them to Mr. Gilbert, Under Secretary of the Treasury, and Secretary Mellon, and that newspaper notices were being given to the press reading as follows:
> "In view of the inquiries which are being received in regard to the new silver dollar, the Director of the Mint desires to state that the Philadelphia Mint is now proceeding with the coinage of the dollar and that the new coin will be available on or about December 30th. The sword which appeared on one of the models submitted does not appear on the coin."

The press release was issued on the afternoon of December 24 (Saturday). A letter from Moore to Fraser adopts the same version of events as the press release: "As you doubtless recall a broken sword appeared on one of Mr. Francisci's models, showing the 'bellicose eagle.' News of it reached the public and it seems to have caused considerable discussion. However, the broken sword does not appear on the Peace Dollar, and at the suggestion of the director of the mint the more passive bird was taken instead of the other." Commission advisors Daniel French and Herbert Adams agreed with the decision. The work necessary to correct the problem was considerably more involved than simply using a different design.

Although the recommended final design with the eagle grasping a broken sword was preferred by the artists and everyone who had seen the models, the public and now Treasury officials wanted nothing to do with a broken-sword dollar. The situation was very awkward: articles and photos promoting the new dollar were appearing daily in newspapers around the country; de Francisci was publicized as the coin's sole designer. The director of the Mint (and other officials) had seen the approved obverse and reverse models but nothing else. Only members of the commission and their advisors had seen the other competitors' designs, including de Francisci's alternate reverse. This alternate sketch model showed an eagle ripping a sword to pieces, but the design's lettering was awkward and no one now wanted anything to do with a sword on the coin. The eagle looking toward the sunrise and holding an olive branch in its talons was generic and "not a portrait of any particular eagle." It was liked by the commission, whose members obviously thought the broken sword added to the symbolism. An eagle quietly looking into the distance was consistent with those on the quarter eagle, half eagle, and eagle gold coins, and although it was not an exciting design, it was certainly peaceful and acceptable.

Late on December 22, Fraser, Moore, and O'Reilly discussed what could be done to correct the "broken sword" problem. There was no time to make a plaster model of another design and have coins struck bearing the 1921 date; the reverse hub was already being cut from the electrotype. Director Baker was on his way to San Francisco at the time and it is probable that Mint staff telephoned him as O'Reilly requested. Fraser sent Baker a follow-up telegram at 2:24 a.m. December 23:

> If you deem it advisable under the present criticism the broken sword could be removed from the hubs before dies are made. That would leave the design as it was originally, simply a peace coin. It would also obviate all criticism from the broken sword idea. I should like this as well without the sword.

The director, having no way to see the altered design, depended on the good judgment of Moore and Fraser for changes to the reverse of the new coin. Mary O'Reilly prepared a memorandum for Undersecretary Gilbert:

> The accepted model for the reverse of the Standard Dollar bears at the base of the Eagle a device representing a broken sword. As a

result of a published description of the model numerous protests against the use of this device are being received.

Mr. Fraser, the sculptor member of the Fine Arts Commission, has suggested in a telegram received this morning that the broken sword be removed from the model.

Mr. Charles Moore, the Chairman of the Fine Arts Commission, has also suggested that the broken sword be not used as a part of the design.

The dies have not yet been made at the Mint, and I have the honor to request instructions in regard to proceeding with the preparation of the same.

Gilbert agreed with the suggestions and ordered the change made immediately. Modifying the reverse hub would be difficult, but it would solve the broken-sword controversy, and prevent public relations problems that were bound to occur if a different sculptor's reverse design were substituted. The administration, the Mint, the commission, and the sculptor could all avoid embarrassment, and the newspapers could continue their feature articles and photos. Modifying the hub was also quicker than remodeling the original design and cutting a new hub—this would have been impossible to do before the end of the year.

MORGAN SAVES THE PEACE DOLLAR

Early on the morning of December 23, de Francisci was asked by Fraser to go to the Philadelphia Mint and supervise removal of the broken sword from the hub. Morgan was going to do the die-cutting work, but it was important to have de Francisci there to approve the results. Superintendent Styer later recalled:

Mr. Francisci personally visited the Mint and remained the greater part of the day while the Engraver was cutting the broken sword out of the dies. . . . I feel it was important to have him here while the Engraver was removing the broken sword from the dies, and to obtain his approval after its removal.

The meticulous work was done under magnification with very fine engraving tools—not the kind of thing de Francisci or Fraser was skilled at doing. Only the steady, experienced hand of George Morgan could turn the situation from failure to success. Morgan had to do more than remove the broken sword, he had to strengthen the rays, then cover as much of the re-engraving as possible so that the change was not noticeable. Part of the work was done on the hub and part on the master die. To help hide the alteration, he extended the partial olive branch, which was partially obscured behind the broken end of the sword, back to the original part of the branch. He also removed the piece of stem protruding to the left of the eagle's talon and sharpened the leg.

In late afternoon Mary O'Reilly sent a letter to Secretary Mellon:

> I have the honor to submit models [samples] of the proposed designs for the Standard Silver Dollar.
>
> A slight alteration of the design for the reverse, as originally submitted, has been made in order to eliminate the broken sword, and the modified design is submitted for your approval.
>
> The model as now submitted has the approval of the Fine Arts Commission, and is in compliance with the requirements of the law.
>
> *Respectfully,*
>
> *R.T. Baker, Director of the Mint*

The samples were likely lead "splashers" or small plaster casts, there being no time to harden the hubs and make dies. Undersecretary Gilbert approved the new sword-free reverse and the mint continued preparing master and working dies. Baker wired his approval on December 24.

The models illustrated below, which de Francisci later insisted were the originals, differ somewhat from the 1921 coins. The obverse tiara has two bands on the model and one on the coin; subtle hair detail evident on the model is missing on the coins, with even the best Proofs lacking detail in the center of the design. This is consistent with the original cast delivered to the Mint and approved by Fraser. On the reverse, it appears de Francisci took a copy of his broken sword model and altered it in imitation of the changes Morgan had made at the Mint. However, he did not use a coin as a prototype, and got the mountain peak and olive branch wrong. The rays were originally broad and flat at their base near the rim, and became narrower toward the tip. The coin shows the rays as simple lines cut more deeply into the die near the rim. Mint engraver Morgan touched up the lettering and in doing so, created the "slant-top A's" used inconsistently on the reverse of 1921 coins.

Morgan's work was of such high quality that it took more than 85 years for anyone to detect the alteration on the 1921 coins.

| Obverse Cast | Reverse as Issued |
| Models | |

| Obverse | Reverse |

Top, 1921 Peace dollar: obverse cast sent to the mint and reverse as issued. Bottom, models *(courtesy Smithsonian Institution, Archives of American Art)* for the Peace dollar. These were likely made by de Francisci for public relations purposes since they do not match the 1921 design as issued.

1921 PRODUCTION—HIGH RELIEF

The Mint staff used the Janvier reducing lathe to produce high-relief hubs, master dies, and finally working dies for the coining department. The fine, raised lines visible on some Uncirculated coins are evidence of the haste with which the reductions were made. There was no time to make extensive trial strikes or to test the presses for best pressure and die-spacing combination. Any press-setup trials were probably evaluated on the spot and then tossed into the discard bin. Using a new high-relief design without proper testing was very risky, and it is a credit to the Mint staff that the first production coins turned out as well as they did.

The director wanted as many coins as possible produced before the end of the year. Accordingly, Philadelphia Mint Superintendent Freas Styer sent a telegram to Director Baker in San Francisco on December 28 to announce commencement of Peace dollar coinage: "First Peace dollar struck at eight thirty this morning. Coining successfully."

Anthony de Francisci was also in attendance as the first high-relief coins of his design were stamped by the presses. The first specimen was reserved for President Harding, and the sculptor was also able to reserve a few specimens for himself. After returning home from the mint, de Francisci sent a telegram to Mary O'Reilly:

> Inspected first issue today, mint. Unable purchase few specimens. Paid upon promised fifty coin packet due mail January 5th. Fraser and I appreciate sooner delivery. Is it possible? Recd telegram thanks.

These coins were to be sent by Morgan, to whom de Francisci had previously given $50.

The *New York Herald*, on learning there would be no broken sword on the new dollars, published a chortling editorial taking full credit:

No Broken Sword

It is gratifying to learn from Washington that the new silver dollar, about to be minted in commemoration of the Conference on Limitation of Armament, will not have upon it the design of a broken sword.

The protest made by THE NEW YORK HERALD last Wednesday against the use on an American coin of something generally accepted as the symbol of defeat, disgrace or abjuration may have called the attention of the responsible authorities to a grave error. If such was the case THE NEW YORK HERALD is glad to have prevented the issue of a coin which would have misled foreigners as to the attitude of this peace loving but not pacifistic nation.

Congratulations are due to those in Washington who were quick to acknowledge that it would be a mistake to represent the sword of the United States as broken.

With coining beginning two days later than assumed in prior numismatic literature, the Mint was either more efficient than thought in striking the new dollars, or it produced fewer than officially reported, or some of the coins were actually minted in 1922. Treasury sources state that 1,006,473 dollars were struck in December 1921, and allowing the four days from the 28th through noon on the 31st for work, the coining department averaged more than 250,000 coins per day during the last week of December. This is an amazing output when one considers complaints about die breakage. The *New York Times* reported that 856,473 were struck in 1921 and other sources mention approximately 800,000. Whatever the correct final total, Baker must have given a big sigh of relief upon reading Styer's telegram; he didn't realize his problems were just beginning.

Simultaneous with production of the 1921 circulation coins, engraver Morgan had Sandblast and Satin Proofs made. The Proof dies were from the same hubs as production dies but made with greater care in impressing the design, and the coins were struck on a medal press. Also, while the coining department was busy, Morgan created new 1922-dated high-relief hubs similar to 1921's in anticipation of continuing the high-relief design into 1922. He took a 1921-dated hub and changed the date to 1922. Changes were also made to the rays and hair, the lettering was narrowed and made more rounded, the outline of the portrait was strengthened, and all the A's on the reverse were made slant-topped. The reverse hub was slightly damaged above the eagle's right talon during alteration. This version was used to create master dies from which were struck the 1922 high-relief Proofs and failed production trial pieces. Overall, these 1922 Proofs—Morgan's touched-up version—may be the best rendition of the Peace dollar to leave the mint: they had sharp lettering, detailed modeling of the hair, and good delineation of the eagle. These were likely first made during the last week of December but almost certainly before January 8, 1922.

By midweek, after hearing from the coining department about problems with die failure and striking quality on the 1921 dollar coins, Morgan began looking for ways to improve die life and strengthen design details. The old 1878-type dollar dies had routinely struck 200,000 coins per die pair; now the coining department was getting less than 25,000 coins per die pair. Since the high-relief design also did not strike properly with one blow from the press, an obvious solution was to reduce the relief. One of the frequently mentioned excuses for reducing height of the Peace design was that bankers complained the coins did not stack properly. Considering that Morgan had decided by January 3 to reduce the relief and none of the 1921 dollars were released until later that week, comments by bankers could not have been the primary cause for the design change.

Production difficulties with the new silver dollars were documented in a handwritten note located in the commission's files. An unknown but obviously "inside" observer says:

After experience in striking silver dollar, Mint reports relief too great and distribution of areas brings highest relief on each side in center of coin and to attempt to drive the metal into this part of design necessarily brings fin to outer edges and breaks die. Dies can be made to stand only about one hundred tons to square inch. The design is so distributed in circle that in making coin the metal is drawn away from the top and bottom and driven laterally to sides of coin resulting in decided difference in thickness which mars appearance of finished coin and interferes with stacking. Changes which appear necessary could be made in dies without greatly changing design and could be made by engravers of Mint after consulting artists if such consultation is deemed necessary. End quote. Director of Mint has held up all coinage. He suggests that new model be made by artist with lower relief. ~~This~~ There can be no change in design. The lower relief will permit better definition in lettering—letter U in word trust should conform to lettering on reverse—same letter should not be made two ways.

Uneven thickness and a fin along the rim were the two primary problems that plagued the high-relief Peace-dollar design and required the search for a replacement. As requested by the sculptor during the first striking of the coins, engraver Morgan shipped 50 of the regular-issue coins to de Francisci on January 3 as well as sending a separate letter:

Today by American Express I sent to you 50 of the Peace Dollars.

I know you will be disappointed, but the pressure necessary to bring up the work was so destructive to the dies that we got tired of putting new dies in ———.

In changing the date to 1922 I took the opportunity of making a slight change in the curvature of the ground. I anticipate at least 20 tons less pressure will be required to bring up the design ———. This should double the life of the die. I will send to you an early strike of the 1922.

The 50 silver dollars arrived on January 5. According to Teresa de Francisci in an interview sometime after the artist's death in 1964, "Anthony was so certain he would lose that he told his artist friends, 'I'll give you a silver dollar if I win.' Then, when he did win, we ordered 50 pieces from the mint—and he gave them all away to keep his promise. He never even kept one for himself."

Morgan's letter clearly says he had already altered the 1922 dollar's "curvature of the ground" and that he would send a sample from the first batch, but the coins had not been struck as of the letter's date. Morgan was referring to the 1922 high-relief hubs, although experience had already shown that high-relief dies were unsuitable for coinage and it would make no sense to repeat December's problems. (He could not have been referring to the "normal" 1922 low-relief design familiar to modern collectors, because that design had not yet been created.)

De Francisci may never have received the promised 1922-dated dollar. He replied to Morgan on January 5:

> I have received your letter and the coins. Thank you very much for both.
>
> I had to agree with you in being disappointed over the results of the first strikes. However, considering the speed we both had in this work the result seems rather satisfactory.
>
> Now, Mr. Morgan, I have to disagree with you emphatically in regard to changes in the curvature of the ground. If the relief of the coins is too high and the required pressure to bring it about, too destructive to the dies. [sic] I feel sure that it can easily be overcome in a more artistic way—that is to produce another hub, with a lower relief and after changing the year to 1922 leave the rest untouched.
>
> I am taking this matter up with the Fine Arts Commission and hope you will receive instructions to this effect very soon.

De Francisci wrote to Commission of Fine Arts secretary Hans Paul Caemmerer the next day. He did not indicate any reaction to seeing a 1922-dated coin, and a reaction would have been expected given the changes. He also wrote about the 1922 issue in the future tense.

> I have received a few of the Peace Dollars from the Philadelphia Mint and although the rush in which this coin had to be produced was too great to give a very perfect result, either artistically or mechanically, I feel now that something must be done since we will have more time for the 1922 issue. Primarily, I would suggest and with emphasis, that if possible, to forbid the Mint engravers from touching in anyway the dies or hubs of said coins.
>
> A letter from Mr. Morgan which I enclose herewith states his intentions to do more changes, small in mechanical gain but very damaging to artistic values. That is regrettable because unnecessary.

The Mint's chief complaint is the height of the relief of the liberty head. Mr. Fraser and I have agreed that in order to overcome that mechanical hindrance to reduce the general relief of the coins by machine—a very simple process—a new hub would have to be made but the result, surely pleasing, would justify my work and the ideals and prestige of the American Fine Arts commission.

De Francisci makes three important points in his letter: (1) the 1921 coins were adequate but not as good as they could have been due to haste, (2) he and Fraser had discussed the problems and felt defects of the 1921 coins could be corrected for 1922 because there was time to make adjustments, and (3) Morgan intended to make changes for 1922 and he should not be allowed to do so. De Francisci apparently did not realize that Morgan had already made a unilateral change in the design. The sculptor assumed that there would be time to reduce the relief on the dies for 1922, had spoken with Fraser about the coins, and was probably not aware that the Mint had actually begun work on the 1922 design.

The general public got to see the new 1921 Peace dollars on January 4 with 75,000 released at the Federal Reserve Bank in New York. Each customer was limited to one coin so that its supply could be distributed to the greatest number of people. There was also concern that speculators would try to get their hands on large quantities of the new coin and then resell them at a profit. Newspapers mentioned long lines of people eager to get one of the new coins. A reporter even asked a New York Federal Reserve Bank employee about rumors that the coins would not stack properly, whereupon the employee got 10 of the new coins and stacked them just like the old dollars.

Director Baker, still on his western mint tour, had a few of the new coins shipped to him in San Francisco. On visiting his hometown of Reno, Nevada, the local newspaper waxed proud:

Baker Brings New Dollars to His Reno Friends

Reno is the second city in the West to feast its eyes on the new 1921 Peace dollar, and fittingly so because the coin's creator, Raymond T. Baker, Director of the Mint, is a Reno man. Mr. Baker arrived from San Francisco this morning with three of the new dollars in his vest pocket. He brought them to as many of his closest friends here.

The Liberty head, of a design differing somewhat from the old head, is on the coin and on the reverse side is the American eagle surveying his surroundings from a mountain peak with an olive branch clutched in his talons. The word "peace" is engraved beneath the eagle.

Approximately 900,000 peace dollars of the 1921 date were coined in the Philadelphia mint, according to Mr. Baker. There was no coinage of this issue in the San Francisco or Denver mints. Having started his western trip before the coins were turned out, the director sent East for some of them after his arrival in San Francisco. A few of them he gave to his friends there, keeping three as souvenirs for Reno. The new dollars now are in circulation in the East, Mr. Baker said.

Perhaps the most meaningful commentary on the Peace dollar was from Fraser in an interview published in the *New York Tribune* on January 5, 1922:

> The new design follows the ideals urged by Saint-Gaudens and others concerning richness and suggestiveness for our coins. President Roosevelt gave much attention to this subject when the new twenty-dollar coin was struck in his Administration. I recall that after the design for that piece was accepted, the reduction of it and in the coinage the bas-relief was unsatisfactory and had to be changed so as to get away from the ordinary standards and raise it in its suggestiveness and richness. The design of the peace dollar conforms to this ideal.

To Fraser, the new dollar was the conclusion of work begun in 1905 by his mentor, Saint-Gaudens, and President Roosevelt to raise the artistic level of America's coinage.

1922 PRODUCTION—HIGH RELIEF

Comments in Mint and commission files indicate the Peace dollar dies did not simply develop fine cracks with use over a period of time as is commonly opined. Instead, they failed suddenly and had to be replaced. Thus, almost as soon as 1921 Peace dollar production began, it appears that engraver Morgan attempted to redesign the dollar to improve striking characteristics. Fraser, whose original role was "following the coin through the Mint," as Moore had commented on December 20, now appeared to be supervising and advising the mint employees as if he were Baker's surrogate. With Baker out of town and Undersecretary Gilbert in Washington, Morgan's first attempts to reduce the coin's relief were taken on the engraver's own initiative.

Morgan appears to have used the high-relief 1922 hub and made careful changes to the design to strengthen lettering, hair detail, and other aspects of the design, including reducing the width of the border (or rim). The engraving staff created working dies from Morgan's revised design and began making test strikes around January 5, 1922—the day after the 1921 dollars were released in New York. New high-relief dollar dies were shipped to the other two mints on January 6 in anticipation of initiating production. Superintendent Styer also sent samples to the director's office. This is likely the source of most of the 1922 Proof examples known to modern collectors:

> As per your request I am enclosing herewith two Peace dollars, one of the coinage of 1921 and one of 1922, with reduced border, sand blasted and finished to show all details of the work. I am also enclosing two other pieces, one of the coinage of 1921 and one of 1922, both being bright pieces, for comparison. I will thank you to return these coins when they have served your purpose.
>
> We have just tried a stack of twenty pieces of the coin with the reduced border against twenty coins of the old design and find very little difference between the two stacks, the "Peace" dollars being very slightly higher than the old.
>
> For your information will say the dies shipped to San Francisco and Denver are similar to those from which the coins of 1922 herewith enclosed were struck.

The "sand blasted" pieces referred to are sometimes called *Matte Proofs* using the high-relief designs. The two "bright pieces" were probably what would now be called *Satin Proofs*. The fact that quantities were available for stacking and that "dies shipped to San Francisco and Denver are similar" indicates that Morgan felt these would be the normal circulation coins for 1922. The "early strike of the 1922" coin, referred to in Morgan's January 3 letter to de Francisci, probably would have been one of these high-relief pieces struck in early January, although it was never sent. Of the 35,401 high-relief 1922 Peace dollars reported produced for die testing purposes, all but a few examples were supposed to have been melted. No examples were struck at Denver or San Francisco.

The exchange of letters between Morgan and de Francisci created more difficulties than it solved. The Commission of Fine Arts, learning of the coinage problems, attempted to reassert its leading position on the Peace dollar and ran head-on into the acting director of the Mint:

The Bureau has been advised through the telephone by the Fine Arts Commission that Mr. Morgan has been in communication with Mr. Francisci in regard to change of design of the Peace Dollar.

Absolutely no authority whatever has been given for the slightest change to be made in the design of the Peace Dollar.

I would suggest that no communication be addressed to Mr. Francisci in regard to the changes which may later be considered until the matter has been submitted to the Director and his decision reached.

It is understood that a mechanical adjustment has been made in the blanks in order to permit the coins to go through the weighing machines, but that such change does not involve the slightest alteration of the design.

To Mary O'Reilly, the correspondence between Morgan and de Francisci was unauthorized and violated Mint rules. All orders relating to coinage originated with the director's office and as acting director she was not prepared to allow an employee and an outside artist to dictate changes to the Peace dollar. Meanwhile, the commission wrote to Baker's office asserting its prerogatives:

In accordance with your suggestion made at the time the design of the Peace Dollar was under consideration, will you now refer a Peace Dollar of 1921 to the Commission of Fine Arts for examination and report as to the mechanical results attained at the United States Mint; and also will you direct that no changes shall be made in the hub before the Commission make their report?

I enclose a copy of a letter from Mr. Morgan.

At the Philadelphia Mint, Fred Chaffin from the Mint Bureau in Washington, who was there on administrative duty as chief clerk, had a conversation with George Morgan, and then wrote to O'Reilly:

Am sending under separate cover the 5 pieces requested—and am enclosing herewith letter received from Mr. Francisci by Mr. Morgan. It seems Mr. F. left the cash to pay for his coins with M. and when he sent them to him he referred to the design which brought this reply. Have cautioned Mr. M. not to do any ~~letter~~ writing to anyone relation to this design.

Will you please return this letter. . . .

[Note below]

Don't you think the Sand blasted pieces are fine[?]

The coins Chaffin sent were probably Sandblast Proofs dated both 1921 and 1922. This would establish that at least five specimens were sent to the director's office, plus the four earlier specimens. Difficulties with the new dollar design were outlined in a letter from Styer to Baker on January 6. Notice the similarities with Moore's conversation notes, above:

I beg to submit for your consideration certain changes, which we find from experiments and experience in coining the newly designed silver dollar should be made in the design to make it suitable for coining.

I have gone into this matter thoroughly with the Engraver of this mint and he says "That while the model of this coin as made by Anthony de Francisci and approved by the Fine Arts Commission as the best of those in competition is a fine work of art, it is not in its present condition suitable for coining. The relief is too great and its distribution and areas are not wisely planned. The highest relief on each side is in the center of the coin and to attempt to drive the metal into this part of the design of necessity brings a fin to the outer edge and breaks the die. Dies can be made to stand only a certain pressure, viz: about one hundred tons to the square inch of surface, and any pressure beyond this is sure to result in destruction of the die. The design is so distributed in the circle that in making the coin the metal is drawn away from the top and bottom and driven laterally to the sides of the coin, resulting in a decided difference in thickness, which mars the appearance of the finished coin and interferes with stacking."

The changes which appear necessary to us to bring it nearer the coin relief could be made in the dies without greatly changing the design and could be made by the Engraver of the mint after consulting with the Artist designer, if such consultation is deemed necessary.

As you are aware, changes similar to those proposed by the Engraver were necessary and made on the double eagle, the quarter, dime and one-cent with the approval of the artists who made the models for these coins after experiments disclosed the necessity for such changes.

You will also appreciate that the short time in which we had to make our reductions, hubs, master and working dies and producing the coin in the year 1921 did not permit of experimenting. In fact we had time to make but one reduction of either side of the model, and the working dies were struck from that hub and master die.

I am convinced with a few changes that could be made in the dies which would not materially change the design, much better results—both as to making these practical for coining purposes and improving the appearance of the coin as well—can be obtained. It is impossible to make a perfect coin from the present design.

I would thank you for your views on this subject as soon as possible.

Unfortunately for the Mint, Morgan's 1922 high-relief coin was not acceptable. The relief was still too great for efficient coinage, and Morgan was not in full command of the intricacies of the Janvier reducing lathe and so was unable to mechanically reduce the relief. Acting director Mary O'Reilly issued orders to cease work on the 1922 Peace dollars on January 10:

I beg to confirm telephone conversation of this day requesting you to discontinue all the work on the preparation of dies for the 1922 silver dollars. . . .

It is understood from your letter of January 6, 1922 that the relief of the model from which the dies were prepared for 1921 coins is too great, and its distribution and areas are not wisely planned; that the highest relief on each side is in the center of the coin and to attempt to drive the metal into this part of the coin brings a fin to the outer edge and breaks the die, and that this results in a decided difference in thickness which mars the appearance of the coin and interferes with stacking. It is also understood that the change is necessary to bring the model nearer to coin relief, and that such change could be made at the mint without changing the design, after consulting with the designer.

In accordance with your suggestion over the telephone it has been decided to take the matter up with the Fine Arts Commission with a view to procuring from Mr. Francisci a new model of lower relief. In doing this it is understood no change will be made in the design of the coin. As soon as this Bureau has conferred with the Fine Arts Commission you will be advised what further steps are to be taken.

O'Reilly kept Baker, who was still in Reno, updated via telegram:

Experiments with nineteen twenty two[–dated] dies like those sent Denver, San Francisco show relief still too high. Absolutely necessary have no change whatever in design. Have today wired Denver, San Francisco not to start regular coinage until further instruction. Taking up matter with Fine Arts Commission tomorrow. Transportation requests at Denver.

Superintendent Styer sent Fraser a brief report on January 11:

> Test of pressure required [for] nineteen twenty-two[–dated] [co]ins to coin. . . . Still more than expected and [more than it] should be. Will proceed with reduction of relief on both sides as suggested to Engraver and report progress to Director Friday [January 13].

The last sentence indicates that Morgan proceeded with yet another 1922 version on orders from Styer. During the first half of this period Baker was out of town, which left much of the government decision making in the hands of Freas Styer, who had been superintendent of the Philadelphia Mint for only six months. Taking into account that nearly three weeks were occupied with Morgan's revised designs, it is possible that several versions were created, tested, and discarded. This would explain the relatively large number of dies used and the small number of coins produced.

While the coining department was trying to strike dollar coins, Baker had spoken with Fraser and Moore. There had been more than enough problems with the new coin, as Moore noted:

> The Commission has had much difficulty in getting the designs out of the Mint and into the hands of the artists; but the mechanism is not at all perfected, let alone being oiled. We shall have all we can do to get results from the Mint authorities so that the work of the artist shall be expressed adequately in the coin itself. There have been many unfortunate circumstances connected with the production of the Peace Dollar, most of which were due to haste.

Public comment about yet another design problem was something no one wanted. If anyone on the commission (besides Fraser and Moore) knew about Morgan's redesign work, nothing was recorded in the minutes or surviving commission correspondence. It is possible de Francisci was kept in the dark about the status of the redesign until it became necessary for the Mint to request his help.

The commission's minutes for January 13, 1922, reflected the uncomfortable circumstances affecting the new silver dollars: "It is necessary to make certain mechanical adjustments in the dies. The mint reported that it is desirable to lower the relief to permit stacking at the banks and give greater distinction to certain portions of the coin. These changes will be made by the mint in cooperation with the designer of the coin."

The relief-reduction experiments were not going well and by January 19 the situation must have looked bleak. Styer wired Denver Mint superintendent Grant, "Unable to say when dollar dies will be shipped. Forwarded one cent obverse dies today." It was clear that the artists could not be given control over production matters; however, it was equally clear that the Mint's revised design was not acceptable. Acting Director O'Reilly again ordered all work stopped on January 20.

It appears that the first trial strikes of high-relief 1922 dollars, possibly including all of the 35,401 test dollars R.W. Julian reported, were sequestered while Morgan worked on a lower-relief version.

1922 Production—Medium Relief

The experimental relief debacle had cost the Mint more than three weeks of production time—long enough to have struck nearly 5 million coins. At this point, near the end of January, matters became critical and Fraser, de Francisci, and the commission were called in. Superintendent Styer wrote again to the director on January 24. This time he included three examples of a new, medium-relief version begun on January 11. These were a Sandblast Proof, a bright or "Satin" Proof, and a normal coin, the last piece struck before the dies failed:

I beg to submit herewith three Peace dollars struck from the die reduced in relief.

You will notice the head is lower in relief and slightly larger. It is placed a little lower in the circle.

On the reverse side all the lettering has been strengthened and the rock reduced in relief. All these changes are absolutely necessary and were arrived at after considerable experimenting.

I am now convinced, after we struck 3200 pieces that the eagle on the reverse side must be lowered.

As you suggested, Mr. Morgan got in touch with Mr. Fraser over the 'phone and asked him to come over tomorrow. He said he had engagements that would not permit of him coming tomorrow but he expects to leave for Washington Wednesday evening and would see you there. He approves reducing the relief of the eagle and said he believed it should be reduced. In fact, he told Mr. Morgan to do what he considered necessary. He may be able to stop here on his way back to New York.

The bright and sand-blasted pieces were of the first strike and the coin marked "3200" was the thirty-second hundredth piece struck—the last before the die sunk.

Mr. Morgan will immediately go to work on the reverse side of the hub.

Fraser saw Baker on Thursday, January 27, in Washington and apparently was given one or more of the new medium-relief pieces to take with him and examine in detail. He wrote to Charles Moore on the 29th indicating his rejection of Morgan's latest re-work attempt:

> Since I saw Mr. Baker on Thursday I have very carefully inspected the new dollar. I find that such an amount of work has been done by the engraver that the artistic value has been reduced to a point that makes it impossible for me to accept the finished coin as representing what the Commission of Fine Arts passed as the model for the new dollar.
>
> Not only has the artistic value been lowered, but it has been changed in design (all the massing taken out of the hair, and lines run through it), which, as I understand it, is against the law.
>
> The only solution of the difficulty is to reduce the design to the required relief, and allow no engraver to touch the surface of the die, except at the rim; or if the letters, for instance, required sharpening, this should be done only in the presence of the artist. We must insist on this if we are ever to have an artist's work show in our coinage. If some work on the coin is imperative to aid in manufacture, this should be done with the artist at the engraver's elbow.

Medium-relief Peace dollar design prepared by Philadelphia Mint engraver George T. Morgan.

Thirty years ago reducing machines were not sufficiently developed to reproduce the artist's model, so it was necessary to employ engravers to retouch the dies to look as much as possible like the artist's work. The Janvier machine has made this work unnecessary. When properly handled, it reproduces the artist's model with absolute fidelity, and any hand-work on the die is getting away from the work of the artist, and should not be allowed, except in the presence of the artist.

As you know, we have tried in vain to carry out this idea for the last twenty years. I can see that it is due to the fact that the engravers who are still working at the Mint, feel that the work is incomplete without some touch from their hands. Naturally, in the case of the broken sword, which was removed, that had to be done in the die only because of the lack of time. Any change not in the die should be done on the models, so that the character remains the same all over the coin.

I realize that all of the work done on this coin has been at breakneck speed, to comply with the wish of Mr. Baker, but now that the 1921 coin has been minted, I think we should see that the work is properly executed for once. A very short time would be required to cut the die for the head side, as the hub for the eagle has already been done. I hope that it has not been worked over by the engravers.

De Francisci met Fraser and Morgan at the Mint on Monday, January 30, to examine coin samples and decide how to proceed. Discussions took several hours and de Francisci left without making a decision about what should be done or his role in the work.

1922 Production—Low Relief

Three days later, on February 2, de Francisci wrote to Director Baker:

After a few hours of deliberation at the Mint Monday afternoon we came to the following conclusions: Primarily, that I should rush to the studio and remodel the obverse in lower relief. In the meantime Mr. Morgan is trying another reduction hoping that the result will be satisfactory from the mechanical standpoint and that no further retouching will be necessary, however, he had scant hopes of success in this method, considering my model faulty in coin relief; therefore, I felt it a necessity to reconstruct my relief while Mr. Morgan is busy with the new trials.

> I expect to deliver this new model to the mint on Saturday with Mr.
> Fraser's approval. No doubt you will authorize me the trips to Phila.
> for the delivery of the model and later for the inspection of the hub.

Forty years later, de Francisci summarized the final events (as he recalled them) leading to production of the low-relief Peace dollar. His recollections seem to sidestep creation of a new low-relief model:

> I was then advised by the Secretary of the Mint, Baker, to go to the
> Philadelphia Mint and assist the Chief Engraver to reduce the
> height of the relief—a process, mostly mechanical, achieved under
> skilful care with the aid of the Janvier pantograph. The changes
> were accomplished within a few days, and all the subsequent
> mintage of the coin have been produced with the revised dies.

The artist delivered his new low-relief models on February 6, then visited the mint every day during that week until the hubs had been cut and checked. Mint engravers had been working with one of the Janvier machines since 1906, but had not learned the subtleties of its operation required to produce the finest reductions, or consistently modify relief. An unfortunate aspect of having Fraser and de Francisci at the mint was that neither had experience or detailed knowledge in operating a Janvier reducing lathe. Except for making suggestions and critiquing the results, neither sculptor was qualified to improve the work. Had a technician from Tiffany's or Medallic Art been called in, the 1922 low-relief coins might have turned out noticeably better than they did.

The 1921 obverse and reverse designs were completely remodeled by de Francisci, including revising the shape and distribution of rays on both sides. Photos of the original 1921 models and de Francisci's recreated reverse model differ in many details from the 1922 low-relief versions and confirm that new models were made.

New hubs were made for circulation coins under the supervision of de Francisci and Fraser. The resulting dies had much lower relief than the 1921 versions with some loss of detail on the obverse, particularly at the junction of the lettering and field. The primary trouble area was at the center of the head where the hair was not well defined; however, Fraser seems to have insisted on this when he refers to "massing of the hair" in his correspondence. On the reverse the change in relief was somewhat less successful, possibly because the original reverse was already in lower relief than the obverse, and further changes made the lettering and eagle's feathers less distinct. Three noticeable details of the new reverse were the lack of connection between olive branch and eagle's talon, three rays below the word ONE instead of four, and the presence of two hills to the right of the word PEACE rather than three.

Limited production was begun to test the new low-relief dies. These first coins are true "trial strikes" since their purpose was to test dies under simulated production circumstances. In the week between February 6 and 13, thousands of silver dollars could have been produced. About one hundred thousand per day were struck on February 13 and 14—the total quantity may never be known unless Mint die records from the period are located. Apparently the low-relief design was performing satisfactorily: by February 9 Baker was telling the press that full production would begin within days. Reluctant approval came from Fraser by telegram on February 14:

> To avoid delay will accept new dollar under protest. Hair over ear not raised to level of strand on each side as we desired. Cheek bone good. Lettering good. Hair must be raised over ear on new dies being made. Coins already struck can be put out.

The Philadelphia Mint officially began production of low-relief Peace dollars on February 13, followed by Denver on the 21st and San Francisco on the 23rd. The low-relief Proof coins share similar characteristics with the trial strikes and were probably made during this same time period. Mint records indicate that at least one low-relief Proof was sold on March 1, so the coins must have been struck on or before that date. Some pieces were likely made for Baker's approval before February 14.

Fraser's acceptance of the low-relief dies freed the Mint from interference by Fraser and de Francisci. Presumably, they used this occasion to make dies for the branch mints and correct the defect on the reverse hub by adding a piece of stem to connect the olive branch and the eagle's talon. The hair on the obverse portrait was also altered to better define the strands over the ear. The consistently "flat" appearance of nearly all 1922 dollars suggests that a second new hub was made by the Mint staff right after the commission's oversight ceased. The author consulted professional sculptor and medalist Heidi Wastweet about the difficulties of cutting high-quality hubs and master dies using a reducing lathe. She indicated that a mismatch between the tracing stylus and the cutting head in the Janvier could easily produce the poorly defined lettering common on 1922 Peace dollars. De Francisci's 7.5-inch models have a rather low angle between the top of the lettering and the curved field of the coin when compared with the old Morgan design. Careful control over the Janvier lathe would have been required if the relief was to be reduced while also maintaining apparent sharpness of the lettering.

The low-relief dies proved to be satisfactory for quantity production and it appears that at this point no one cared about the flat, lifeless results.

With samples approved by Fraser, the Philadelphia Mint was in full production, and working dies were soon sent to the branch mints in Denver and San Francisco. The first batches of dies were probably from the trial strike hubs, with the disconnected olive branch. Philadelphia Mint staff added mintmarks for Denver and San Francisco and shipped dies as soon as Fraser accepted the design. A new Mint director, Frank Edgar Scobey, was confirmed on March 7, 1922. Scobey was one of President Harding's closest friends and poker buddies. The appointment was purely personal; Scobey possessed no special qualification for the office. Fortunately, during the 18 months he was director of the Mint, he did little damage. By fortuitous circumstance he avoided the problems associated with the Peace dollar, while taking credit for increased production.

The extra work performed by de Francisci is supported by the sculptor's ledger entry for 1922 where he lists income of "$1,750—P. Dollar." This total included $1,500 for the finished models—$750 for each side accepted by the director of the Mint. The remaining $250 was payment for assisting in design modification for the 1922 low-relief coins. He also charged the Mint $80 for the five days in February that he helped supervise the new hubs.

It should be further noted that many details of the low-relief design resemble the so-called original plaster models more closely than do the 1921 varieties. Similarities are evident in the shape of rays on both obverse and reverse and the style of the lettering, particularly on the reverse. These details support the conclusion that the 1922 low-relief coins are direct reproductions of new models, and that the so-called 1921 reverse model was created after production of the 1921 coins had begun.

By June 30 the Mint could boast of producing more than 410,000 of the new dollar coins per day. Although the Mint continued to refine the low-relief design to improve production, this was the last substantive design change to leave the Mint until 1934.

De Francisci, his work on the new dollar finally complete, recorded his income and expenses for the project and moved on to other commissions.

PRODUCTION CONTINUES

It is unlikely that anyone outside the Mint (except Moore, Fraser, and de Francisci) saw the experimental medium-relief dollars from late January 1922. Mint Director Baker, already stung by design and production problems, would not have wanted yet another public flap. He likely wrapped everything up under the title of "design adjustments for better production" and left the matter to disappear quietly. Morgan and the rest of the staff were probably embarrassed by the attempted improvements and had no desire to draw attention to the condemned coins. The aborted high-relief silver dollars from early 1922 were just so much scrap metal and melting them was the only option available to Mint officials. A few Sandblast Proof pieces survived in the director's office or at the Mint. These might have been retained as souvenirs, later finding their way into private collections or circulation.

After negative criticism of the broken sword and high-relief production problems, enthusiasm for the Peace dollar amongst the commission and Mint director evaporated. The last letter with a positive tone was the one written by Moore on December 20—after that there was a sense of frustration. It is as if everyone involved wanted to get production started and move on to other things. Commission advisor Daniel Chester French, referring to the broken-sword design, admitted "I fear that the jury that passed on the designs for the Silver Dollar will have to confess that it made a mistake, for I believe that the broken sword can only be interpreted in one way—as a symbol of defeat. As I was one of the jury, I should like to interpret it in some other way if I could." Of the many small but significant improvements that could have been made to the design while testing the low-relief 1922 dies, few seemed to have been accomplished.

The *Annual Report of the Director of the Mint* had this official comment on the new coin:

> The "Peace dollar" takes the place of the old design of the standard silver dollar, which was first issued in 1878. This coin commemorates the declaration of peace between the United States, Germany, and Austria, exchanges of peace treaty ratifications having been made in Berlin on November 11, 1921, and in Vienna on November 8, 1921, and peace having been proclaimed by the President of the United States on November 14 and 17, 1921, respectively. No special Congressional authority was required for the change in design of the silver dollar, since the law permits changing the design

of any of our coins not more frequently than once in 25 years. The design of the "Peace dollar" was selected by the Fine Arts Commission from models submitted by a number of prominent sculptors, and is the work of Anthony de Francisci.

On the obverse is a female head emblematic of Liberty, wearing a tiara of light rays, and the word "Liberty"; on the reverse is an eagle perched on a mountain top, holding in its talons an olive branch, witnessing the dawn of a new day; the word "peace" also appears. Other mottoes and inscriptions are as required by the coinage laws. The design for the silver "Peace dollar" was approved in December 1921, and 1,006,473 pieces were executed by the close of the calendar year. Subsequent coins of this design will bear the year in which made. At the close of the fiscal year on June 30, 1922, a total of 24,701,473 of the new design coins had been struck.

In a similar vein, the Commission of Fine Art's report states:

The Silver Peace Dollar.—At the request of the Director of the Mint this Commission undertook to secure a design for a silver dollar to commemorate the proclamation of peace by the United States, on November 14, 1921, ending our participation in the World War. Eight leading medalists were invited to enter a competition, and as the result Anthony de Francisci was selected to design the coin. The silver dollar enters scarcely at all into circulation in the northeastern portion of the United States, where the retirement of soiled bills keeps the currency in reasonably good condition; but in other portions of the country the demand for the silver dollar is large and steady. Some 800,000 of these coins were minted and circulated in 1921; and the total issue since then to the end of February, 1926, is 168,879,473.

The Commission regards the silver coins of all denominations as important means of fostering among young people especially a feeling for design by familiarizing them with good examples. The effect is the more efficacious in that it is unconsciously exercised. The entire silver coinage has now been changed under the advice of the Commission.

Although the report describes and illustrates many medals and commemorative coins approved by the commission, the Peace dollar is not one of them.

James Fraser continued as sculptor member of the Commission of Fine Arts while pursuing his career and promoting the work of his talented wife, Laura Gardin Fraser. He was to remain one of America's most respected and honored sculptors through the balance of his life. Fraser played a major role in bringing the Peace dollar to the public. He met with Director Baker on several occasions, sent the initial competition announcement, hosted the design jury, oversaw completion of the original models, aided in approval of the alternate reverse, supervised production in 1921, supervised both the Mint's and de Francisci's creation of the low-relief variety, and gave final approval to the 1922 design. This is a striking amount of work for someone who is barely mentioned in previous accounts.

For many reasons—all seemingly acceptable at the time—the Mint, the commission, and de Francisci maintained a unified fiction about the whole design selection, alteration, and production process. By reinforcing the idea that it was bankers' objections that caused the 1922 design change, and by not mentioning the experimental coins at all, their good intentions have muddied the numismatic waters for nearly a century. The origin of this "information blackout" was likely Undersecretary Gilbert who, according to Mary O'Reilly, did not "wish to give publicity to [the] change hence issued newspaper notice [in] your [Baker's] name stating sword which appeared upon one of the models submitted does not appear on coin." An insular bureaucracy took measures to protect itself and in doing so involved two of America's best sculptors in its deliberate deception.

The low-relief coins were eventually produced by the hundreds of millions, and like their predecessor silver dollars, sat in vaults—legal backing for the paper currency of commerce.

The ANA committee fussed and complained about being excluded from much of the Peace dollar selection process. However, if Brenner, Henderson, and the others had known all that occurred in December and January, they may have been thankful they were *not* involved.

Anthony de Francisci, his wife Teresa, and their daughter Gilda lived quietly in their New York flat. His commissions were somewhat irregular and teaching provided a reliable income base for the family. The public recognition and increase in commissions one would have expected for the designer of the United States' premier silver coin never seemed to materialize. The large, majestic, allegorical commissions for building pediments and statuary usually eluded him; most assignments were relatively small. His name quietly slipped from the commission's "short list" of medalists. His creative style seems to have reached its peak in the late 1920s. He won the coveted J. Sanford Saltus Medal for accomplishment in medallic sculpture from the American

Models submitted by Anthony de Francisci for the 1938 Jefferson nickel competition. Small-diameter electrotypes of these designs exist, but are not products of the U.S. Mint. *(Smithsonian American Art Museum)*

Numismatic Society in 1927. His medals, bas-relief, and other works show superior craftsmanship and excellent subject representation, yet from the 1930s onward they consistently lack the expressiveness that the best of his peers brought to their work. His sculpture documented rather than inspired. De Francisci gave coin design one more try in the 1938 competition for the Jefferson nickel. His design met the competition's creativity-stifling requirements, but was not selected as the replacement for Fraser's Buffalo nickel.

During World War II he served as a translator in the Army's Censorship Office for the War Department. He appeared on television on May 4, 1954, in a CBS-TV program for children, explaining how medals and bas-relief were made. His last commission was for design of the 1964 New York World's Fair medal—a dull, pedestrian creation.

The Peace-dollar design sputtered along from 1921 through 1928, when recoinage of the Pittman Act silver was completed. An audit of some of the Philadelphia Mint vaults in June 1936 showed there were still 154,800 1921 Peace dollars sitting in storage along with nearly 150 million other silver dollars.

PEACE DOLLARS, 1934–1935

Coin collectors have long noticed the sudden increase in production of silver coins beginning in 1934. After languishing for much of the previous dozen years, demand for coins seemed to jump, pushing the mints to work hard to keep up the pace. In part, commercial demand was increasing, but the government was also producing more coins because it was profitable to do so. By forcing large quantities of new coin through the

Federal Reserve System to commercial banks, the appearance of greater prosperity was carried to the man on the street. The reasons for striking silver dollars in 1934 and 1935—coins that had no commercial use and were not wanted by merchants—are embedded in the Roosevelt Administration's attempts to pull the nation out of depression and the political involvement in Western states' silver-mining interests.

From World War I to 1934 the market value of .9999 fine silver was marked by a sharp increase in price followed by a long decline. The boom in silver prices during and immediately following the war was caused by European countries making large purchases of war materials from India and China. Payment was required in silver as that was the metallic currency accepted in local trade. Silver prices were also pushed upward by a general increase in industrial and commodity prices, and (later) U.S. purchases of domestic silver under provisions of the Pittman Act of 1918.

By 1919 the market price of silver was high enough to threaten its use in U.S. subsidiary coinage, and the Treasury Department took steps to prevent wholesale export of silver dollars. Bills were introduced in Congress to reduce the fineness of U.S. coins or to remove silver from them all together. In March 1920 Great Britain was faced with having the bullion value of its silver coins exceed their face value by 30 percent. The prospect of speculators melting coins forced the British government to reduce the fineness of coins from .925 (sterling) to .500. Over the next decade, 32 countries followed suit in debasement. Silver prices collapsed in 1921 after several countries changed their policies for use of silver in coinage. From 1921 to 1932, more than 541 million ounces of this demonetized silver was sold on the world market. Without international government purchases of silver for coinage, and the end of the Pittman Act domestic purchases at $1.015 per ounce, the average price plunged from $1.019 in 1920 to $0.631 in 1921.

But the market price of silver did not stop there; it continued to decline. In 1929 the average price of fine silver was $0.529, in 1930 it dropped to $0.382, in 1931 the average was $0.287, and in 1932 an ounce of silver cost just $0.279. The historic low of $0.245 was reached in December 1932. At that point the standard silver Peace dollar was worth less than 19 cents in bullion! At these price levels, few American silver mines could be operated profitably, and the cost of extracting silver from gold and copper ore—the primary source of domestic silver—was prohibitive at the fixed price of $20.67 per ounce of gold.

By late 1933, the U.S. economy seemed to be slowly responding to stimuli from the Roosevelt Administration's monetary and employment policies. Modern coin collectors place considerable emphasis on the Gold Surrender Order of April 5, 1933, and subsequent Treasury Department regulations. Yet, for a typical working man and his family, gold played little role in personal finance. The government's action in removing gold from commercial circulation combined with issuance of up to $3 billion in United States Notes—both planned by a numismatist, then-secretary of the Treasury William Woodin—brought a significant increase in the money supply while adding flexibility to the Federal Reserve System.

In Western states, silver and copper mining interests saw an opportunity to improve their personal financial situation, while claiming to aid economic recovery and increase the money supply. Miners and politicians had been trying to boost silver use for many years. Some Western companies, such as the Pedley-Ryan Investment Company (later called the Cow Gulch Oil Co.) of Denver, Colorado, produced one-ounce silver tokens dated 1933 in anticipation of selling them to small investors. (Inevitably, such schemes failed to attract many purchasers and the remnants found their way into collectors' hands, listed in the Hibler and Kappen catalog of so-called dollars.) The primary advocate of aid to silver mining was a senator well known to numismatists: Key Pittman of Nevada. Pittman had engineered an amendment, known as the Thomas Amendment, to the Agricultural Adjustment Act of May 12, 1933, which permitted the government to purchase newly mined domestic silver. After modest lobbying by Pittman and other silver-mining representatives, President Roosevelt issued an executive proclamation based on the Thomas Amendment on December 21, 1933, which required the government to purchase all domestically produced silver at $0.6465 per troy ounce.

Although American producers were given a very generous price for their product (the open market price was approximately $0.41), it was also a good deal for the government. The method used to pay for the purchases of newly mined silver was unique among New Deal financing schemes. The executive order stated that only half of the silver purchased was to be coined. The order, however, made no mention of the fact that the silver was to be coined at $1.2929 per ounce, which was exactly twice the price at which the silver was purchased. (This is the bullion value at which a silver dollar contains one dollar in precious metal.) The government, therefore, could pay for all of it by coining only half of the newly mined silver it purchased, and would have a seigniorage (profit) of 50 percent remaining. Further, the secretary of the Treasury was permitted to coin the seigniorage as well, rather than returning it to the general fund. This more than doubled the quantity of coin which could be struck from a given cost of silver. By this method, the government converted bullion costing an average of $0.6465 into legal coin with a face value of $1.2929 if struck as silver dollars, or $1.38 if struck as subsidiary silver. In effect, this was "free" money plucked off the financial tree planted by the late Treasury secretary William Woodin. Some of the earliest silver deposits were paid for in silver dollars, and 1934- and 1935-dated dollars were ostensibly produced for this purpose, but this was soon changed to permit payment by government check. Silver producers no more wanted the bulky dollar coins than did the general populace.

New domestic silver purchased amounted to approximately 1.5 million ounces per month. From this silver, 7,021,528 dollars were coined in 1934 and 1935. Under authority of the Silver Purchase Act of June 19, 1934, the Mint struck an additional 53,029 standard silver dollars in 1935. This used a total of 5,447,409 ounces of fine silver purchased from domestic mines at a cost of $3,537,278.50 (out of approximately 8.5 million ounces purchased from U.S. mines before July 1934). An additional 22.7 million ounces was acquired before passage of the Silver Purchase Act, at $0.50 per ounce, in repayment of war debts. The remainder was used for subsidiary silver coinage, which was issued in large amounts from 1934 onward, and as backing for paper currency. The decision to strike a few million silver dollars was an obvious political favor to Senator Pittman and his silver-state colleagues. The dollar coins were something impressive to show their constituents. But it also reinforced the Roosevelt Administration's decision *not* to reduce the silver content of the standard dollar as had happened with the gold dollar. For a short time in 1936, consideration was given to producing more silver dollars. Dies were made and sent to the Denver Mint. However, by the time secretary Henry Morgenthau had approved issuing Proof sets for coin collectors in April, he had decided against producing more dollar coins.

A prior agreement by the president to accept up to $200 million in additional silver in repayment of war debts at the rate of $0.50 per ounce further added to the silver stockpile. During the last half of 1933 this allowed Great Britain to pay off a significant part of its debt by acquiring silver in India for less than $0.40 per ounce and reselling it to the United States for $0.50 per ounce. The "nationalization" of silver purchasing in 1934 provided further support for Western silver producers by paying above-market rates for the pure white metal.

By January 1937 Mint engraver John R. Sinnock believed there would be no need for more silver dollars in the future and certified the destruction of master dies and hubs. For unknown reasons, the Philadelphia Mint retained seven reverse dies (numbers 14, 15, 16, 18, 21, 23, and 26) in the coining department, and the Denver Mint retained 32 reverse dies.

During World War II, the Treasury's stockpile of unused silver found critical importance in uses as diverse as a new five-cent coin alloy, solder for aircraft and electrical parts, and wire for nuclear research. The Manhattan Project built a uranium processing facility in Oak Ridge, Tennessee. The purpose was to enrich uranium with the U-235 isotope, which could then be used in a weapon. The facility, called Y-12, contained several large racetrack-shaped isotopic separators or "calutrons." These used giant electromagnets to deflect the U-238 atoms into one collector and slightly lighter U-235 atoms into another. Normally the electromagnet windings would have been made from copper wire, but copper was a critical war material. Because silver has slightly better electrical conducting properties than copper, and was not on the critical war materials list, the Oak Ridge scientists borrowed 14,700 tons of fine silver from the Treasury. This was used to make the necessary wire and bus bars for the calutrons. After the war, most of the silver was returned to the Treasury Department.

Commercial demand for silver dollars increased during World War II, with approximately 50 million pieces entering circulation between 1941 and 1943—more than 10 times the quantity released during all of the 1930s. Although Treasury officials had no figures on the quantity melted, an internal report stated, "we assume a large part of this silver went into the melting pots. Eastman Kodak Company, one of the largest users of silver, is said to have met a large part of their needs through the melting of silver dollars." The Act of December 18, 1942, permitted melting of silver dollars that were considered unfit for circulation, and during 1943 and 1944 the Treasury recovered 36 million ounces of metal from an estimated 46 million badly worn and mutilated dollar coins.

Hubs, Dies, and Coins

All coins produced by the mint are struck from hardened steel dies, which in turn are incuse copies of the master hub. During the era of the Peace dollar, this hub was made from the original design models using a device called an engraving/reducing machine (or "lathe"). Regardless of the time, skill, and care spent by a medallic sculptor in creating a coin model, the final look of the coining die will be determined by the hands that guide the reducing machine. With proper care, these temperamental yet relatively simple machines are capable of producing an amazingly sharp, beautiful engraving. Although there are variations in technique, the process of creating hubs and working dies has changed very little over more than 100 years.

This section concentrates on how the original design model is converted into the finished master hub. The emphasis is on a better understanding of what de Francisci, Morgan, and Fraser did in late January 1922 to reduce the relief of the Peace dollar, and possibilities for why the resulting coins tend to have poorly defined detail, particularly in the lettering. It may also help readers appreciate the subtleties faced by both Mint and outside engravers when preparing a coin design for production.

Die-Making Sequence

During the period in which the Peace dollar was first produced, the U.S. Mint used a basic process to make design reductions and working dies. If a large number of coins were needed, the Mint followed certain procedures:

1. A plaster model (positive) was made by the sculptor.
2. A copy of the model (negative) was made from the original.
3. A galvano (positive) was made by electroplating the model (number 2 above) to create a copper shell. (Alternatively, a bronze cast of the model was used.)
4. A master hub (positive) was made by mechanically copying and reducing the design on the galvano.
5. A master die (negative) was made by pressing the hardened master hub into soft die steel.
6. A working hub (positive) was made by pressing the hardened master die into soft die steel.
7. Working dies (negative) were made by pressing the hardened working hub into soft die steel.
8. Coins (positive) were struck from the hardened working die.

The extra steps limited the number of times the master hub was used so that wear was minimized on the master hub. It also offered the maximum number of opportunities for touch-up of the design before coins were struck.

Producing a Master Hub

In 1920, the U.S. Mint was using a Janvier engraving/reducing machine purchased in 1906. This was first used to make reductions of the new Saint-Gaudens–designed $20 gold coins. After copying the negative plaster model (number 2 above), a positive galvano is made by coating the plaster model with carbon dust, then electroplating copper onto the model using a solution of copper sulfate. The resulting galvano is a copper shell, approximately 1/16th of an inch thick. It is sometimes filled with solder or plaster to give it strength. The hard copper surface can withstand the friction created by the tracing stylus when the engraving/reduction machine is used, something a plaster model cannot. The galvano is extremely durable and will hold sharp details with minimal wear.

Although there are a number of brands of engraving/reducing machines, they all operate on the same principle as the simple pantograph. A rigid metal rod has a tracing stylus attached to one end and a cutting tool on the other. The rod pivots on a moveable fulcrum so that the distance from the pivot point can be changed by moving the rod to one side or the other, then locking it in place (imagine a simple lever or a child's see-saw). If the pivot point is in the exact center of the rod, as one end is moved a certain distance, the other end will also move an equal distance. As the pivot point is repositioned, the lengths on each side of the fulcrum change in a predictable manner. If the long end is moved a certain distance, the short end will move a much smaller, but proportional distance.

The first step in making a reduction is to calculate the ratio between the sizes of the model and the hub. For the Peace dollar, the ratio between the model and the coin was specified as 5:1, so the ratio of tracing stylus to cutting tool also had to be maintained at 5:1. This ratio is used to determine how to set the gears for the proper speed of the machine. If the gears are not set correctly, there will be visible cutting lines left on the face of the hub. The model-to-coin ratio is also used to determine the size of the tracing stylus and cutting tool. It is important that the cutter be in exact proportion to the tracing stylus. If the cutting tool is too small, then lines produced on the hub will be thinner than they should be; if the cutting tool is too large, the lines will be disproportionately thicker.

Once the correct ratio is selected, the galvano is mounted to the faceplate of the Janvier reducing machine (the large disk near center of the

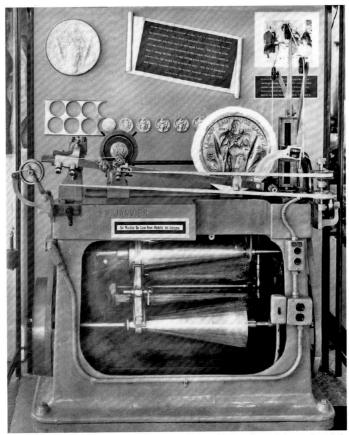

Janvier engraving/reduction machine. The original model (galvano) is on the right; the hub being cut is on the left. There is a die-cut strip from which blanks have been cut just above the hub. To the right is a succession of strikes with increasing detail imparted by multiple blows of the press. *(Smithsonian American Art Museum)*

photo above). A rod of soft steel is mounted to the left of the galvano. The greater the reduction (the smaller the diameter of the coin) the further to the left the die holder is moved.

The reducing/engraving–machine operator selects a tracing stylus based on the smallest detail of the galvano. The tip of the stylus must be small enough to easily fit inside the thinnest lines but no smaller. The chosen stylus is mounted in its holder and perfectly centered on the galvano. A freshly sharpened cutting tool is mounted in its holder and perfectly centered on the steel rod. If the stylus and cutting tool are not perfectly centered, the image in the center of the hub will be distorted. This is especially noticeable when a straight line runs through the middle of the design. Additionally, the tracing stylus and the cutting tool must be correctly matched to

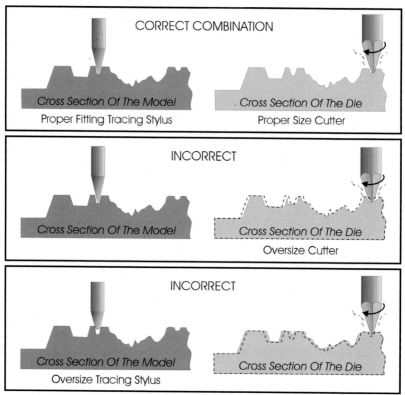

Use of either an incorrect tracing stylus or an incorrect cutter will result in loss of detail and a "flat" look to the lettering. At top, correct combination results in optimal transfer of detail from the model to the hub; center, cutter is too large to engrave details into hub; bottom, tracing stylus is too large to get into smallest areas of model, with the result that the cutter can only approximate the original design.

one another and to the level of detail in the model (or galvano), otherwise important details will be lost (see the illustration above).

Cutting the hub begins in the center of the cast or galvano, and the arm moves downward toward the edge as the model and die rotate clockwise simultaneously. A lubricant, usually light machine oil, is run over the cutting tool to keep steel chips cleared away from the tip. The reducing/engraving–machine motor turns both the galvano and the hub at the same rate. The cutting tool is also turned, but at high speed— somewhat like a dentist's drill. When everything is running up to speed, the arm holding the tracing stylus and cutting tool is gently lowered so the tools touch the galvano and hub surfaces. This begins the cutting of the hub. The gears are then engaged and cutting slowly moves toward the edge of the hub as the galvano and hub slowly rotate.

It can take from 12 to 30 hours of continuous operation to cut the hub in a single pass. The machine cannot be stopped and restarted midway into the cut; if the cut is interrupted, the machine must be restarted at the beginning. For detailed designs, a second or third cut (or "finish" cut) is made using smaller tools for both tracing and cutting. This smoothes larger areas, while transferring the fine detail embodied in the original model.

Hub Quality

The single biggest contribution to low-quality reductions is haste. When the die engraver is under pressure to meet production deadlines, behind schedule due to mishaps, or simply impatient, he will cut corners wherever possible to speed up the process. One of the easiest ways to speed up the process is to use a larger tracing stylus / cutting tool combination. However, this will "dull" the design by missing much of the delicate detail so carefully tended to by the sculptor. Engraving time can also be dramatically reduced by taking fewer finishing cuts, or cutting in only one pass. When dies are cut in only one pass, the high volume of metal removed will prematurely dull the cutter. This produces relatively fine detail in the center but increasingly poor detail toward the rim as the cutter begins to dull.

The size of the cutting tool must be in exact proportion to the tracing stylus. If the ratio is off for the initial rough cut, then the finishing cut will be doomed. If the cutter is too large in relation to the stylus, then the lines will look fat and clear planes will look bloated. If the cutter is small in relation to the stylus, then features will look too narrow. If the gear settings are too fast for the cutter and stylus combination size, then uniform curved lines spiraling out from the center will appear on the hub's surface.

EFFECT ON THE PEACE DOLLAR

The 1921 Peace dollars often show curved line segments near the obverse rays and lettering. It is possible that in the rush to cut hubs, the Janvier was set to too high a speed in relation to the size of the tracing stylus and cutting tool. With a detailed, high-relief model such as the Peace dollar, patience and careful control of the Janvier would have been needed to produce the best-quality hubs. In February 1922, de Francisci, Fraser, and Morgan had to accomplish three things simultaneously: transfer the new model to new hubs, reduce the relief, and maintain detail in the hubs. The first two were accomplished from a new model, as evidenced by the low-relief Proof coins and, to some extent, the trial strikes. However, substantial portions of the original detail appear to have been lost in the process. This is evident in both the obverse hair and in the reverse lettering and eagle's feathers when the circulation strikes are compared to the Proofs. Proofs have better-defined lettering than subsequent issues. The sides of letters, rising from the field to the top surface of the letters, are more nearly perpendicular to the field than on later issues. This makes the letters look more sharply defined. Later coins, speculated to be from a new hub made in mid-to-late February, have letters with gently sloping sides, producing the appearance of the letters merging into the field.

The 1922 relief-reduction efforts seem to have hurt the reverse more than the obverse. Although the 1921 obverse was in high relief, the reverse was originally close to normal coin relief. By reducing it further, de Francisci, Fraser, and Morgan made the lettering very soft and indistinct and eliminated much of the feather detail on the eagle.

Overall Peace Dollar Appearance

A common question among silver dollar collectors is, "Why don't Peace dollars have the sharpness and eye appeal often found in coins of the Morgan design?" When one considers that overall production quality— equipment, die steel, annealing, and so forth—was better than during the 1880s and 1890s, the typical Peace dollar was probably better made that a typical Morgan dollar. The answer is a combination of factors that may not be readily apparent.

One part is the relatively bland, almost featureless design. Large areas have only subtle variation in relief. Where detail could have been included, such as the area over Liberty's ear or the eagle's feathers, de Francisci and Fraser decided to "mass" features rather than clearly delineate them.

Another difficulty is the direct reduction from de Francisci's bronze casts to hubs on the Janvier reducing lathe. Because Morgan was no expert in use of the lathe, and the artists were permitted no hand-retouching of hubs, soft detail and lettering was inevitable. To see an example of this, take a 1921 Peace dollar and examine the eagle's talons and lower leg. Then compare the sharpness of features to the wing feathers. Morgan recut the talons by hand when he removed the broken sword from the reverse hub. The eagle's feathers were left largely as they came from the reducing lathe.

Lastly, Peace dollar dies were not designed with a single radius of curvature as were the old Morgan dies. Thus, they were not basined or polished in the same way as Morgan dollars. Die basining (adjusting the radius of curvature to accommodate differences in equipment and planchet configuration) helped to sharpen the junction between the field and the portrait and lettering. This produced clear separation between field and design, thereby increasing the visual sharpness of the coins. Without this die preparation step and retouching, Peace dollar dies retained their smoother gradation from field to relief. The visual impression is of a "soft" or "mushy" coin. This also accounts for the absence of completely prooflike Peace dollars.

THE LOST 1964-D
PEACE DOLLARS

Coin collectors like a good mystery, and prime among them is the fabled 1964-D Peace dollar. Few U.S. coins, with the possible exception of the 1913 Liberty Head nickel, have been subject to such extensive rumor, supposition, speculation, and fictional anecdotes. The 1964-D Peace dollar ranks as the most mysterious, perplexing, and uncollectible coin of the series.

ADDITIONAL DOLLARS NEEDED

The silver dollar had been a government-produced commercial unit of the United States' monetary system since 1794. It was issued in spurts coinciding with economic and political conditions from 1794 through 1803, 1836 through 1873, 1878 through 1904, and 1921 through 1935.

The last gasp for the standard silver dollar began on February 28, 1963, when Mint director Eva Adams wrote to assistant secretary of the Treasury Robert A. Wallace. Adams was concerned that the budget request for fiscal year 1965 omitted funds for producing new silver dollars.

> The increasing popularity of silver dollars, and the rate at which present supplies are being sent into circulation, brings up the problem of manufacturing additional supplies in the near future.[1]

She suggested that 100 million pieces would cost $800,000 (plus metal) to strike during the first year of restored production. The following years would require about half that quantity due to decreased interest. In addition to funding, Adams noted the following:

> [The] addition of 100 million silver dollars to our coinage workload, because of the size of the coin and the additional manufacturing

problems, would place an almost impossible strain on our manufacturing facilities for fiscal 1965. Production of these coins would substantially reduce the output of other denominations. It is difficult to estimate the precise effect of this production problem, but from a cost accounting approach the cost of 100 million dollars would be equal to the cost of about 1.026 billion cents.

In view of the continuing coin shortages, and since we are approaching our maximum productive capacity, this would be a very poor time to start making silver dollars.[2]

Adams also noted that if the Treasury's stockpile of silver were used only for subsidiary coins—dimes, quarters, and half dollars—it would last for about 16 years. If silver dollars were added, the accumulated metal would last for about 13 years, provided the market price of silver stayed below $1.2929 per ounce, above which point it became profitable to melt dollar coins. For subsidiary silver coins, the market price had to rise to $1.38 before it was profitable to melt them. She concluded by noting that present law required Silver Certificates to be redeemed in silver, but that use of silver *dollars* was not required.

Eva B. Adams, director of the Mint from 1961 to 1969. She initiated the idea of producing more silver dollars to replace those put into circulation during the early 1960s. She also issued the production order on May 12, 1965.

During the next months, negotiations on the political level dominated the silver dollar's future. Western state senators, lead by Senate majority leader Mike Mansfield (D-Montana) wanted more silver dollars struck to maintain the supply and support traditional Western use of the coin. Others wanted to reduce the silver content of the nation's coins, as had been proposed in 1919 and 1933. The Treasury Department wanted Congress to repeal the 1934 Silver Purchase Act and reassured those supporting the repeal that "if more silver dol-lars were needed in the west . . . they would be produced."[3] This seemed to satisfy the majority leader and the Western states' faction favoring silver dollars won out. On April 29, during testimony on H.R. 5389 (a "Bill to Repeal Certain Legislation Relating to the Purchase of Silver and for other Purposes," passed June 4, 1963), secretary of the Treasury C. Douglas Dillon told the Senate Banking and Currency Committee: "Silver dollars will not vanish from circulation. We have a stock of about 81 million which will be issued as required. If and when more are needed, they will be minted."[4] Passage of H.R. 5389 signaled the gradual removal of silver backing from U.S. paper currency. It also authorized issuance of gold-backed $1 and $2 Federal Reserve Notes to replace Silver Certificates.

Senator Mansfield's actions in sustaining use of silver differed little from those of his fellow silver-state senator of the previous generation, Key Pittman of Nevada. Where Pittman concentrated on ways to stabilize the domestic silver-mining market in 1918 and 1933, Mansfield's interest was maintaining use of the white metal in coinage and specifically as circulating dollar coins. Both supported large purchases of silver by the government from domestic producers.

Adams wrote on July 31, 1963:

> As a decision has been made that the Mint should produce silver dollars when the present supply is exhausted, it becomes necessary to determine the procedure for announcing this decision.
>
> It would seem that the Secretary would wish to put out a release, if not, would the White House? Otherwise, could it be announced by the Director of the Mint at the meeting of the American and Canadian Numismatic Associations in Denver during the week of August 6th? About 5,000 persons will be in attendance.
>
> It should be recognized that announcement of a decision to make new dollars would probably have the effect of halting the rapid outflow of old dollars, at least to Collectors. This is extremely desirable, as the supply is low, having dropped from 93,898,733 on January 1, 1963 to 65,416,872 on July 1, 1963, with 10,635,000 going out in July, leaving a total of 54,781,872.
>
> Forty Million of these are held by the Treasurer, to be used to redeem silver certificates at the Cash Room of the Treasury.[5]

In a more detailed memorandum later the same day, Adams outlined alternatives for the dollar's design:

> Regarding the design of the coin, the following alternatives might be considered:
>
> 1. Follow the letter of the law, which provides that, after a coin design has been in effect more than 25 years (as is true with the Peace dollar, made from 1921 to 1935 . . .), the design may be changed by the Director of the Mint with the approval of the Secretary of the Treasury.

In the present situation, the Director feels it would be advantageous to reuse one of the old designs. This would (1) discourage the probably greater interest of collectors, were it a new design; (2) preserve the fine tradition and artistic beauty of the older dollars; and (3) effect savings, as the Mint retains the old dies, thus eliminating preparation of new designs, models, etc.

2. Arrange to have a Design Commission, appointed by the Secretary or the White House, to select a new design through competition among sculptors and artists. This has the disadvantages of (1) more cost, as the winning design must be paid for; (2) the time element, which can be disastrous, as indicated by the history of such contests; (3) inevitable controversy about the design, as indicated by many pending requests for Commemorative Coins; (4) the fact that sculptors and artists favor high-relief designs, making production slow and costly; and (5) the Mint has capable engraver-artists who could, if necessary, produce a new or adapt an old design with proper relief for existing presses to operate efficiently.

3. Retain the present design (commemorative the declaration of peace after World War I) which has never proved popular, and which would require as much adaptation as #1 above.[6]

Wallace prepared his own version of Adams's memorandum for Secretary Dillon, repeating items 2 and 3, and adding the following:[7]

Re-issue the pre-World War I Liberty head design. This would (a) discourage excessive interests of collectors who would probably be more interested in a new design; (b) preserve the fine tradition and artistic beauty of the older designs, and (c) effect savings as the Mint retains old dies, thus eliminating the preparation of new designs, models, etc. [Note added to memo: "1878–1904, 1921"]

His recommendation to Secretary Dillon was to adopt the old Morgan Liberty head design. There was no discussion by Wallace about the old hubs having been destroyed in 1910, and it is unlikely he or anyone at the Mint was aware of this. He also omitted any comments about usability of old dies. Dillon approved the recommendation on September 24 and the matter seemed to be settled.

Many in the Treasury Department disagreed with the decision and some, like Undersecretary of the Treasury for Monetary Affairs Robert V. Roosa, asked, "Do we really have to mint these things? It seems to me quite confusing to get this going now that we're within a couple of months of having the Fed's new notes."[8]

Plans were also moving forward to ration the remaining silver dollars until new ones could be minted. Internal notes indicate that Treasury staff knew the Carson City dollars were worth more than other Morgan dollars, "in excess of $3 each, based on dealers' bids."[9] They were also aware that some other dates of Morgan dollars had a premium, but, "bags of silver dollars with moderate numismatic value will be inter-mixed with bags of low numismatic value and sent to the Federal Reserve Banks in an attempt to avoid publicity regarding the release of coins avidly sought after by dealers and collectors."[10] Wallace prepared another memorandum, which Dillon approved on September 24:

Disposition of Old Silver Dollars

. . . plans for rationing the existing supply of silver dollars; basically it is a plan to mix silver dollars of high and low numismatic value except for the 2-1/2 million with very high value, to be held back for the time being. Preference will be given to Western banks where silver dollars are more likely to be used in circulation rather than collected by collectors. The Treasurer's office would use the Peace dollar, with no numismatic value, in over-the-counter transactions, and for distribution to local banks to avoid speculating runs.[11]

The U.S. Mint began to prepare for striking silver dollars. Deputy director Frederick W. Tate let Fern Miller, superintendent of the Denver Mint, know what was happening. Tate suggested that the Denver Mint plan for dollar production including weighing, blank cutting, and other operations sufficient to strike "approximately ten million dollars per month."[12] He also asked Miller to consider the use of annealed strip or blanks to avoid a production bottleneck caused by insufficient annealing capacity.

Superintendent Miller had Walter J. Judge, superintendent of the coining division, prepare an outline of preliminary work necessary before dollar coinage could be started:

In connection with the stamping of silver dollars, among other con-siderations, the following are items that will have to be taken care of:

1. Die sets for blanking presses, probably two.
2. Strengtheners for rings at punch presses.

3. Discs and segments will be required for upsetting mills.

4. Tools for upsetting mills will be needed.

5. If rheostats on presses are not adequate for slowing down press speed for stamping rate, it will be necessary to make new pinions for those presses used for dollars.

6. Additional tubes for adjusting machines will be required as tubes are available for only four machines.

7. Weights for adjusting machines will be required for the greater tolerance now allowed. The present weights are made for a grain and a quarter tolerance. On hand—five sets of standards, six sets of lights and four sets of heavies.

8. Mr. Jamieson thinks that some type of feeder can be designed for stamping presses to eliminate hand feeding. Work will have to be done on these.

9. If new presses are received in time for the dollar program, dollar fingers[13] will have to be supplied or made here.

10. If finishing or rolling is not adequate, shaving mills will have to be overhauled and set up in adjusting room to avoid excessive scrapping of blanks.

Would appreciate being informed if we may proceed with the above mentioned mechanical work relative to manufacture of silver dollars and, also, if there is to be any change in size or weight of the coin.

Additional personnel will have to be recruited for reviewing of coin, for stamping section and the adjusting room.

It will not be possible to operate all of present presses on account of our present limited annealing facilities.[14]

Miller's plans met with the director's approval, and Miller was also advised that there was to be no change in the dimensions or weight of the dollar coins. Judge noted that there were 32 leftover dollar dies at the Denver Mint:

We have on hand the following dollar reverse dies:

Year 1934—22

Year 1935—5

Year 1936—5

If any change is made on reverse dies, we will, of course, need new reverses as well as obverse dies and collars.

> If Philadelphia can supply us with three sets of dollar tubes and three lower rails for adjusting machines, this will eliminate the necessity of these being made here.[15]

The Philadelphia Mint shipped upsetting machines equipped with dollar tubes and adjustment rails (attachments for shaving blanks to correct weight) to Denver.

Silver for the new coins would have to come from the Treasury's stockpile. Miller was advised that when the silver was purchased, beginning in 1933, the government had paid an average of $0.6197 per ounce. However, the metal had been revalued as backing for Silver Certificates thus crediting the seigniorage to the nation's budget before any coins had been struck. Unlike coins struck with silver from the Bland-Allison or Sherman acts, the Denver Mint could never make a dime of profit on the silver dollars.[16]

On November 21, President Kennedy requested a supplemental appropriation of $675,000 for the Treasury's current budget to provide for the manufacture and shipment of 50 million silver dollars. The funds were to come from transfers within in the Office of the Treasurer. This was considered along with the regular fiscal year 1965 funding proposal which included $1.25 million to produce 100 million silver dollars.[17]

Planning for silver-dollar production came to a halt with the assassination of President Kennedy on November 22, 1963. The mints struggled to produce as much coin as possible to help allay public apprehension about potential economic instability. Mint headquarters focused on design and production of a new half dollar honoring the slain president, and politicians waited to see what kind of a leader President Lyndon B. Johnson would make.

Production of silver dollars again became a political bargaining chip on April 1, 1964, when Senate majority leader Mike Mansfield (D-Montana) and Senator Lee Metcalf (D-Montana) met with Treasury Undersecretary Roosa, general counsel G. d'Andelot Belin, and special assistant Joseph Bowman in Mansfield's office. Both senators had introduced bills that would reduce the silver content of U.S. coins, and the Treasury was opposed because it was likely to increase the coin shortage by encouraging people to hoard the older, full-weight coins. The House of Representatives had also removed funding for minting silver dollars from its version of the appropriations bill, and some in the Treasury Department still wanted to mint dollars to replace the ones it had once held. Both senators wanted silver dollars made to maintain the Western tradition of "hard money." After limited discussion, the Treasury representatives and

Senators Mansfield and Metcalf agreed to a solution. Mansfield would support the Treasury's added appropriation for striking silver dollars and see that the appropriate language was in the final bill. In exchange, he and Metcalf would withdraw support for bills debasing the silver coinage.[18] (Both senators would later support removal of all silver from dimes and quarters.)

One might wonder why minting more silver dollars was so important to Mansfield and Metcalf. After all, they represented a state whose population was only 674,767—41st among the states.[19] Although a "small" state, Montana was one of the few where cartwheels actually served the needs of local commerce. The coins were commonplace in merchants' cash drawers, making their way through business and banking channels much like subsidiary silver. The Federal Reserve Bank branch in Helena, Montana, was consistently among the top three users of silver dollars in the country. The same pattern held through the 1950s, and in fiscal year 1960, the Helena branch distributed 3,950,000 silver dollars, more than any other branch.[20] This consistent local usage helped to affirm Mansfield's insistence on continued production of the coins.

Within a week of the meeting, Director Adams wrote to Wallace.[21]

> It is planned to manufacture silver dollars [of the pre-World War I Liberty head design] only at the Denver Mint. That Mint is located in the section of the country where dollars are actually used for circulating purposes, and collectors' demands will be minimized by producing coins at one Mint only. This approach also precludes the necessity for including dollars in either proof sets (made only in Philadelphia), or uncirculated coin sets (which contain sets from both Mints).
>
> Two or three of the better presses at Denver will be reserved for dollar stamping operations, and will be operated at a reduced rate of speed to minimize wear and tear because of the heavy coin. It is estimated that one press will stamp approximately 150,000 dollars in twenty-four hours, as compared to approximately 190,000 fifty-cent pieces and 190,000 quarters during the same period.
>
> With continuation of [the practice of purchasing nickel strip], our chief bottleneck in producing dollars together with other silver coins, will be in the [silver] strip annealing operation. However, a new strip annealing furnace was put into operation at Philadelphia during the past several weeks which practically doubles the strip-annealing capacity at that plant. This greatly increases our over-all potential for producing silver denominations.

Careful consideration will be given to the production schedule at each mint, with particular attention to avoiding short runs of any denomination at either plant, which make the coins more attractive as collector's items.

With sufficient funds in fiscal 1965, we can operate the Philadelphia as well as Denver facilities around the clock, seven days a week, and, if necessary, can send silver blanks to the Denver Mint for stamping into finished coins.

As the fiscal year 1965 appropriation bill neared passage, a conference committee was set up to resolve differences between the House and Senate versions. Treasury Secretary Dillon wrote to the chairman and members of the Senate Treasury–Post Office Subcommittee:

I wanted to reemphasize the interest of the Treasury Department in securing approval of [$600,000 for the manufacture of 45,000,000 silver dollars.]

While I know you are familiar with our problem, I wanted to reassure you that the Administration feels it important to continue the use of the silver dollar, as it is one of the six standard coins prescribed by law, and is particularly used as an ordinary and traditional medium of exchange in many far western states. Also, use of the silver dollar will, to a great extent in the West at least, alleviate the heavy demands we have had on the quarter and fifty-cent pieces. This eventually will balance out the use of silver, as the minting of enough halves and quarters to substitute for the 45,000,000 silver dollars will take almost as much metal for the same use . . .

Present plans call for the minting of the dollars, if approved, at the Denver Mint only, using an old design, and the 1964 date . . .

If this item is approved in our Appropriation Bill it would be our policy to distribute the silver dollars through the Federal Reserve Banks in the West where they are used as a medium of exchange. We would not use them in redemption of silver certificates at the Treasury.[22]

On July 28, 1964, Congress passed the 1965 Appropriations Bill authorizing production of 45 million standard silver dollars and allocating $600,000 to cover expenses. President Johnson added his approval. Mint Director Adams followed up with authority for Philadelphia Mint assistant engraver Frank Gasparo[23] to produce new dies for the silver dollar:

You are hereby authorized and requested to proceed with the production of silver dollar dies for use at the Denver Mint. The initial order should be for one dozen pair of dies and an additional order will be submitted after we have heard from the Denver Mint. Please also prepare about six collars for this denomination.

Please have the dies and collars delivered to the Denver Mint on or before October 5.[24]

1964-D Peace dollar die.
(Reversed for visibility.)

Oddly, there was no further mention of using the Morgan design for new dollars. Possibly officials, following Wallace's earlier comments, felt the Peace design was unpopular and using it would reduce demand. Also, the existence of old Peace dollar reverse dies might have caused Director Adams to decide to use the Peace design. At present we have a single, blurry photo of a 1964-D Peace dollar obverse die.

The old dies and collars from Denver turned out to be unusable for new dollars.[25] Superintendent Miller placed an order for 50 pairs of dollar dies to be shipped, five pairs per week, and also ordered five extra edge collars to supplement the 30 on hand.[26] "The Philadelphia Mint has prepared a new drift for the subsequent fabrication of dollar collars, and will supply to you five new dollar collars for your initial production."[27] Philadelphia superintendent Michael Sura had examined the leftover Denver dies and advised,

> Confirming telephone conversation with Mr. Neisser we received from the Denver Mint on September 17, 1964, one box containing 32 One Dollar reverse dies. These dies are in poor condition, corroded, pitted and undersized and will be destroyed. It is also considered advisable to destroy all One Dollar collars presently in stock. New collars will be prepared for the minting of the 1964 dollars.[28]

Thus, the 1964 dollars were going to be struck from entirely new face dies and reeded-edge collars.

The first batch of new dollar dies (D-1 through D-5) were shipped to Denver on September 28, 1964,[29] and another set of five dies (D-16 through D-20) on October 19.[30] But by October 28 Miller requested that no more dollar dies be sent, suggesting that nothing more was to be done in the immediate future.[31]

While new dollar dies were being made, the Mint was also experimenting with alloys and layered metal in an attempt to find a substitute for silver in circulating coinage.[32] The shortage of coins was acute and Treasury officials knew they could not keep up with future demand if they had to mint standard .900 fine subsidiary coins. Treasury officials blamed the shortage on coin collectors, coin dealers, and silver speculators, claiming that "10 million collectors" no longer saved one or two of each denomination, but now "have adopted the habit of saving rolls and bags of new coins."[33] The real reasons for the shortage were a large increase in higher-value vending machines, a rapidly expanding economy, increased use of silver in consumer products, failure of large silver users to recycle metal (which led to production shortfalls and increased metal prices), inefficient distribution of coins, and hoarding encouraged by individual apprehension about the world political and military situation.

A DECISION AT LAST

Four months passed with no silver dollars struck and presented to Senators Mansfield and Metcalf. Preparatory work was progressing, but the Senate majority leader was anxious to see the coins issued. Secretary Dillon prepared a confidential memorandum for President Johnson, stating in part:

> [Senator Mansfield] was certainly led to believe that they would be minted. It was simply assumed by all concerned that if the funds were appropriated, they would be used. Therefore, it appears to me that Senator Mansfield is justified in feeling that he has had a commitment that the dollars would be made.
>
> . . . The coin shortage, however, persists, and we simply have not felt justified in cutting down production of badly needed nickels, dimes, quarters and 50¢ pieces to mint dollars that will not stay in circulation . . . The possibility of the coin shortage delaying production was not mentioned or discussed with Senator Mansfield.
>
> In these circumstances I feel that if Senator Mansfield insists that the dollars be minted, we must mint them. However, I believe that minting the dollars will expose him and the Administration to serious criticism on at least two grounds.
>
> First, we—and he—will be criticized for minting dollars that are not needed, at a time when there is a real need for other circulating coins . . .
>
> Second, even if . . . these dollars were put into circulation only in the Western states, they would not remain in circulation in Mon-

tana or anywhere else. There is very little question but that they will simply be bought and hoarded by coin collectors or others. The effect will be to waste $45 million of needed silver.

The Treasury ran out of silver dollars (except for $2,800,000 of very high numismatic value still held at the Treasury) on March 25, 1964. So far as we know, silver dollars are not now a circulating medium of exchange. In a few localities in the country, such as in Las Vegas casinos, they are still being used, but special steps have been taken to ensure they are not carried away . . . Virtually all of the approximately 480 million silver dollars now outstanding have been hoarded by various groups and people around the country. In the six months previous to March 25, 1964, 45 million silver dollars were issued by the Treasury, and they simply vanished . . .

I expect to see Senator Mansfield tomorrow and go over all this with him again. If, in spite of these facts, he still wants us to go ahead, I will tell him, unless you feel otherwise, that we will mint and distribute the dollars sometime this spring.[34]

This certainly sounded like a death blow to the 1964 dollar. The secretary of the Treasury had nothing good to say about striking more silver dollars and felt it would be a waste of bullion that could better be used to make subsidiary coins.

But that did not account for the majority leader's tenacity. A deal had been struck the previous April, and Mansfield had lived up to his part of the bargain. He had kept his word, and now he wanted his constituents in Montana to see that the Treasury would keep its word. That was the way of the West. On March 25, 1965, Mansfield wrote to Secretary Dillon about the much-promised silver dollars.

I am once again calling to your attention the question of the minting of the 45 million silver dollars requested by the Administration, authorized by the Congress, and funds appropriated for the same.

It is my understanding that at least in certain areas of coinage the shortage is considerably less severe that it has been in recent months and it would be my hope, therefore, that the minting of the silver dollars would get underway as soon as possible to the end that this matter can be settled.

I know that you and the President are aware of my great and personal interest in this matter and I know also that you are fully cognizant of what this means to the State of Montana.

I would appreciate your immediate attention to the matter to the end that the 45 million silver dollars authorized and appropriated for by the Congress will be undertaken as expeditiously as possible.[35]

It was obvious from the senator's letter that he wanted the coins minted and wanted it done soon. President Johnson certainly understood the situation and was acutely aware of the political favors in play. But Johnson had more to deal with than silver dollars. On April 1, 1965, Secretary Dillon resigned and the president nominated Henry H. Fowler as the new secretary of the Treasury. He was quickly confirmed, assuming office on April 4.

Senator Mansfield wrote to Fowler about the silver dollars on April 2, the day he was nominated, and Fowler replied on the 16th:

Secretary Dillon discussed this matter with me before he left the Treasury Department and expressed hope that this matter could be worked out to your satisfaction . . .

I am sure you can imagine how much I must absorb in a very short time in order to reach decisions on the pressing issues of silver, the new coinage alloy and how soon we can proceed with the manufacturing of silver dollars. I want you to know, however, that I am fully aware of your position on silver dollars, and hope very much that something can be worked out.[36]

Wallace provided a memorandum to the secretary the same day. In it, he reinforced that the coin shortage "has a bearing on our decisions with respect to new coinage alloys." He also noted:

The actual facts of the situation are that we have not resolved the issue of whether we need the 40 million ounces of silver involved to help protect our existing coinage during our changeover to a new alloy. In addition, we would be severely criticized for issuing silver dollars because they would not circulate, but would instead be snapped up by speculators and hoarders not only because the silver alone is worth a dollar, but also because they would be expected to have a very high numismatic value.[37]

By May 6, Secretary Fowler was being bombarded by memoranda from his staff. Special assistant Joseph M. Bowman wrote in part:

During the last several months I have had several conversations with Senator Mansfield about our failure to mint the silver dollars. Several months ago, in compliance with the President's instruction to Secretary Dillon, I met with Mansfield and told him that we would mint the silver dollars if he made the decision that the Treasury do so, and at that time advised him of the difficulties involved, e.g., that numismatic magazines were already advertising these unproduced silver dollars for $2.50 a piece, and that the portion of the 45 million silver dollars which would be released in Montana would last only 3 days. Earlier, Mr. Valenti (White House) met with Mansfield and had substantially the same conversation. Mansfield advised me that he would not make the decision or take the responsibility in this matter, that Treasury had made the commitment, and that it was Treasury's decision. However, he said that he wanted the silver dollars minted.[38]

Meanwhile, Wallace wrote to Fowler the same day advising that, "It is now too late in the fiscal year to complete the minting of these silver dollars." He also noted that the president was soon to recommend a new coinage alloy, and that the mint wanted to "reprogram the $600,000 for additional equipment" to help ameliorate the expected hoarding of silver coins.[39] Thus, Director Adams's interest was no longer in producing the required coins, but in securing use of the $600,000 previously appropriated for silver-dollar expenses. The same memorandum also revealed that Assistant Secretary Wallace had met with Mansfield on April 13:

Secretary of the Treasury Henry "Joe" Fowler gave approval for the Mint to produce silver dollars in May 1965 although he personally recommended against it.

I told him that I wanted him (Mansfield) to be aware of the real problems and probable criticism the treasury faced if it minted silver dollars at this time with the coin shortage already at a critical stage. Mansfield told me that he realized that the problems we faced were serious. He said, however, that he had made this promise in Montana during the last campaign, and that Lee Metcalf had another race next year, and that he wanted the silver dollars minted. I suggested to the Senator that the June 30 date of expiration of last year's appropriation was rapidly approaching and that perhaps we could lobby for an additional appropriate if the dollars were not minted before the expiration of the appropriation. He said that he did not think we could get this approved in Committee.[40]

Assistant Treasury secretary Joseph W. Barr was copied on the memorandum and he and Secretary Fowler went to visit Mansfield the next morning, hoping to get the senator to agree to delay minting silver dollars. They knew that if Mansfield would agree to request that available funding be extended into the next fiscal year, this would effectively kill the entire project.

While the coin inventory is far from satisfactory, it is possible that we can take some chances and shut down the production of pennies (and possibly nickels) in the Denver Mint and begin production of the silver dollars in approximately four weeks.

Because of a statutory shutdown of the Mint at the end of June, we can get about a three weeks production during the month of June. It will take approximately another two to three months in fiscal year 1966 to complete this production run.

. . . we can tell Senator Mansfield there will unquestionably be a great public outcry when these coins are minted. . . . However, the commitment was made in good faith and we intend to live up to our part of the understanding with the Congress.

[Finally], we might as well make it clear to Senator Mansfield that this action will be interpreted by many as an attempt to bribe the western silver block in an attempt to support our coinage recommendations. There is nothing we can do about these allegations and we are prepared to take them. Our intention is simply to live up to an honorable commitment delivered in good faith.[41]

The meeting was held, but the Montana senators held firm. There was nothing more the secretary could do. Mansfield expected the Treasury to uphold its part of the bargain. He and Metcalf had long ago withdrawn their support for debasement of the silver coinage, and were prepared to support recommendations for complete removal of silver from U.S. coins. But they wanted the silver dollars struck.

Fortunately, the Mint had been preparing for silver-dollar production for nearly a year and had dies, collars, and other equipment ready for use. On May 12, director of the Mint Eva Adams issued orders to Denver Mint superintendent Fern Miller to begin trial production:

> You are hereby instructed to proceed with the striking of trial pieces, on a production-run basis, of a proposed issue of silver dollars bearing the 1964 date. Precautions should be taken to assure that the striking of these trial pieces conform with applicable provisions of law and the Mint regulations, in the event they should not be approved for release to general circulation.[42]

The phrase "production run basis" meant the coining department was to simulate actual production runs of the coin using normal presses and striking large numbers of trial pieces. The Philadelphia Mint had already struck 30 test pieces and forwarded two to headquarters in Washington, D.C. They were stored in the office safe of Mint headquarters technologist Howard Johnson.[43] President Johnson announced commencement of silver-dollar production, the first in 38 years, in a May 15 press release:

> Last year, the Congress appropriated $600,000 to the Mint for the manufacture of 45 million Silver Dollars.
>
> The minting of these Silver Dollars was necessarily postponed while the Mint devoted its facilities to the production of other coins to overcome the coin shortage that developed in 1963–64.
>
> This course was followed because it is possible to use paper currency in place of Silver Dollars, but there is no substitute for smaller coin.
>
> It has always been my intention to carry out the will of Congress as soon as feasible. Substantial progress has now been made in bringing the supply of small coin into line with demand. Consequently, I have directed the Mint to proceed with the making of Silver Dollars, up to the amount authorized by the Congress, during the remainder of the current fiscal year, ending June 30.
>
> They will be distributed in the areas of the country where the Silver Dollar has traditionally been used as a medium of exchange.[44]

President Lyndon B. Johnson announced renewed production of silver dollars on May 15, 1965. The press release actually triggered the end of any possible silver dollars for the next five years.

With a persistent coin shortage in place, a date freeze in effect, upward pressure on the price of silver, and Congress considering removal of silver from all coinage, the Treasury Department acted on the orders of Congress. Nearly every administration official connected with the situation understood its futility. Coin-dealer advertisements were already offering $7.50 per coin for the new dollars, and it was agreed they would vanish into speculators' hands the day they were released.

DENVER IN ACTION

The Denver Mint, in search of additional space for presses, had converted a large storage building it owned (formerly a power substation for the Denver Tramway Corporation) into a press room. It was equipped with 12 large and 4 small ammunition presses, provided by the Department of Defense and reconfigured by Mint mechanics to strike coins. With passage of Public Law 88-580 "Retention of '1964' on All Coins" on September 3, the date on coins was fixed at "1964," and use of .900 fine silver would cease at the end of June 1965. After 173 years as a standard metal for U.S. coinage, silver would be replaced by copper-nickel clad layered material. But for a while, silver dollars still had a chance of being produced.

Michael P. Lantz, a Denver Mint employee at the time, tells what happened in an article in the September 16, 1996, issue of *Coin World:*

> In May, William Summers, assistant superintendent, Coining Division, received a call from Mint Headquarters in Washington, authorizing him to start production of the 45 million silver 1964-D Peace dollars. William Steinmetz, foreman in the press room, was put in charge of setting up the presses for the production run. The tramway press room was selected to be used to stamp the dollars, as it was easy to secure, and the presses could develop the tonnage necessary to stamp a silver dollar.

Collars, feeding tubes, and other mechanical parts were on hand. Ten pairs of dollar dies were shipped to Denver on May 10, 1965, and received by Denver Mint superintendent Fern V. Miller the next day. Additional collar dies were shipped a few days later. The obverse and reverse dies were both numbered 26 through 35 inclusive.[45] The mint made most of its own blanks at this time, so cutting dollar blanks was not a problem. Miller had the departments for melting and refining and rolling and cutting working on silver-alloy strip and blanks long before she received Adams's order for trial production.

Eight hundred ninety-one ingots of .900 fine silver were delivered by the melting and refining department. Each ingot measured 1.5 inches by 12 inches by 5 feet and weighed approximately 5,040 troy ounces (420 troy pounds).[46] Employees of the rolling and cutting department rolled silver strip of the correct thickness, then cut 3,994,050 ounces of dollar blanks. With each blank weighing 0.8594 ounce, that was 4,647,487 blanks.[47] After weighing, annealing, cleaning, and removing defective blanks, 2,784,987.5 troy ounces of blanks remained (3,240,618 pieces).

It appears that a few setup trial pieces were struck on May 13 and 14.[48] This is consistent with Mr. Lantz's comments in his article:

> The first day of set-up work for the new dollars was slow, as everything on the press seemed to need to be changed. William Steinmetz later told me that it was like building a new press, as everything had to be modified for the dollar.
>
> The first days, production was slow. Very limited numbers of dollars were struck. None were turned over to the Cash Division which shipped coin to the Federal Reserve Banks. All of them were secured in the tramway building under lock and seal.

Superintendent Miller ordered 10 more pairs of dollar dies on May 14.[49] Production trials began on May 15 and continued through May 24.[50] The converted ammunition presses were set up in dual mode—two coins were struck at the same time. Planchets were manually fed into tubes on either side of the press much as had been done when the first Peace dollars were made in 1921. Lantz reported that a pressman named Tom Tani struck the first 1964-D Peace dollar after the press was set up. (Tani would later strike some of the first Eisenhower dollars.) Production improved the next day and a second press was configured to strike dollars. For trial production, only about 1,576,809.7 ounces of blanks (1,834,780 pieces) were prepared for use by being run through the upsetting mill. None of the blanks were damaged in this operation, so more than 1.8 million planchets were ready for final adjusting and striking. Out of this quantity, 277,065.3 ounces (322,394 planchets) were used in minting the trial pieces.

The Bliss ammunition presses shown below were the type on which the silver dollars were struck. Each press, which could develop 250 tons of pressure, was set up to strike two coins at once (dual mode) at approximately 120 tons. The planchets were fed into the press through a conical tube. The press operator filled the two tubes from a rack where the planchets had been placed on edge to be checked for defects. They were

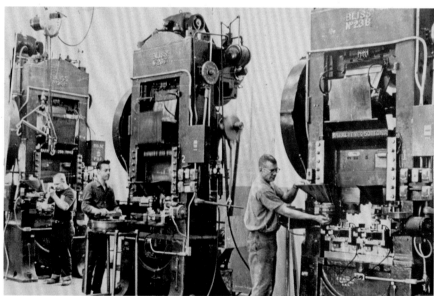

Converted Bliss ammunition presses of the type used to strike 1964 Peace dollars. Pictured left to right are die setter Walter Mattson (shown inspecting a die), press operator James Mattrews (who is preparing to dump a scoop of planchets into a feeding tube), and press operator Mel Osborn (left hand on top of a feeding tube). The presses shown above were set up to strike four quarters with each blow.

also oiled lightly to help prevent sticking in the feeding tubes. Finished coins were checked first by a foreman, and after the press was running properly, checking was done by the press operator.[51]

Acting coiner William Summers provided a breakdown of the process steps taken in handling the silver-dollar trial strikes. Along with a description of the processes, he included a diagram with the weight of silver alloy at each step. The number of each step in the following list corresponds to the numbers on the diagram, shown on page 95.

Production, handling and storage of dollars blanks and coins.

1. Rolling and Cutting.

    Blanks punched out of strip dropped into open tote box. These were emptied into open gondolas. When filled, the gondolas were taken to Process Weigh.

2. Process Weigh.

    Blanks in open gondolas were dumped into an open weigh tub, weighed, and poured into open tote boxes and taken to Blank Annealing. A sample was removed from each gondola for checking the individual blank weights. Blanks in an open gondola pan were sent to be weighed.

3. Adjusting—Sample Test.

    The open pan sample of blanks was poured into an open shaker tray and hand fed into feeder tubes at the automatic scale. The weighed blanks were returned to Process Weigh in an open pan.

4. Blank Annealing and Cleaning.

    Blanks in open tote boxes were charged into an annealing furnace which discharged the blanks into an open quench tank. Blanks were raised out of the quench tank in an open scoop and poured into cleaning equipment. The cleaning line discharged the blanks into an open gondola. When filled, the gondola was locked and moved to the balcony of the press room for upsetting.

5. Upsetting Mills.

    Locked gondolas were emptied into a locked chute which discharged through a gate into an open pan at the upsetting mill. The mill discharged blanks into an open gondola. When filled, the gondola was locked and taken to Process Weigh or to Adjusting.

6. Process Weigh.

Upset blanks in locked gondolas were dumped into an open weigh tub and from the tub into a locked gondola. The gondolas were taken to the Coin Press room.

7. Stamping.

Unadjusted upset blanks were poured from locked gondolas onto open shaker trays and hand fed to coin press feeder tubes. Dollars discharged into open catch boxes at the presses. The catch boxes were emptied into small open tote boxes. When full, the tote boxes were emptied into lidded gondolas. At the end of each stamping day, all coins and blanks were placed in locked gondolas. The gondolas of coin were stored in a vault at night. When the gondolas were filled with coin, they were locked and taken to be weighed.

8. Process Weigh.

Coins in locked gondolas were dumped into an open weigh tub, weighed, and then into locked gondolas. The gondolas were placed in a vault while waiting to be adjusted. The gondolas were not removed until they were transferred to the Cashier's vault and taken to Blank Annealing. A sample was removed from each gondola for checking the individual blank weights. Blanks in an open gondola pan were sent to be weighed.

9. Adjusting.

Upset blanks in locked gondolas were emptied into open shaker trays and hand fed into feeder tubes at the automatic scales. The scales discharged the blanks into small pans which were emptied into open gondolas. When filled, the gondolas were locked and sent to Process Weigh. Condemned blanks were dumped in open tote boxes and returned to Process Weigh.

10. Process Weigh.

Upset adjusted blanks in locked gondolas were poured into an open weigh tub and then into locked gondolas. The gondolas were sent to both the coin press room and the south end of the building—where they were stored. The open tote boxes of condemned upset blanks were poured into an open weigh tub and then into a locked gondola. The gondola was returned to the Melting Division.

11. Stamping.

Upset adjusted blanks in locked gondolas were poured into open shaker trays and hand fed into coin press feeder tubes. Dollars [were] discharged into open catch boxes at the presses. The catch boxes were emptied into open, small tote boxes. When full, the small tote boxes were emptied into standard tote boxes covered with cloth. At the end of each stamping day all blanks were gathered up and placed in locked gondolas. All coins were put in the standard tote boxes and placed in a vault to await reviewing.

12. Reviewing.

Adjusted coins in tote boxes were removed from the vault and dumped into open bins atop the review table. Coins passed across the table on a traveling belt and [were] discharged into an open tote box. The filled tote boxes were covered with cloth and returned to the vault. They remained in the vault until being transferred to Process Weigh.

Orders were received to cease production.

13. Process Weigh.

Adjusted, reviewed coins in tote boxes were removed from Reviewer's vault and poured into locked gondolas. The gondolas were placed in the Cashier's vault. Locked gondolas of unadjusted coin were removed from a Coiner's vault and placed in the Cashier's vault. Cut blanks in open tote boxes were poured into locked gondolas.

14. Cashier's Vault.

All coins were moved in locked gondolas from the coining Division to the Cashier's vault. One gondola of coin was removed from the Cashier's vault to the mutilating machine.

15. Mutilator.

About one-third of the coins from a locked gondola were mutilated in the presence of two witnesses. Receives orders to stop mutilation and melt up all coin as soon as possible. All coins were returned to the Cashier's vault in locked gondolas.

16. Cashier's Vault.

All locked gondolas were removed from the vault and escorted to the Melt Room, where they were turned over to representatives of the Melting Division. I, the undersigned, Acting Superintendent of the Coining Division of the United States Mint at Denver, Colorado, do hereby attest to the foregoing procedure having been followed in the striking and handling of the recent trial strikes of silver dollars.[52]

Between steps 9 and 10 (along the right side of the diagram) there is an apparent shortage of adjusted blanks. After step 9, the weight of blanks is 1,480,809.70 ounces, yet after step 10 there are only 181,065.30 ounces of metal. The box to the left of step 10 has no number in Summers's diagram, but the title "M&R" suggests that 12,000 ounces of adjusted upset blanks were melted at this point. That would leave 1,468,809.7 ounces of blanks remaining. Of this, it is likely that 1,287,744.4 ounces (1,498,422 blanks) were never transferred to the tramway building for use in the presses, and were not struck as coins. Also note that steps 5 through 8 on the left are upset, but unadjusted blanks. As such they might not have met legal coinage standards and would likely have been destroyed even if permission had been given to eventually release the other dollar coins. All the coins in steps 9 through 12 were fully upset and adjusted, which suggests they could have been released if production was approved.

Superintendent Miller called the pieces "model coins" which would be consistent with her later assertion that the pieces were trial or experimental pieces. It is presumed that a small number of samples, possibly from the setup tests on May 13 and 14, were sent to the Mint director's office in Washington. None of the dollars were shipped to Federal Reserve Banks or otherwise distributed.

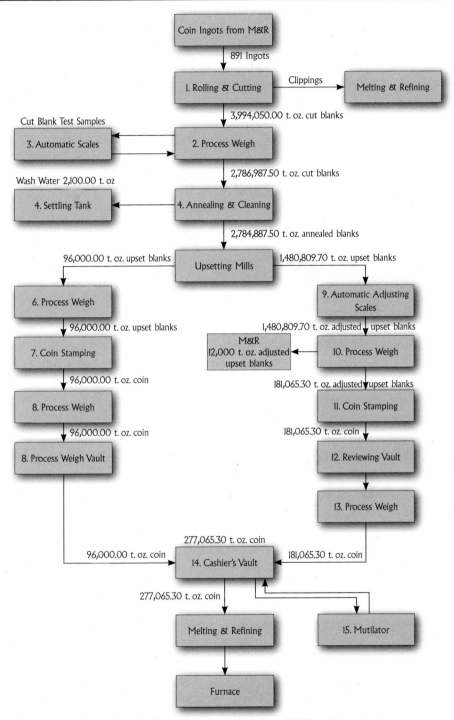

Coin Ingots from M&R

891 Ingots

1. Rolling & Cutting — Clippings → Melting & Refining

3,994,050.00 t. oz. cut blanks

Cut Blank Test Samples

3. Automatic Scales ← → 2. Process Weigh

2,786,987.50 t. oz. cut blanks

Wash Water 2,100.00 t. oz

4. Settling Tank ← 4. Annealing & Cleaning

2,784,887.50 t. oz. annealed blanks

96,000.00 t. oz. upset blanks — Upsetting Mills — 1,480,809.70 t. oz. upset blanks

6. Process Weigh

9. Automatic Adjusting Scales

96,000.00 t. oz. upset blanks

1,480,809.70 t. oz. adjusted upset blanks

7. Coin Stamping

M&R
12,000 t. oz. adjusted upset blanks ← 10. Process Weigh

96,000.00 t. oz. coin

181,065.30 t. oz. adjusted upset blanks

8. Process Weigh

11. Coin Stamping

96,000.00 t. oz. coin

181,065.30 t. oz. coin

8. Process Weigh Vault

12. Reviewing Vault

13. Process Weigh

277,065.30 t. oz. coin

96,000.00 t. oz. coin — 14. Cashier's Vault ← 181,065.30 t. oz. coin

277,065.30 t. oz. coin

Melting & Refining

15. Mutilator

Furnace

Information in the table was copied from William Summers's original diagram. The only changes are the addition of a box for step 13 and the full title for step 9, "Automatic Adjusting Scales."

The coins were not counted or bagged, although sample canvas bags had been made.[53] Approximately 2/3 of the new coins were sent through the reviewing process, where

> adjusted coins in tote boxes were removed from the vault and dumped into open bins atop the review table. Coins passed across the table on a traveling belt and [were] discharged into an open tote box. The filled tote boxes were covered with cloth and returned to the vault. They remained in the vault until being transferred to Process Weigh [where they were then transferred to the Cashier's vault].[54]

This is as close to being released as any of the coins got. Because all accounting of the coins was done on a weight basis, the exact quantity of coins struck cannot be determined. Information released by the Mint during congressional testimony said that approximately 300,000 silver dollars were struck,[55] but that was changed on June 15, 1965, in a memorandum to deputy treasurer William Howell, who was concerned about the dollars appearing in the Denver Mint's annual accounting:

> The following information was presented to the House Banking and Currency Committee in connection with the hearings on the new alloy legislation:
>
> "A large number of silver dollar trial strikes were made at the Denver Mint, but the pieces were not counted and bagged, or delivered to the cashier, as finished coins. All trial pieces have been melted as required by Mint Regulations.
>
> "The Mint controls its values during experimental and other operations as a weight basis, rather than a piece-count basis, and the trial strikes did not reach the final stage of being counted and bagged. However, from our control records of the number of troy ounces of materials that were processed in the press room, it is estimated that approximately 316,076 pieces were processed. The dollar trial strikes were dated 1964."
>
> In view of the manner in which the trial strikes were handled, there is no possibility that any silver dollars will appear in the Denver or related Treasury accounts.[56]

Although the letter above seems to correct congressional testimony, the coining department records from William Summers show that 277,065.3 ounces of planchets were struck into dollar coins. This would have produced approximately 322,394 coins. An internal Denver Mint accounting memorandum broke out expenses by function for the silver dollar project and concluded, "Approximate number of strikes melted 322,000." There is no record of this August estimate being released to the media, although it differs from Summers's report by only a few thousand pieces. With a discrepancy of more than 6,300 pieces between Summers's weight of struck dollars and the Mint's initial estimates given to Congress, it is the author's inclination to accept a quantity of 322,394 based on weight as the number of 1964-D trial pieces struck.[57]

Further, Director Adams estimated that one press could produce approximately 150,000 dollars per 24-hour work day. Since the coins were struck during only one shift, daily production would not have exceeded 50,000 pieces per press. During the eight work days of trial production, one press could have struck about 400,000 pieces. When it is considered that there must have been frequent stoppages to adjust the presses and make other changes, production of approximately 322,000 coins is consistent with reported mintage from May 15 through May 24.

The Denver Mint was not alone in the silver-dollar project:

> Mr. Campbell [from the Philadelphia Mint] called and gave the following information:
> Blanking die sets will be ready in 5 or 6 days.
> Philadelphia will start shipping dollar blanks to Denver in about 5 days after they start blanking, or about May 26 or 27. It will take Philadelphia about 10 or 11 days to roll the silver dollar metal. Philadelphia will make 15,000,000 silver dollar blanks and Denver will make 30,000,000.
> Philadelphia will need a hundred coin bins to ship blanks.[58]

END OF THE PEACE DOLLAR

Almost as soon as production was announced by the president, members of Congress raised objections. They were led by vocal Massachusetts representative Silvio O. Conte, who had vigorously opposed the coinage appropriation, and now saw minting the coins as a complete waste of money and silver. He further opposed the 40 percent silver Kennedy half dollar as a waste of metal and a sop to silver-producing states. Conte introduced a bill on May 19 that specifically prohibited production of silver dollars after passage of his bill. Publicity about the new dollars in the midst of a "coin shortage" also brought negative criticism to the

Mint and Treasury Department from ordinary citizens. All the predictions of public objections made by Secretary Dillon came true, and Senator Mansfield must have finally realized that Montana's silver dollars were never going to be released. Congressional opposition to striking silver dollars was so strong that when the next hearings were held concerning the proposed Coinage Act of 1965, the dollar coin was omitted from the list of denominations.[59]

Director Adams, testifying before a hastily called congressional hearing on May 24, stated that approval was given for striking trial pieces, but not for production for official release. "They are in the status of trial pieces which can be melted down because they are not ever for circulation."[60] As House committee members grilled Adams and other Mint and Treasury officials, they seemed to gradually understand what had happened. The Treasury and Mint said they were trying to follow the 1964 law ordering production of 45 million silver dollars. With time running out to strike coins, the Mint began testing dies and presses. Even if they could not produce all of the required coins by the June 30 deadline, they could at least make a start at complying with Congress's wishes.

One plan had been to strike between five and seven million pieces by June 30 and then ask for an extension to make the rest. Based on Director Adams's comment that one press could strike 150,000 dollars during a 24-hour day, and Mr. Lantz's observations that two presses had been setup to strike dollars, the maximum capacity would have been 300,000 pieces per 24-hour work day. If the Denver Mint operated seven days a week, with three eight-hour shifts per day, and assuming twenty-four working days from May 25 to the June 20 scheduled closure, then a maximum of 7,200,000 silver dollars could have been produced by the end of fiscal year 1965. Accounting for normal press stoppage due to die changes, maintenance, and accidents (such as die clashes and stuck planchets), the five to seven million production target was reasonable.

Evidence supporting this plan includes the congressional testimony on May 24 and a teletype from Miller on May 17:

> We wish to place our order No. 23-65 for the following. 300 pair of dollar dies with the delivery rate of 70 pair weekly. 100 dollar collars. We need 25 immediately and the remainder as soon as possible.[61]

This is further supported by Miller's teletype request on May 18 to stop shipment of cent, nickel, dime, quarter, and half dollar dies.[62] Obviously, the full production capacity of the Denver Mint was going to be shifted to silver dollars.

However, the coin shortage, rising price of silver, and depletion of Treasury metal stock made the entire enterprise look foolish. Constituents were writing letters to members of Congress demanding to buy the "rare" new dollars so they could resell them at a profit. Coin-collector publications were running ads from coin dealers offering to buy the new dollars at a significant premium. The Treasury Department must also have realized that if Conte's bill became law, they could be stuck with a relatively small number of 1964 silver dollars for which there was a huge speculative demand. Adding a million or so new dollars to the 2.3 million Carson City dollars already saved because of their collector value would only multiply the Treasury's problems. The new Peace dollars had become nothing more than another method for speculation in silver prices and coin values.

Telephone calls ordering a halt in all operations relating to the silver dollar went to the Denver and Philadelphia mints on the afternoon of May 24. Denver Superintendent Miller immediately reinstated her previous die order, cancelled the dollar die orders, and added a request for 500 more quarter dies—probably planning to use the dollar presses for quarters.[63] A press release on May 25 explained the decision to the media:

Treasury Decides Against Producing Silver Dollars

The Treasury today announced that it has decided against the minting of any new silver dollars at this time.

Last year, in response to a Treasury request, Congress appropriated $600,000, an amount sufficient to manufacture 45 million silver dollars.

To carry out the expressed intent of the Congress, the Treasury recommended to the White House that the United States Mint be authorized to begin production. It was on this recommendation that the White House announced May 15th, that production could begin.

Since that time, however, members of the Congress who, by reason of their Committee assignments, have a direct and responsible interest in the United States coinage, have strongly urged the Treasury not to proceed with the production of these dollars. After conferring with the White House, the Treasury has therefore determined that the Mint will not make any of these dollars at this time.[64]

The 1964-D Peace dollar was dead as a circulating coin.

The day after Adams's encounter with Congress, a memorandum arrived from the office of the treasurer:

> Is there any chance that any silver dollars recently produced on an experimental basis might show up in the accounts of the Denver Mint as minted dollars, and thereafter appear on the Daily Statement and Circulation Statement? If so, this would be disastrous and in my opinion some way must be found to prevent it. Will you please let me know.[65]

Thus began the Mint's obsession with secrecy and desire to wipe out all trace of the coins' existence. The new dollar coins were immediately sequestered as Mint officials circled the wagons to avoid further embarrassment. On May 26 orders were received by Superintendent Miller to destroy all the trial strikes.[66] A committee of Denver Mint officers gathered to begin melting the 1964-D Peace dollars. All signed a statement that read,

> We the undersigned do hereby attest to the fact that six gondolas containing trial strikes of silver dollars were delivered by representatives of the Coining Division to Mr. Vern H. Owen, Foreman of the Ingot Melting Section, in our presence on May 26, 27 and 28, 1965; that the contents of these gondolas were kept constantly under our surveillance until they were destroyed by melting and casting into ingots; that all such trial strikes delivered on a given day were actually melted on that same day without the necessity of keeping any unmelted pieces under our control between working shifts; and that, in our opinion, there is absolutely no chance that any of the trial strikes so delivered could have escaped destruction in the melting furnace.[67]

> /Signed/

> *Vern H. Owen, James A. Drekle, Ronald E. White.*

> *Witness to complete melting /signed/:*

> *James J. McLaughlin, Henry W. Riddick, F.V. Miller.*

To further remove traces of the inconvenient coins, all the working dies were mutilated at the Denver Mint on May 28, rather than being shipped back to Philadelphia. This involved 50 obverse dies (number D-1 through D-50) and 6 reverse dies (number D-1, D-4, D-5, D-6, D-12, and D-13). For reasons presently unknown, the reverse dies shipped to Denver earlier in the month, numbers 26 through 35, were not included on the destruction list.

Everyone connected with the project had to sign a statement saying that none of the coins were in their possession and all they had seen had been destroyed. The statement, dated June 11, 1965, included the signatures of 35 employees and read,

> Whereas we, the undersigned employees of the Denver Mint, were assigned to the various processing and handling operations necessary for producing blanks and trial strikes of silver dollars in accordance with the projected plans for eventually manufacturing silver dollars, we wish to state for the record that none of the blanks or trial pieces were removed by us, either individually or collectively, from their normal channels, locale, or containers; that we have no knowledge of other persons having done so; that none of the blanks or trial strikes are now in our possession; and that above-normal security procedures were followed in handling this experimental material.[68]

Officials were concerned enough about possible "leakage" of a coin or two from the trial production that they contacted former employee Larry V. Truitt and obtained a sworn statement that he did not have, and had never had, one of the coins in his possession.[69] Some members of Congress wanted to be sure this did not happen again. Representative William P. Widnall (R-New Jersey), calling the 1964 Peace dollars a "fiasco," stated during Coinage Act of 1965 hearings, "I am going to offer an amendment to flatly prohibit the coinage of silver dollars for a period of five years from the effective date of this act."[70]

The cleanup continued into the summer of 1965. On August 2, Miller reported that her facility had spent $19,332.67 for overhead and $11,955.27 for labor to make 6,203,879 ounces of blanks (approximately 7,196,500 blanks) and the trial pieces.[71] On August 3, Philadelphia Mint engraver Frank Gasparro received orders to destroy 40 pairs of partially fabricated Peace dollar dies that remained in his department.[72] The remaining 28 test pieces struck at Philadelphia were put through rollers and then melted.[73] The two pieces sent to Washington remained there until 1970. Researcher David Ganz interviewed Mint technologist Howard Johnson in 1973. He reported that Johnson told him that in the spring of 1970, "When we destroyed these in Washington, there were four people present. We put it through our rolls and I demolished them."[74]

From the number of completed dies, those in production and the large quantity of blanks manufactured, it is apparent that plans were well along for full-scale production of at least five to seven million 1964-D Peace dollars.

President Johnson did not want the coins produced but he could not countermand the will of Congress. He could, however, use his political skill to manipulate the situation to his favor. The presidential announcement ensured the coins would both be struck—following Congress' direction—and never released, thus complying with the sentiment of Congress and the general public. Had the Treasury Department wanted to mint 1964-D dollars, it would have been done quietly beginning in late 1964. Public announcement would have been delayed until the end of the fiscal year. At that time opponents would have been powerless to have millions of coins melted.[75] In effect, Secretary Fowler and President Johnson used publicity and negative criticism generated by the production announcement to bypass Senator Mansfield and kill the project.

Although there would be no Peace dollars for politicians, collectors, or speculators, and no new pieces would see circulation, de Francisci's venerable bit of idealism had one final gasp before it expired. In the months leading to approval of legislation authorizing the Eisenhower dollar, Mint Director Mary Brooks wrote to Nicholas G. Thornton, superintendent of the Philadelphia Mint:

> Subject: Experimental Trial Strikes. 80/20 silver copper clad on core of 20/80 silver copper for one dollar coins.
>
> . . . in the presence of your Trial Strike Committee, you are authorized and requested to blank, anneal, upset and strike ten (10) one dollar coins using U.S. Peace coinage dies.
>
> Two (2) one dollar coins should be transmitted to this office by Mr. Macellaro with a form #601.[76]

Demoted from coinage to surrogate, the Peace dollar design met its end when the 10 experimental pieces were later crushed and melted, on Director Brooks's order. Ironically, the coin meant to symbolize a lasting peace after the Great War for Civilization became a testing object for a dollar coin honoring one of the soldiers who brought an end to the next Great War.

KNOWN SPECIMENS AND SPECULATION

Records indicate that all planchets coined into silver dollars were melted at the Denver Mint. The situation is similar for the 28 pieces once held in Philadelphia and 2 pieces held in Washington. No other coins have been acknowledged as being in possession of the Mint or Treasury, and there are none in the Smithsonian National Numismatic Collection.

Nonetheless, the absence of open, forthright disclosure by the Mint and Treasury in 1965, and the lack of a per-piece count of the coins, has created considerable suspicion among coin collectors. Rumors and assertions about the existence of 1964-D Peace dollars are commonplace, with a number of notable collectors and dealers claiming to have seen or been offered examples. With that in mind, it may be useful to examine some of the ways one or more 1964 Peace dollars could have survived.

Official Holdback—Approval Samples

It is conceivable that examples were held back from destruction by Treasury officials. These could have been additional samples from the Philadelphia tests or setup trials made in Denver on May 13 and 14. In past eras, pre-production samples were commonly sent to the director's office in Washington. Notable examples include the 1922 high-relief Peace dollars, 1922 medium-relief Peace dollar trial strikes, and the Sandblast Proof pieces of 1921 and 1922. All of these were initially prepared as samples for the director and Treasury officials to examine. None appear on bullion or mintage accounts and the total quantities were so small that the silver could easily have been lost in normal clippings and wastage. Most appear to have been paid for by Mint headquarters staff.

The 30 specimens struck in Philadelphia would have been expected to serve this purpose, and likely were made on a medal press as had been done in the past. (Absent any post-striking treatment, these would qualify as Satin Proofs in today's collector language.) Were the Denver test pieces mixed with others, or were they shipped to Washington for comparison with the Philadelphia samples?

Official Holdback—VIP Specimens

It is possible that specimens were reserved from either the Philadelphia or Denver tests for prominent persons connected with the 1964 Peace dollar. These coins might have been given to the president, Senator Mansfield, Secretary Fowler, or others. Historically, pattern or experimental examples have been provided to certain officials as part of their design approval process or as special favors. (This is similar to the approval samples noted above.) However, in all instances the author has identified, prominent persons were provided with the first *production* pieces, not trial or setup test pieces. This was the case in 1877 when President Hayes purchased a pair of pattern silver dollars (William Barber and Morgan designs). In March 1878, the president was given the first production piece off the new dies. In 1921, the first production Peace dollar was reserved for President Harding—not the first setup or test piece.[77]

The Mint's lack of complete disclosure and secretive attitude in the past makes it impossible to discount either of the official holdback possibilities.

Sanctioned Distribution as Souvenirs

As a footnote to the 1964-D Peace dollar story, there is a persistent tale that sometime during the trial production period employees were allowed to buy two of the dollars, but were later told to return them. These were intended to be souvenirs or mementos of silver-dollar production. Any such distribution must have occurred during the final days of trial production, just before officials could have certified the design and presses ready for full-scale manufacture. The standard story says that many of the 1964 coins were returned but since they were simply thrown into a bin, no one verified that the coins returned were actually 1964 specimens and not some other date of Peace dollar. Dumping these recovered coins into one of the tote boxes would have preserved the correct metal weight, provided all the coins distributed were retuned one-for-one. Variations of the story claim that one or more 1964 silver dollars were spent in a local bar. Some versions claim the story was verified by Superintendent Miller or that it was told to someone by her.

Nothing in available documents indicates that this kind of distribution took place. There are no known records of employees paying for coins, or of them being returned and the payment refunded. There are no signed statements from anyone claiming this distribution occurred. Superintendent Miller and other senior staff signed sworn affidavits that no coins were released in any manner. This anecdote might be a distortion of how employees purchased Kennedy halves on the release date in March 1964. Michael Lantz's article notes that any sale or distribution of 1964-D silver dollars prior to their official release by the Treasury department was both contrary to Mint policy and possibly illegal.

Unofficial Holdback

During setup tests and trial production, dollar coins were frequently moved about in open or unlocked tote boxes and gondolas. All the coins were accounted for by weight only—there was no physical count of the coins. Thus, it was possible for any employee having access to the Tramway Building to remove one or more coins from a tote box or gondola. The missing coin(s) could have been replaced with common 1924 (or other date) silver dollars readily available in bright, new condition. It would have been important for the number of replacement coins to both exactly match the count of pieces removed, and visually resemble the 1964 coins. Employees of the coining department were detail-oriented men with acute awareness of differences between one bit of stamped metal and another. Considering differences in design and overall fabric, the 1964 dollars may have had a very different "look" to them than their 1920s or 1930s cousins.

With no physical count of coins having been made, replacement would have kept the coiner's bullion account balanced, so switching a few coins might have been relatively easy. However, getting replacements into the Tramway Building and then removing 1964-dated dollars would probably have been much more difficult. The Tramway Building had been selected for trial production because it was relatively easy to secure. Employees were searched on entering and leaving and were not permitted to enter with bags, lunch boxes, or anything that could be used to hide coins. This was routine procedure at the Denver Mint, and a separate building made it simpler to implement for the Peace dollar project. There are no security or Secret Service records of any employee being caught with unauthorized materials entering or leaving the Tramway Building.

The affidavit signed by employees was likely aimed at this possibility. The fact that it was signed by all employees who William Summers identified as having worked on the project suggests that these were the only ones who had sufficient access to allow the coins to be switched. It is probably impossible to determine if anyone else had access to the new coins.

This substitution scenario was the only one mentioned by the Mint's attorney in 1973 when he issued an opinion about ownership of any 1964 Peace dollars that might surface.

Unofficial Removal

With all metal weights recorded and matching through the coining process, it is unlikely anyone could have simply stolen a coin or two. The process weighing scales were sensitive to the tenth of an ounce—far less than the weight of one coin. That leaves the possibility that one or more members of the destruction team removed coins after they had been weighed but before they were destroyed in the Ingot Melting Section by superintendent Vern H. Owen.

This would have required a very unusual degree of collusion between the six Denver Mint officials present, including the superintendent. In addition to Mint representatives, Superintendent Miller stated, "I might add: Mr. Osborne, Mr. Blake and Mr. Allen of the Secret Service dropped in a couple of times during the operation."[78] This would make quite a crowd of people, several of whom would likely have had to conspire to remove coins. Unfortunately, William Summers's metal weights do not tell us what the silver weighed after it was melted. Mint attorney Carl Landis stated that metal was also weighed after the coins were melted, and pre- and post-melting weights were equal, but he provided no substantiation. Considering normal tolerances in handling precious metals, it is extremely unlikely that pre- and post-melting weights of more than six million ounces of silver were identical. If they were, it would suggest some sort of adjustment to the actual weight was made. Although very remote, this possibility cannot be entirely eliminated.

LEGITIMACY

Little was publicly said about 1964-D Peace dollars for almost eight years.[79] In that time the new Eisenhower clad-composition dollar was issued, with a 40 percent silver edition made for collectors. The diameter was the same standard 38.1 millimeters as the ill-fated 1964 silver dollars. The mushy blandness of Eisenhower dollar coins could have inspired greater awareness of collectors who longed for what might have been in May 1965.

A press release was distributed by the Bureau of the Mint on May 31, 1973. It briefly outlined the history of the 1964 Peace dollar in the same language used in prior releases. However, it added new sentences to the final paragraph:

> All of the trial strikes for this proposed 1964 dollar were ordered destroyed under the strict supervisory and accounting procedures required by Mint regulations. None reached the final stage of being counted, bagged and issued by the Mint's cashier as finished coins. Should anyone have such trial Mint-struck pieces in his possession, they are the property of the United States which it is entitled to recover since the pieces were never issued.[80]

The new, threatening language originated with Mint attorney Carl A. Landis, who had been reading the Mint's subscription copy of *Numismatic News Weekly*. A front-page article titled "Answer the '64 Dollar

Question And You Can Be $3,000 Richer" caught Landis's attention.[81] In it coin dealer Robert "Bob" Cohen of Bladensburg, Maryland, was described as having run an advertisement in the April issue of the ANA's magazine, *The Numismatist*, offering to buy 1964 Peace dollars for $3,000. The article claimed, "His research leads him to believe that 100 or more of the coins—and perhaps as many as 300—were spirited out of the Denver Mint in 1965, during the brief period when they were being struck."[82] Later, the article claimed, "The seven-year statute of limitation now has expired, and hobby observers are watching closely to see if any of the coins start to surface."[83] Cohen is also reported to have said that his theory was bolstered by a noticeable increase in the number of dollar planchets appearing on the market since 1965. He claimed that planchets and coins were removed by the same persons.

With hobby attention now focused by the article, Landis prepared an opinion for Roy C. Cahoon, assistant director for Public Services. After reviewing the article's basic content and a few facts about the 1964 silver dollars, Landis cited the case of "United States v. Barnard, 73 Fed. Supp. 531, United States District Court, Western District, Tennessee, on July 22, 1947, which held a $20.00 double eagle gold piece, dated 1933, which was purchased by the defendant Barnard in good faith for $900.00 from a collector of rare coins, was not issued as money or currency, but was personal property which could be recovered by the United States."[84]

Landis said the Barnard case was so apt and suited to the circumstances of the hypothetical case involving a 1964-D silver-dollar trial strike that he quoted at length from the court's opinion. Landis's conclusion, which was incorporated into the last paragraph of the May 31 press release, was,

> It is my opinion that circumstances at the Denver Mint in the instant case indicated that a 1964 silver dollar trial strike, though purchased by a rare coin collector in good faith, was not issued by the Denver Mint as money or currency. It is personal property of the United States, which the United States is entitled to recover, where all such strikes were carefully weighed before and after they were melted into bullion and the weight remained the same, thus indicating that the strike involved was stolen from the Mint by substitution of a planchet or a dollar coin of earlier date.[85]

This appears to represent the Mint's sole basis for threatening to "recover" any 1964 Peace dollars; it is not without some obvious flaws. The most apparent is that Landis claims the planchets and coins were weighed both before and after melting and the weight was the same.

However, available documents, including William Summers's sworn affidavit and Superintendent Miller's destruct affidavit, say nothing about the weight of metal after melting. With six gondolas filled with coins and blanks having been melted, it highly unlikely that before and after weights would be been exactly equal. Summers's letter indicates that 2,100 troy ounces of silver were lost just during the annealing and cleaning processes. The Denver Mint's internal accounting showed that a total of 6,203,879 troy ounces of blanks (and presumably including coins) were operated on by the Mint for silver dollars.[86] Landis's claim that melting this much metal was done without loss is a considerable stretch of credulity.

A second problem is that the Barnard case occurred at a time when witnesses could be brought to testify to their actions and documents they had produced. Although this may have been true in 1973, by the early 21st century most potential witnesses are dead, and the available documents are hearsay.

Lastly, Mint Bureau records of 1933 accounted for double eagles by the piece as well as by weight and included a complete trail from coining department to vaults to Assay Commission, Smithsonian, and other destinations; this was not the case with the 1964 silver dollars.[87]

There are quite a few renowned American coins whose circumstances of origin are unclear. Besides a multitude of specimen, Proof, and other pieces with special surfaces, examples include the 1913 Liberty Head nickels and 1884 and 1885 trade dollars. The 1913 nickels are particularly apt examples because we know that no pieces of this date of the Liberty Head design were authorized. Working dies were made as part of routine Mint procedure but no orders were given to strike coins from these dies. The new Buffalo design was adopted on December 18, 1912, and the new Buffalo nickel approved for production on February 18, 1913. Seven years after the Liberty Head nickel was abandoned, in 1920, advertisements began to appear in hobby publications offering to buy 1913 Liberty Head nickels. In subsequent years the five known Liberty Head nickels have been written about, publicly displayed, and sold and bought at auction and through private sale more than a hundred times. At no point has any claim been made that the coins are illegal to own.

1964 Peace Dollar Appearance

Given the 28-year gap in silver-dollar production and destruction of hubs and master dies in 1937, it is likely 1964 Peace dollar details differed noticeably from low-relief varieties of the 1920s and 1930s. The new edge collars would also differ from the old ones and might more closely resemble the edge on an Eisenhower dollar than any prior Peace dollar. Additionally, when one considers that Philadelphia Mint engraver Gilroy Roberts and assistant engraver Frank Gasparro had fully mastered the Mint's reducing-lathe technology, it is reasonable to expect that inscriptions and other details would be better defined than on the 1922 or later pieces. A final difficulty in imagining a 1964 Peace dollar is that engraver Sinnock destroyed the hubs in 1937, which would have forced the Mint to use models, casts, or galvanos for future production. We don't know which set of design models were used, assuming any of the ones remaining at the Philadelphia Mint were suitable. We also do not know if changes were made to improve striking. The Mint had a 1921 high-relief obverse cast that had been used for the 1921 coins. There was no usable 1921 reverse cast or model because the reverse hub had been recut by George Morgan to remove the sword. De Francisci's 1922 low-relief models could have been used; however, we have no photos or other information about them so details of design and relief may not match normal Peace dollars. The closest we can come to visualizing these last models are the 1922 low-relief Sandblast Proofs sent to Washington for approval.

The only portion of the 1964-D coins that we have any reliable descriptive information about is the edge. Engraver Roberts prepared new edge collars for the dollar coins and these, evidently, differed from those last used in 1935. Presumably, these new collars were not discarded when the Peace dollar was abandoned, but were later used on experimental and early-production Eisenhower dollars in 1970 and 1971.

Unless someone donates a "stray" genuine 1964-D Peace dollar to the Smithsonian Institution, it is unlikely that anyone except a few Treasury officials and a dwindling number of former Mint employees will ever see one.

A low-resolution photo of the obverse die was recently discovered, but it lacks sufficient detail for more than general confirmation of the 1964 design.

5

PEACE DOLLAR
DESIGNS

The Peace dollar design was the last step in the evolution of United States coinage from static 19th-century formalism to a more dynamic and diverse representation of America. The changes began in 1907 and 1908 with redesign of the four gold denominations, followed by the cent in 1909, the nickel in 1913, and the dime, quarter, and half dollar in 1916. All of these coins trace their ancestry to the Cornish, New Hampshire, studio of Augustus Saint-Gaudens, his students, and assistants. Each of the coin designers of this era either worked directly with Saint-Gaudens or was heavily influenced by his style and late neo-classic view of sculpture. Beginning with President Theodore Roosevelt's push for changes to America's circulating coins, the first decades of the 20th century saw a consistent attempt by artists and politicians to express the unique character of America on its coinage.

Objectively, the most truly "American" coin design of this era was James Earle Fraser's Buffalo nickel. Its unique theme is carried front to back, linking the bison and Native American images in their interdependence (at least for those tribes living on the Great Plains). Second place goes to Adolph A. Weinman's Liberty Walking half dollar, with a flag-draped American icon striding confidently toward the sunrise and the reverse featuring an assertive eagle watchful and controlling of America's territory. Weinman's dime, combining concepts of liberty, strength, and unity, is more cohesive than most designs, yet none of the dime's symbols are American in origin or derive immediately from America's deeper character. Both Fraser and Weinman spent several years working with Saint-Gaudens, and later both were teachers of and mentors to Anthony de Francisci.

Other designs, though they were vast artistic improvements over the banal design work of past Mint engravers and remain popular with collectors, are of more European and classical Greek derivation than American. Bela Lyon Pratt's half and quarter eagle obverses ceremonially stylize a war chief of one of the nations of Native Americans, yet do not bring us any closer to the subject or its meaning. His eagle reverses simply copy (with minor corrections) Saint-Gaudens' $10 eagle and fail for the same reason as its prototype. Saint-Gaudens' designs, though beautiful in their own right, struggle to connect to the American spirit. The magnificent double eagle obverse, showing Liberty (actually *Victory* from the General Sherman Memorial in New York City) striding boldly forward holding the torch of justice, depends on the trite introduction of the U.S. Capitol building for its national connection. The $10 gold eagle uses the portrait from the same head of Victory but attaches an incongruous Native American war bonnet to the portrait. The effect is simultaneously striking, beautiful, and silly.

The Peace dollar's theme is clearly stated in its official name: "Peace dollar." It is the only circulation coin of the United States that was given a title before it was designed. Anthony de Francisci's composite portrait of Liberty is both homage to its predecessors—particularly *Victory*—and a reflection of the less formal, more engaging America that followed World War I. To his credit, he did not *copy* the sample bust Fraser provided; he adapted it to the tenor of the time. As a portrait, it is as well modeled as the prototypes but also possesses an individuality and personality that prior Liberties lack. Here, Liberty is both an ideal and a person—identifiable by the viewer as readily as the figure on the Red Cross poster by Howard Chandler Christy, yet having no specific name other than Liberty or Freedom or some deeply felt ideal. This approach to his subject is similar to Adolph Weinman's treatment of Liberty on the 1916 dime, where the portrait is more youthful and vigorous than its predecessor. The alternate reverse, with its active eagle and symbolism, carried forward America's post-war attitude. Regrettably, this eagle and its connection to the obverse were lost when an innocuous standing eagle was selected. The reverse, as minted, is a bland cousin of the other standing eagles on coins of the time. It is so insipid that even adding the word PEACE to the other inscriptions does nothing to strengthen the effect. The poor creature has had most of its feathers shorn in the name of "redesign for lower relief" and begins to approach the level of squab instead of bald eagle. Noted art interpreter Cornelius Vermeule, writing

The Spirit of America **poster for the American Red Cross, 1919, by Howard Chandler Christy.**

in his book *Numismatic Art in America,* maintained a somewhat different opinion of the Peace dollar:

> Dependence on ideas worked out by Saint-Gaudens fifteen years earlier saved the coin from artistic mediocrity, for enough of the master's style has filtered through in his familiar iconographic types of Liberty and the eagle to ensure an interesting if not great coin . . .

The obverse is weak, because an element of prettiness permeates the head of Liberty—an emptiness of face, an elaboration of hair, and an overall glossiness that adds up to nothing beyond the thick rays, the meaningless locks out behind, and a vapid lower jaw.[1]

Although some have suggested that the prototypes go back to Greco-Egyptian coins, the sculptor was not a student of numismatics, knew little of ancient coinage, and probably had never seen a Ptolemaic coin.

In notes prepared for a speech, de Francisci good-naturedly said,

It is a fact I know very little about the science of numismatics. In spite of the brilliant monographs on coins that I receive once in a while from Mr. Newell, Mr. Noe, or the late Mr. Wood, I must confess the knowledge of the history of coins is scant. The reason is that I have found no time to delve into such a fascinating field; I couldn't.

For years I have been under the delusion that I am a sculptor and it seems that delusion still persists. But while I do not know much about [the] history of coins I do know that if [it] had not been for sculptors we should not have coins as we know them. Mr. Noe would be out of a job and Mr. Newell, out of a hobby.[2]

Considering the experience and qualifications of the sculptors participating in the Peace dollar competition, a legitimate question is: "Were de Francisci's designs really the best?" The designs of only two other

Like the obverse design on the Peace dollar, the designs on the Winged Liberty dime and the Buffalo / Indian Head nickel personify the ideals of the time.

competitors are known to exist; of these, one entrant appears to have ignored the competition's requirements and the other submitted stale, recycled designs. Compared to these two samples (and they are very limited and somewhat speculative samples), de Francisci's sketches look remarkably fresh and original.

We know from de Francisci's personal papers and later comments by his wife that he harbored reservations about his designs and wondered if they really were the best. We also know by inference that at least one competitor, Robert Aitken, was displeased with results of the competition, and, more particularly, with not being promptly notified of the results.

> Two different men have more or less complained lately that they have never heard anything officially from the Commission, and it seemed to me in one case particularly that it would have been much nicer if the Secretary's office had sent notifications immediately.
>
> The particular one is in the case of the competition for the peace dollar. I met Mr. Aitken at the Club a couple of days ago and his hair was rather standing on end over the competition generally for some reason, but the particular thing that seemed to be worrying him was that none of the competitors except—I suppose—the winner, had had any notification of its result at all, except by what they saw in the papers.[3]

De Francisci's design sketches fall into two distinct groups: allegorical and literal. The allegorical designs focus on peace-giving rituals such as presenting a sword to a goddess, holding a dove of peace, breaking a sword, or the removal of conflict by a winged creature such as Pegasus or Liberty. The allegorical designs were apparently intended for the coin's obverse although none of them meet the competition's requirement for a "head of Liberty." These may be as much "working out of old ideas" as serious attempts at a dollar obverse design. There was a great deal of "cross-pollination" among several of the New York sculptors. They contended with one another in many of the same design competitions and it is not surprising that some of their designs resemble each other. This is particularly apparent in de Francisci's work and his admiration of Weinman's creative prowess and technique. (Virtually the only personal letters de Francisci kept were those sent to him by Weinman.)

All the literal designs use an eagle as required by the competition and were suitable for use on the reverse. Yet it is evident de Francisci was searching for something different from the usual Saint-Gaudens-style bird. He tried several variations on a flying eagle, including one flying directly toward the viewer. His standing eagles—static, requiring description of their inaction—are simultaneously inoffensive and safe: perfect refuge for Mint bureaucracy's preservation.

DESCRIPTION OF THE OBVERSE

The obverse of Anthony de Francisci's Peace dollar features a large, profile head of the goddess Liberty. Her long hair is combed back and the tresses are coiled into a bun at the crown of her head. Several locks of hair are loose and blown backward by a breeze. On her head is a tiara projecting rays of light—the liberty of thought—into the world. The bust occupies most of the diameter of the coin. Just inside the upper rim is the word LIBERTY, widely spaced and partially overlaid

Obverse portrait prototypes, top left to bottom right: Teresa de Francisci, profile taken for a newspaper feature; *Nike Eirene* medal by Saint-Gaudens; original Peace dollar obverse; cast of final design.

by the light rays. The motto IN GOD WE TRUST is placed horizontally, with Liberty's neck dividing the phrase. Beneath the portrait is the date 1921.

There are no sketches known of the obverse portrait so we don't know what Miss Liberty looked like before the plaster model he entered in the competition. With his wife, Teresa, available as a model, it is likely that de Francisci did his preliminary work directly in clay or plaster. The competition's specifications were clear and the sculptor's vision needed little working out once he had decided on the approach. The sketch model submitted for the competition was based on the sculptor's previous impressions of the goddess and the profile of his wife.

After the competition was awarded, de Francisci used a bust of *Victory* by Augustus Saint-Gaudens (supplied by James Fraser) to help get the portrait the way the commission preferred. The *Victory* bust was similar to Saint-Gaudens's 1907 design for the one-cent coin and the medal *NIKH-EIPHNH* (*Nike-Eirene*—"Victory-Peace") from 1902. The profile portrait of Teresa de Francisci appeared in many newspapers just after the new coin was released. Feature writers promoted Teresa as the model for the new dollar and encouraged their readers to believe the portrait of Liberty was really Teresa's portrait. Since few readers had seen the new coin, and the papers were prohibited from printing photos of it, imagination took over and some stories deteriorated into fiction. De Francisci's final Liberty portrait differs from the prototypes in several important ways: the forehead is more nearly vertical, with a well-defined eye ridge above the nose; the nose is shorter in proportion to the face; the chin is narrower, with a slightly smaller overbite. The sculptor's earliest training was in Italy, where the sculpted portrait tended to be less massive than the French style favored by Saint-Gaudens. Overall, the Peace dollar Liberty is lighter, more youthful, and less formal than its predecessors, although not as bold.

This obverse was paired with the original reverse. Unfortunately, this combination distributed the highest portions of the head opposite the highest portions of the eagle. This arrangement could not have produced well-struck coins while retaining higher-than-normal relief. Contributing to the appearance of weak striking is the lack of fine detail in the hair above the ear. This area is somewhat better defined on the original cast than on the best of the coins, although it is this "massing of the hair" that Fraser stated was preferred. The missing detail is therefore a part of the design concept combined with poorly made reductions and incomplete striking.

DESCRIPTION OF THE ADOPTED REVERSE

Undersecretary Gilbert selected the adopted reverse after public objections to the "broken sword" design forced removal of the emblem from the hub. This design features an eagle resting on a mountaintop, wings folded, looking passively toward the rays of a new dawn of peace; in its talon is an olive branch. Along the upper rim, partially encircling the eagle, are the words UNITED STATES OF AMERICA and just below that, in letters of the same size, is the motto E PLURIBUS UNUM; the value ONE DOLLAR is placed horizontally and split by the eagle's legs and wings; at the lower rim on the mountain is the word PEACE. Rays of light come from behind a distant range of mountains or hills, symbolizing the dawn of a new era of peace. It was important to keep the base of the rays well away from the edge to prevent die cracking in this area. The distant mountains act as a buffer between the rays and the edge; for this reason they were altered several times throughout the design's lifetime. During the last-minute changes in December 1921, Morgan tightened the composition by building a second olive branch from remains of the broken sword.

De Francisci may have included the word *Peace* in his designs because he thought it augmented the concept of the broken sword. However, in at least one letter he stated, "The legends—United States of America, E Pluribus Unum, In God We Trust, date, Liberty, one dollar & peace were required by the federal bill."

Adopted reverse, top left to bottom right: $10 gold coin reverse by Saint-Gaudens; Ptolemaic Egyptian eagle; Verdun medal by de Francisci; $5 gold coin reverse by Bela L. Pratt; reverse as issued.

The adopted reverse was not mechanically compatible with the obverse. The bulk of the eagle's body and wings lies directly opposite the highest portions of the obverse portrait. This inhibited metal flow into the recesses of the dies and produced coins with weakly struck centers. Reducing the relief on new models in 1922 helped, but did not completely solve the problem.

Conceptually, this design is related to Saint-Gaudens's eagle of 1907 and Bela Lyon Pratt's version used on the quarter and half eagle reverses of 1908, but without the fasces, intertwined olive branch, and forward-striding stance. Rays were used on the Saint-Gaudens double eagle (both sides) and appear in several of de Francisci's sketches for the new coin. The Peace dollar eagle's direct ancestor, however, is the sculptor's 1920 Verdun City medal. Both of the Verdun reverse designs include standing eagles holding olive branches in their beaks. The version illustrated above bears a strong resemblance to the adopted reverse bird, although the Verdun variation, with its forward stride, seems both stronger and more protective. (The rooster represents France, to whom the American eagle is bringing peace.) Compared to the alternate reverse, this design lacks movement and emotion. In Daniel Chester French's words, it is a "passive bird."

The Peace dollar's eagle is the last in the 20th-century lineage of confident symbols perched on American coinage since 1907. It was succeeded by a parade of pathetic, bland, and sickly birds of mediocre caliber. The Washington quarter (1932–1998) has an eagle more closely resembling a bat hanging from a vine than a symbol of power. By 1948, the Sinnock-Roberts design honoring Franklin had evaporated the eagle to a barely-noticed "chicken nugget" of uncertain provenance. The Kennedy half dollar's semi-heraldic eagle can be excused due to the expedience of its breeding. However, its successor on the Eisenhower and Anthony dollars may be the worst American eagle ever officially created. The feeble, "pesticide-ravaged" creature attempting a soft landing on Earth's moon is completely free of majesty or character; it makes one wish for Ben Franklin's honest turkey. For the American public, the eagle's redemption began only with the Sacagawea dollar coin of 2000. For numismatists—at least those with well-lined wallets—assorted commemoratives and the gold and platinum bullion pseudo-coins offered an earlier peek at what coinage artists might accomplish for the future. Gentle as it is, de Francisci's peaceful American eagle commands an imperial presence compared to its successors.

COLLECTING
AND GRADING
PEACE DOLLARS

WAYS TO COLLECT PEACE DOLLARS

As with other types of coins, Peace dollars encourage the collector to decide what their collection will contain once it is complete. This is a decision that can be guided by the openings in coin albums, or by using specialized lists, or collectors can invent their own ideal sets of Peace dollars.

For some, the Peace dollar is but one specimen (or sometimes two) in a type set of coins by denomination or era. A type set of silver (and non-silver) dollars can be both impressive and an important historical guide to past and present monetary policy and political issues. By acquiring coins of a specific era, such as the coinage renaissance from 1907 to 1921, an entirely different perspective of America's history can be obtained.

But for many Peace dollar collectors, the first goal is to complete the entire set of 24 coins by date and mint. Fortunately, high-quality, attractive Peace dollars are still available at reasonable prices, making this one of the few "complete sets" that most collectors can realistically aspire to assemble. In circulated condition, a complete set might actually be more difficult to assemble than an Uncirculated set. This is because although most Peace dollars did not actively circulate, those that did enter commerce were often used until heavily worn. A really nice set of matched, undipped, original coins in Extremely Fine condition could be a significant challenge to assemble. While there are several coins that are difficult

PEACE TYPE SILVER DOLLAR
COLLECTION STARTING 1921

1921 1 MILLION	1922 51.7 MILLION	1922-D 15.1 MILLION	1922-S 17.5 MILLION	1923 30.8 MILLION
1923-D 6.8 MILLION	1923-S 19 MILLION	1924 11.8 MILLION	1924-S 1.7 MILLION	1925 10.2 MILLION
1925-S 1.6 MILLION	1926 1.9 MILLION	1926-D 2.3 MILLION	1926-S 7 MILLION	1927 848 THOUSAND
1927-D 1.2 MILLION	1927-S 866 THOUSAND	1928 360.6 THOUSAND	1928-S 1.6 MILLION	1934 954 THOUSAND
1934-D 1.6 MILLION	1934-S 1 MILLION	1935 1.6 MILLION	1935-S 2 MILLION	

Collector board for Peace dollars produced in 1939 by Whitman Publishing Co. The board has an opening for each coin issued plus an extra opening to show the reverse design. Approximate mintage is shown below each opening.

to find in high grades, there are no "show stoppers" equivalent to 1916 Standing Liberty quarters or 1893-S Morgan dollars. (The Proof coins are extremely rare and might be the focus of wealthy collectors, but most will settle for a nice set of circulation-strike Peace dollars.)

The first collector albums or boards for Peace dollars were produced by Whitman Publishing Company in 1939. Later, Whitman and other companies introduced folder-type albums and more expensive albums with clear slides covering both sides of the coins. Albums and folders are available for complete date-mint sets and some versions of type sets; however, storing and displaying more specialized collections is up to the ingenuity of the hobbyist.

A couple of Peace dollars are also part of any silver type set, whether it is limited to 20th-century issues or extends backing to the 19th and 18th centuries. With 1921 dollars being the only high-relief coin that is readily available to collectors of average means, this can be an eye-catching example to include in any type set.

In recent years, the growth of interest in silver-dollar die varieties has given collectors new aspects of the hobby to explore. Organizations such as VAMWorld.com and the Society of Silver Dollar Collectors provide resources for research and a place where collectors can share their newest discoveries. Popular variety guides (including *The Comprehensive Catalog and Encyclopedia of Morgan & Peace Dollars*, by Leroy C. Van Allen and A. George Mallis; the *Cherrypickers' Guide to Rare Die Varieties*, by J.T. Stanton and Bill Fivaz; and *The Official Guide to the Top 50 Peace Dollar Varieties*, by Jeff Oxman and David Close) have attracted a rapidly growing body of collectors who are seeking Peace dollars by die varieties. As with other coins, the collector who is patient and looks for the best quality and condition for his or her investment will likely be rewarded with the greatest personal, and later financial, satisfaction.

Another important aspect of collecting Peace dollars is the decision whether to collect raw or certified coins. At present, nearly all of the highest-quality specimens have been certified by one of several third-party authentication and grading companies. However, there is always the chance that a quality coin will turn up that has been hidden away, and there could still be unknown hoards of coins in existence that could produce some new gems to the delight of collectors. If you decide to acquire raw coins, however, there are some things to look out for. First, condition: it can be difficult to detect lightly circulated coins that are being sold at "discounted" prices as Uncirculated. Second, authenticity: unfortunately, there are unscrupulous people in the hobby who attempt to modify coins (altering the date on a common 1923 coin to 1928, for example) so they can be sold as scarcer varieties for more money. Third, surface manipulation: coins are also being dipped and/or artificially toned to make them look better to inexperienced collectors. Purchasing a certified coin does not always guarantee that a coin hasn't been dipped or artificially toned, but it does provide some level of assurance that the coin is genuine and that its stated grade is reasonably accurate. For certified coins, it is widely accepted by most collectors that PCGS and NGC provide the most consistent grading of Peace dollars, and for this reason the population figures stated in chapter 9 use data supplied by both companies. This is not to say that other companies do not grade properly, but in the case of Peace dollars, PCGS and NGC have graded the majority of certified coins anyway.

Weakly struck coins plague much of the Peace dollar series, particularly coins produced at the San Francisco Mint. A poorly struck Peace dollar is most evident in weak or missing hair detail over Liberty's ear on the obverse, and lack of feather detail on the eagle. A fully struck, lustrous Peace dollar, on the other hand, can be a thing of wondrous beauty!

Peace dollars were minted at three different United States Mints: Philadelphia, Denver, and San Francisco. Coins from Philadelphia do not have a mintmark, while those from Denver and San Francisco carry a very small "D" or "S," respectively, on the reverse of the coin just under the ONE, at approximately the 8:00 position.

Assembling a set in Uncirculated (or Mint State) grades is not difficult, but a set in MS-65 and higher is a huge challenge due to the lack of Gem specimens in some of the San Francisco issues, particularly the 1924-S, 1925-S, 1928-S, and 1934-S. The 1934-S is widely considered the key to the series, even though 1925-S and 1928-S are rarer in MS-65. The 1921 issue, for its high-relief design, and the 1928-P, for its low mintage, are other keys in the series that are widely sought.

PEACE DOLLAR VALUES

The value of a Peace dollar, like other silver coins, depends on three factors: the bullion value of silver, numismatic premium, and grading-authentication cost.

Bullion Value

Each uncirculated standard silver dollar, including all Peace dollars, contains 0.77344 troy ounces of pure silver, with the balance of the coin made up of copper (used as alloy to improve durability). Circulated silver dollars have lost some of their silver content due to wear and will have somewhat less precious metal. The price of silver is determined by commodity market trading. These markets provide a means for industrial and speculative buyers and sellers to agree on prices and exchange commodities such as silver, pork bellies (used to make bacon), corn, soy beans, gold, oil, and many others. Potential buyers and sellers offer commodities and the price fluctuates during the trading day as agreements are made. Generally, if there are more sellers of silver than buyers, the price will decline until someone finds it attractive, and they will offer to buy at that price. Likewise, if there are more buyers and demand increases, sellers will hold out for higher prices.

During the day, prices are published as the "spot" price for silver. At the end of the trading day, a final or "close" price is published. The bullion value of a silver dollar is calculated by multiplying the spot or close price times the weight of pure silver. If silver closed at $25.00 per ounce, the value of bullion in a silver dollar would be equal to $25.00 times 0.77344 ounces, or $19.34. Bullion dealers usually pay about five percent less to cover their expenses and profit. It is helpful to know the approximate bullion value of a coin so a collector can determine if a seller is asking too much for common-date pieces.

Numismatic Premium

In addition to the bullion, collectors place a numismatic value on coins. This is simply the amount collectors are willing to pay (or a dealer wants to charge) for the "collectability" of a coin. Very common dates of Peace dollars, such as 1922 or 1923, might sell for a few dollars over bullion value except for extremely well-preserved examples or popular varieties. Prices for these coins will fluctuate considerably as the price of silver changes. Less-common dates, such as 1921 or 1928-P, might have numismatic premiums many times the bullion value, to the point where the silver component of the price is negligible.

Numismatic premium is essentially created by supply and demand. A commonly available coin with low demand from collectors will have a low price. If demand should suddenly increase, sellers will charge more for their coins and the price will increase. A very scarce coin with limited collector interest may sell for little more than a common date if there is little demand for it.

One of the features of numismatic cycles is the promotion and resulting price increase of particular date/mintmark or variety combinations. Owners of large quantities of a particular variety promote it as a rare or very scarce coin that is currently underpriced. The publicity increases demand and sellers hold out for higher prices. Eventually, the pool of buyers is exhausted, and demand declines along with prices. Buyers at the increased price are stuck with coins that can be sold only at a large discount. The saga of the 1950-D nickel, described in Q. David Bowers's *Expert's Guide to Collecting and Investing in Rare Coins* and elsewhere, is a classic tale of demand-driven sales.

Authentication and Grading Premium

When independent authentication and grading of coins became popular in the 1980s, it added another factor to the price of a coin. When bullion and numismatic value were the only factors, collectors could easily determine if they were overpaying or underpaying for a coin. Now, however, owners of independently graded coins (housed in plastic holders commonly called "slabs") expect to recover not only the bullion and numismatic value, but also the money spent to have a coin certified as authentic and independently graded. As with most human activities, many companies provide such services and there is a concomitant range of costs associated with "slabbing" a coin.

A practical example may help in understanding the components of a Peace dollar's value. An ordinary, somewhat bagmarked 1922-P dollar in Uncirculated condition will have a bullion value of $19.34 when silver is at $25.00 per ounce. When found in a dealer's stock book or 2x2-inch holder box, the coin might be priced at $45.00. The same 1922-P coin housed in a major grading company's plastic slab and graded MS-62 might be priced at $55.00.

Source	Cost to Collector	Item Cost	Added Cost
Raw coin	$19.34 + 5%	$19.34	Bullion value
Dealer's 2x2 holder	$45.00	$25.66	Added numismatic value
Grading service slab	$55.00	$10.00	Added certification cost

It should be evident that the numismatic premium might be justified by supply and demand—and the convenience of buying only one example and not a roll of 20 coins as the dealer might have done. However, paying an additional $10 does not improve the coin or add much value to it. For common-date pieces, such services offer little real value unless there is a special purpose for having the coin in a slab.

This changes if the collector is acquiring scarce or rare Peace dollars or ones that are in exceptionally nice Uncirculated condition, such as MS-65 to MS-70. Having a coin independently evaluated (by a third party other than buyer or seller) provides assurance that it is not counterfeit or altered. Here, the difference of a single grading point can also mean hundreds of dollars in the asking price.

QUALITY OF STRIKE

Several factors affect the ability of a coinage press to bring up the full design from the working dies. The amount of pressure applied is of primary importance, and for Peace dollars this was approximately 100 tons per square inch, although sources vary from 80 tons to 120 tons. The disparity may have more to do with inconsistent equipment calibration than actual differences in pressure.

A second but much overlooked factor is the hardness of the planchets on which the design is struck. When silver alloy is correctly softened, or "annealed," it will take a good impression from the dies at the minimum pressure necessary for a fully struck coin. This results in better-looking coins and longer die life, with less need to remove and repair or resurface dies. If, however, the planchets are too hard, the extra pressure necessary to bring up the full design will result in early die failure and incompletely struck coins.

GRADING PEACE DOLLARS

Grading Peace dollars follows the rules for most other coins; however, Peace dollars are most often downgraded due to weak strikes, as well as marks on Miss Liberty's cheek and neck. Certain issues also have flat luster, which is most evident in the fields. Natural toning will not affect the grade, unless the luster is adversely affected. Intentional design softness and weakly struck coins combine to make grading Peace dollars something of a challenge.

The following grading standards are excerpted with permission from *Grading Coins by Photographs*, second edition (Bowers, 2012).

Circulation Strikes

MINT STATE (MS-60 TO 70)

Illustrated coin: 1923. MS-65.

Obverse. At MS-60, some abrasion and contact marks are evident, most noticeably on the cheek and on the hair to the right of the face and forehead. Luster is present, but may be dull or lifeless. At MS-63, contact marks are extensive but not distracting. Abrasion still is evident, but less than at lower levels. MS-64 coins are slightly finer. Some Peace dollars have whitish "milk spots" in the field; while these are not caused by handling, but seem to have been from liquid at the mint or in storage, coins with these spots are rarely graded higher than MS-63 or 64. An MS-65 coin may have minor abrasion, but contact marks are so minute as to require magnification. Luster should be full and rich on earlier issues, and either frosty or satiny on later issues, depending on the date and mint.

Reverse. At MS-60 some abrasion and contact marks are evident, most noticeably on the eagle's shoulder and nearby. Otherwise, comments apply as for the obverse.

ABOUT UNCIRCULATED (AU-50, 53, 55, 58)

Illustrated coin: 1934. AU-50.

Obverse. Light wear is seen on the cheek and the highest-relief areas of the hair. The neck truncation edge also shows wear. At AU-58, the luster is extensive, but incomplete. At AU-50 and 53, luster is less but still present.

Reverse. Wear is evident on the eagle's shoulder and back. Otherwise, comments apply as for the obverse.

EXTREMELY FINE (EF-40, 45)

Illustrated coin: 1928. EF-40.

Obverse. Further wear is seen on the highest-relief areas of the hair, with many strands now blended together. Some luster can usually be seen in protected areas on many coins, but is not needed to define the EF-40 and 45 grades.

Reverse. Further wear is seen on the eagle, and the upper 60% of the feathers have most detail gone, except for the delineation of the edges of rows of feathers. PEACE shows light wear.

VERY FINE (VF-20, 30)

Illustrated coin: 1934-D. VF-30.

Obverse. More wear shows on the hair, with more tiny strands now blended into heavy strands.

Reverse. Further wear has resulted in very little feather detail except on the neck and tail. The rock shows wear. PEACE is slightly weak.

FINE (F-12, 15)

Illustrated coin: 1921. F-12.

Obverse. Most of the hair is worn flat, with thick strands blended together, interrupted by fewer divisions than on higher grades. The rim is full.

Reverse. Fewer feather details show. Most of the eagle, except for the tail feathers and some traces of feathers at the neck, is in outline only. The rays between the left side of the eagle and PEACE are weak and some details are worn away.

Proofs
PF-60 TO 70

Illustrated coin: 1921. Satin Proof.

Some Sandblast Proofs were made in 1921 and a limited issue in 1922 in *high relief*. These are rare today. Seemingly, a few Satin Proofs were also made in 1921. Sandblast Proofs of 1922 have a peculiar whitish surface in most instances, sometimes interrupted by small dark flecks or spots. There are a number of impostors among certified "Proofs."

Obverse and Reverse. Proofs of both types usually display very few handling marks or defects. To qualify as Satin PF-65 or Sandblast PF-65 or finer, contact marks must be microscopic.

7

ERRORS, HOARDS, COUNTERSTRIKES, AND ARTIST'S SAMPLES

ERRORS

An error on any coin as large as the Peace dollar is bound to be spectacular—a few such errors, in fact, are ranked in *100 Greatest U.S. Error Coins* (Bowers, Camire, and Weinberg, 2010). Like all coins, Peace dollars were subject to damage and misstriking during production. Yet coins showing significant errors are extremely difficult to locate. Most of this scarcity is the result of careful inspection at the mints before coins were counted and bagged.

After silver dollars were struck, they fell into a bin in the pressroom. The bins of coins were then dumped on a reviewing table that included a conveyor belt. As the coins moved along the reviewing table, women employees, called "selectors," removed any coins that were improperly struck. The same highly experienced women also inspected and weighed gold coins, rarely missing a defective piece. By the time the conveyor dumped its contents into another bin destined for the counting room, approximately half a percent of the minted Peace dollars had been removed due to defects.

The few error coins that made their way into bags represent the less obvious categories: slight end-of-strip, cracked planchets; blank planchets; and limited off-center strikes. The photos below illustrate some of the best Peace dollar errors presently known. Errors like these can bring substantial prices, particularly when authenticated by PCGS or NGC.

Very weakly struck set-up piece, approximately 30 percent off center. A faint outline of Liberty, with the portrait shifted high on the planchet, is visible.

Weakly struck set-up piece with normal centering. Here, the extreme peripheral devices—including the S mintmark and enough of the date to determine it was struck from a 1922 die—are beginning to show, but there is almost no trace of the main devices. The wedge-shaped marks on this and the previous piece were formed by the junction of the back of Liberty's neck and hair. This was the highest point on the low-relief Peace dollar obverse die (lowest point of the design on the struck coin).

The finest known off-center Peace dollar is this 1922-S specimen struck 15 percent off-center and graded MS-65 by PCGS. An off-center strike occurs when the planchet is not fully in the coining chamber when the dies come together. Examples can have partial reeding or blank edges, depending on striking circumstances. This type of error should have been obvious to Mint inspectors and removed before coins were counted and bagged.

Defective and damaged planchets are somewhat more readily available than other dollar-coin errors, although all are quite rare. This spectacular 1922-P was struck on a cracked planchet that might also have come from the end of a strip of silver alloy. This crack extends nearly half the coin's diameter.

Another cracked planchet—this one is on a 1922-S. The crack is somewhat shorter, about a quarter of the coin's diameter. The close-up view (of the edge of a 1922-P dollar) clearly shows a crack running through the thickness of the coin. Note also the slight distortion of the coin's profile.

Edge clips are also among the more readily available Peace-dollar errors. On this example, a slight but noticeable edge clip (lower left on obverse; upper left, reverse) interrupts the rim on a 1922-S dollar. More noticeable examples probably occurred during production but were removed by sharp-eyed selectors who inspected silver dollars just after minting.

Details of 1922 clipped planchet, obverse and edge.

This 1922-P coin was struck on a planchet cut from the end of a coinage strip. The strip was not full thickness at the end, producing a planchet that was somewhat thinner than normal on one side. This resulted in insufficient metal to fill the dies and a design that seems to face toward the edge of the coin.

These photos show the obverse, reverse, and edge of a very rare partial-collar piece. The planchet was not completely seated in the collar at the time the coin was struck. Thus, only a part of the edge is reeded; the part outside the collar is plain. Notice the misshapen rim on both sides. The coin is slightly larger than normal and not perfectly round.

The 1922-S dollar shown here bears the effects of both an edge clip and a partial collar. Uneven pressure caused asymmetrical distortion of the coin.

Normally, only planchets of the correct size enter the coining press. But occasionally a planchet (or possibly an already-struck coin) of a smaller diameter gets mixed with normal planchets in the press's feeding mechanism. The result is a spectacular error with the design struck on a planchet far too small for it. The example here was struck on a quarter-dollar planchet of correct weight. Errors such as this should have been easily spotted by inspectors and it is amazing that this one slipped through.

This 1923-S dollar was struck on a silver-alloy planchet whose metal was not fully fused. Called a "lamination error," its metal lies in two or more layers that are only partially attached to the rest of the coin. In some instances, the layers remain attached to the coin; in others they fall off, leaving a rough depression and a gap in the design. This could occur due to poorly mixing the copper and silver in the metal strip from which the planchet was cut, or to mechanical stress from rolling improperly softened metal.

Lamination errors such as this are common on silver-copper-manganese alloy five-cent pieces made during World War II, but are rarely found on large, .900 fine silver coins such as Peace dollars.

On the left is a 1921 coin struck on a planchet that was outside the normal, reeded-edge collar. Called a "broadstrike" by collectors, this very rare error is typified by weak, distorted lettering and features. This image was made so that the plain edge (the annulus, or ring, surrounding the coin) is also visible. On the right is a 1925-P dollar that was struck through a fragment of thick cloth or similar material. This might have been a piece of canvas bag or part of a work-man's glove. The tremendous pressure generated during striking impresses some of the material's texture into the coinage metal, while simultaneously distorting the design.

SILVER DOLLAR HOARDS

Unlike coin collections, which have some sort of overriding organization, a hoard is a more-or-less random accumulation of coins. Silver-dollar hoards typically consist of large numbers of bags of dollars acquired from time to time with little regard to date, mintmark, or condition. With most silver dollars not actively circulating, the preponderance of silver-dollar hoards consisted of Uncirculated coins.

The original owners of these hoards usually were mistrustful of banks or the government, or had some personal or political compulsion to accumulate large quantities of otherwise readily available coins. Unlike gold coins, whose metal had substantial value, silver dollars commonly contained less silver than indicated by their face value. Thus, if the hoarder was "investing" in silver, he would have done better to buy pure metal on a commercial market than to save coins. Although this might be a rational approach, it is not what appealed to Ted Binion or LaVerne Redfield when they filled their private stashes with bags of silver dollars.

Hoards of dollars are not as commonly encountered as gold-coin hoards. This is possibly because the coins did not actively circulate or their physical bulk made hiding them from prying eyes much more difficult. While nearly all silver-dollar hoards included some Peace dollars, none are known to have been composed exclusively of this design.

The three largest and best-known silver-dollar hoards—Redfield, Binion, and GSA—are discussed in the following pages. Although each consisted primarily of Morgan-type dollars, Peace dollars were also included. Other hoards, such as the Continental-Illinois Bank hoard, included few, if any, Peace dollars.

Hoard coins that remain in their original distribution packaging tend to be worth more to collectors for their historical and human-interest stories than are coins that have been removed.

LaVere Redfield Hoard

LaVere Redfield acquired significant wealth through brilliant investing in oil and other stocks subsequent to the stock-market crash in 1929. He was known to be a bit eccentric and did not trust the government—and was especially mistrustful of banks. It is believed that because of this skepticism he moved to Reno, Nevada, with the goal of being close to banks and casinos that dealt in large numbers of silver dollars. He traveled around Nevada as if he were a pauper, wearing old, torn clothes and driving a beat-up pickup truck. Few knew of his wealth until after his death, in 1974, and the subsequent discovery of the silver dollars.

Redfield amassed a fortune in silver dollars, at one time holding more than 600,000 of them. A robbery at his home resulted in the loss of approximately 100,000 pieces (100 bags). After his death, more than 400 bags (400,000 coins) of silver dollars were discovered when the Treasury Department seized his house. The bags had been carefully hidden behind a false wall, probably after the earlier robbery.

Redfield also stored food in the same area and, at one point, some cans of peaches had burst and sprayed juice over the coins. Some of this is visible on the coins that were encapsulated, showing up as small spots.

Many high-quality Peace dollars were a part of his hoard, and in some cases pushed previously very rare issues, such as 1926 coins from San Francisco, back to the middle of the rarity scale. Bags of 1925-S and 1928-S coins were found as well, although in lesser quantities than the 1926-S. There were also a few bags of 1934-S dollars, making them only slightly more common. In addition to that, a few bags of high-quality common dates were found.

The entire hoard was purchased by Steve Markoff in early 1976 for $7.3 million. Markoff employed a clever marketing strategy to slowly release the coins into the market so as not to flood populations of some of the higher-quantity issues. As a result, dispersion of the coins actually resulted in a stimulation of the market.

Examples of packaging for Redfield-hoard coins. Left, plastic case with black insert (not from Paramount). Only Redfield-hoard coins have the name "Redfield" on the insert. Right, a Redfield coin graded and encapsulated by NGC. Note the "Redfield" name on the label.

Most of the coins were housed in holders measuring 3 x 3-1/2 inches; these holders had a red insert that was labeled "Paramount International Coin Corporation" and included the Redfield name. These also read "Mint State 65," although the coin might not meet that standard today. Holders with a black insert are the same but say "Mint State 60." Many of the Paramount Redfield coins have since been graded and encapsulated by NGC, PCGS, and ANACS, with a notation on the holder attributing them to the Redfield collection. Redfield holders distributed by Paramount (with the "Paramount" name on the holder) include the following:

- Black holder, no grade, "Redfield Collection"
- Black holder, MS-60, "Redfield Collection"
- Red holder, MS-65, "Redfield Collection"
- Green holder, MS-65 Plus, "Redfield Collection"

Note that Paramount used the same holders, but without "Redfield" on them, for other silver dollars.

Redfield coins in original, intact holders are considered somewhat more desirable than those in secondary packaging; however, they are often priced lower due to the condition of the coins. Blanchard & Company also put coins into plastic slabs labeled "Redfield" (see below).

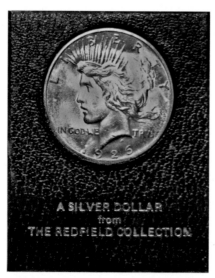 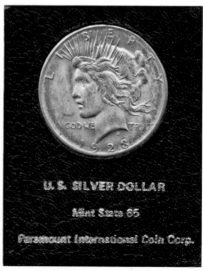

Redfield Peace dollar in a plastic holder from Blanchard & Company and a coin in a non-Redfield holder from Paramount. Holders without the Redfield name were from Paramount's ordinary inventory and bring little premium.

Ted Binion Hoard

The Binion family owned the Horseshoe Casino in Las Vegas. The founder's son, Ted Binion, had a strong belief that paper money was not a reliable source of wealth and therefore chose to collect silver dollars that circulated through his casino. During the 1950s and 1960s he accumulated more than 100,000 Morgan and Peace silver dollars. He stored them in a freezer under the casino before building a more secure vault hidden underground in the desert. The builder of the vault was accused of Binion's death in 2000 and was discovered attempting to transfer the coins from the vault a few days after the homicide.

Binion's hoard was obtained by Goldline International for the sum of more than $3 million. The firm then employed NGC to grade, certify, and encapsulate the coins. These entered the market for the first time several years ago, and are housed in special holders denoting that they came from the Binion collection.

Approximately half of the coins are Peace dollars, and to date only the 1922 and 1923 issues from Philadelphia are available for purchase. Some are very high-quality coins, graded as high as MS-67. They are slowly being introduced into the market in an attempt to keep prices stable and at their current levels, and it is not known what other issues may become available in the future as the dispersal continues.

A 1922 dollar from the Ted Binion hoard.

General Services Administration (GSA) Hoard

As open-market silver prices rose during the early 1960s, collectors and speculators began withdrawing large quantities of silver dollars from Treasury vaults. By March 26, 1964, the Treasury's inventory was down to approximately three million coins, most of which had been struck at the Carson City Mint during the 1880s. To prevent inequitable distribution of these pieces to speculators, Treasury secretary C. Douglas Dillon suspended redemption of silver dollars for paper currency, and later transferred the coins to the GSA for public sale.

Over the next years, GSA held a series of minimum-bid public auctions for the coins. Pieces were sold individually, with limits on maximum ordering quantity. Although most of the three million coins were Morgan-design pieces from the Carson City Mint, several thousand Peace dollars of mixed dates were included. These were sold in the "mixed circulated" and "mixed uncirculated" categories for $3 each. The coins were packaged in soft plastic holders that also included a gray plastic token. The pliable holder was contained in a dark blue envelope. The example illustrated was later independently graded by NGC, which accounts for the imprinted band at the top.

A 1922-P dollar from the GSA hoard in its original flexible plastic packaging.

COUNTERSTRIKES

A counterstrike is made by selecting a Peace dollar (or other coin) as the host, then using new dies to impress a commercial, political, or private message on the coin. Usually, this results in damage to the host coin due to flattening of the design opposite the counterstrike. Peace dollars were popular as host coins because of their ready availability and low cost compared to other dollar-size coins.

In October 1978, numismatist and researcher Mel Wacks designed a special counterstamp for Peace dollars to commemorate the Camp David Peace Accord. The idea for a counterstamped coin occurred to him while he was watching television news coverage of the event. He quickly sketched out a design and sent it to a California company along with instructions and a quantity of Peace dollars, this being the obvious choice for a host coin. Dies approximately the size of a nickel were made and a small quantity of incuse test strikes was produced. (All design elements on the counterstamp die were raised.)

Unfortunately, none of the tests were successful. Wacks then contacted Adam Cool in New Jersey, who was able to cut new dies and successfully stamp 1,000 Peace dollars with the commemorative design in relief. To avoid excessive flattening of the obverse, the coins were apparently placed on a thick sheet of leather or possibly lead during application of the counterstrike. Although these uniface counterstamps are most often seen on the reverse of Philadelphia Mint coins dated 1922 and 1923, Wacks provided original rolls of dollars without regard to date.

The Camp David commemoratives were announced in a press release. Resulting publicity, particularly a mention in the *New York Times*, produced stacks of orders culminating in a complete sellout. Specimens can be found in original cardboard frames and in third-party grading holders. These are the most commonly found counterstamps of a single design.

Wacks sent examples of his personal commemorative to President Jimmy Carter ("It will be placed in the National Archives"), President Anwar Sadat ("Highly appreciating your noble sentiments"), and Prime Minister Menachem Begin ("Your kind gesture is deeply appreciated").

Although this was Mel Wacks's only counterstamp on a Peace dollar, others imitated his initiative. A 1993 counterstamp highlighted yet

Prototype with an incuse design from a California company. Notice the circular cutting marks, possibly done in an attempt to produce a smoother area for the counterstrike. Right: the adopted design on a Kennedy half dollar using cancelled dies by Adam Cool in New Jersey.

another "peace accord." This design is less frequently encountered than the earlier one. In 1995, Continental Coin Company produced examples marking the assassination of Israeli prime minister Yitzhak Rabin.

Although those illustrated here might be among the most interesting Peace dollar counterstamps, other types exist. These are more prosaic, often being little more than dates, or personal names punched into the coin's surface. In most instances, we do not know the purpose or significance attached to these items by their originators.

Counterstamped Peace dollar produced by Mel Wacks to commemorate the Camp David Peace Summit of 1978, and a coin in its original holder.

Peace dollars were also used as the host coin for other private commemoratives. The examples above commemorate a 1993 peace accord and memorialize the assassination of Israeli prime minister Yitzhak Rabin in 1995.

ANTHONY DE FRANCISCI'S DISPLAY SAMPLES

In 1966, Maria Teresa Cafarelli de Francisci, widow of sculptor Anthony de Francisci, donated her husband's papers, account books, photos, and medals to the Smithsonian Institution in Washington, D.C. The documents and photos were transferred to the Smithsonian Archives of American Art, which has an extensive collection of original material by and about American artists. The medals, including a few coins, were placed in the Smithsonian American Art Museum collection. Additional material was donated by the sculptor's daughter Gilda de Francisci Slade. Together, these donations constitute the largest assembly of de Francisci's work in any museum or private collection.

Two 1921 Peace dollars donated to the Smithsonian American Art Museum by Teresa de Francisci in 1966. Top, #1966.51.80 obverse and reverse; bottom, #1966.51.81 obverse and reverse. Note the screw post soldered to one side of each coin. These pieces were attached to the sculptor's portable medal and bas-relief display board. These photos have been enhanced to bring out detail and suppress their black toning. The ink accession numbers written on the coins were removed by conservation staff after these photos were taken.

Anthony de Francisci evidently kept few of the medals he designed. The medallic material Teresa and her daughter donated consisted almost entirely of single-sided bronze casts and electrotypes with a threaded rod soldered on the back. This allowed the pieces to be attached to a display board and taken on visits to prospective clients. These artist's samples were normally gold- or silver-plated and finished so the sample looked like the real thing. Among these display items are two 1921 Peace dollars. Each of the Peace dollars is defaced by having a screw soldered to the coin: reverse on one piece, obverse on the other. This allowed both sides of the design to be displayed.

Since one side of each coin always faced outward on the display, that side quickly tarnished in the New York City air. It appears that de Francisci attempted to keep the dollars shiny by cleaning them with abrasive silver polish. The exposed surfaces of both coins are dull, worn, and scratched. The back sides, where the screw is attached, were protected from further damage and appear to be in original condition. Although both coins are nearly black from sulfur contamination, the protected sides show remarkable sharpness and detail.

Examination of the two protected sides suggest that these very well made specimens were likely part of the original group of 50 sent to de Francisci on January 3, 1922, by Mint engraver George Morgan. The coins are not Proofs and do not have the detail and sharpness of any of the known 1921 Proofs. They also lack the diagnostic characteristics shared by Proofs. However, they have exceptional satin surfaces and crisp detail consistent with coins made at correct pressure from new dies. Had they not been defaced, these two coins might have been among the very finest circulation strikes of this coin produced by the U.S. Mint.

The medallic work of Anthony de Francisci joins other items from the Smithsonian American Art Museum's medal collection on public display in Washington, D.C. These include works by Adolph A. Weinman and Augustus Saint-Gaudens, Paul Manship's Irish coinage designs, and others of interest to numismatists. Museum curators have created an open storage system that allows materials to be accessible for research as well as general viewing by visitors. A large database was also created that provides accurate, meaningful descriptions of the medals and other medallic objects.[1]

OVERSTRIKES

In 1996, several special commemorative items were produced for the 50th anniversary of the *Guide Book of United States Coins* (the hobby's famed "Red Book"). Among these items were 50 three-medal anniversary sets that, although minted, were never distributed. Each set contained one 1-ounce silver round, one overstruck silver dollar (Morgan or Peace), and one gold-plated round. The three were housed in a red display card stamped in gold with the set number.

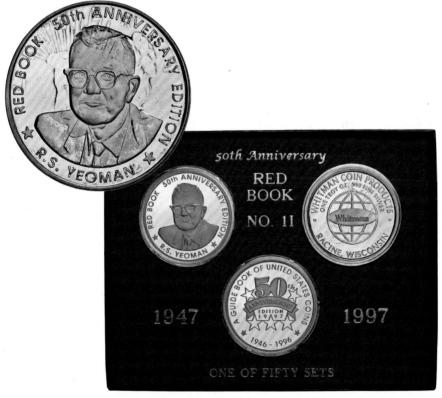

An overstruck Peace dollar commemorating the 50th anniversary of the *Guide Book of United States Coins*. On the obverse, the ghostly outline of Liberty is visible surrounding a portrait of author R.S. Yeoman; on the reverse, the eagle is visible behind the Whitman logo.

PROOFS, PATTERNS, AND TRIAL PIECES

Identification of Proof, pattern, and trial pieces of the Peace dollar design has been a slow process. As noted earlier in this book, the Treasury Department and sculptor suppressed information about difficulties with the coin's original reverse design. The same parties also avoided full disclosure of the pattern and trial pieces made as part of the experiments leading to the final low-relief circulation design of 1922. The following sections identify Proof, pattern, and trial pieces, the diagnostic points relevant to each, and design elements that connect them with circulating coins and with one another.

DESIGN VARIETIES, 1921–1922

As used in this discussion, the term *variety* refers to differences in detail within the same basic design. The term *version* refers to differences created primarily by the method of manufacture. Therefore, Proof and circulation issues of 1921 are different versions of the same design variety.

The following 10 versions of the 1921 and 1922 Peace dollar are evident.

Date	Description	Comments
1921	High relief, circulation	Usually weakly struck, with incomplete hair detail in central obverse.
1921	High relief, Sandblast Proof	Similar to the high-relief circulation design but much sharper strike.
1921	High relief, Satin Proof	Similar to the high-relief circulation design but much sharper strike.

Date	Description	Comments
1922	High relief, circulation	Combines 1922 high-relief obverse with 1921 reverse.
1922	High relief, Sandblast Proof	Similar to the 1921 Sandblast Proof.
1922	High relief, Satin Proof (?)	Similar to the 1921 Sandblast Proof (existence questionable).
1922	Medium relief, circulation	Initial 1922 experimental design. Most melted; one known.
1922	Low relief, trial strikes	Second 1922 circulation design. Used for normal production.
1922	Low relief, Sandblast Proof	Similar in design to the second 1922 circulation design. Surface similar to 1921 Sandblast Proof.
1922	Low relief, Satin Proof	Similar in design to the second 1922 circulation design. Surface similar to 1921 Satin Proof. Sold to Ambrose Swasey, member of the 1922 Assay Commission, on March 1, 1922, by the Mint.
1922	Low relief, circulation	Third 1922 circulation design. Used for normal production.

Observations

1921—PROOF AND CIRCULATION (ALL HIGH RELIEF)

Obverse. *Circulation strikes:* Letters and numerals well defined and slightly rounded on upper surface (not flat). Coronet rays have rounded tips and there is a short ray between rays 4 and 5. Faint internal structure visible on rays 2 and 6. In the motto, the letter V is tall with a pointed base. *Proofs:* Letters and numbers well defined, rounded but nearly flat on upper surface; balance is the same as the circulation coins.

The obverse of the coins examined all had parallel tool marks in the truncation of the neck. These marks are obvious on the Proofs and partially obliterated on the circulation strikes. These are on the original cast delivered to the Philadelphia Mint.

Satin Proofs show multiple die scratches and whorls not evident on sandblasted specimens. The same dies were also used to strike circulation pieces and examples include identical die scratches.

Reverse. The Proof and circulation coins share a defect in the two long rays to the right of the eagle. The three detail images here are from the circulation, Sandblast Proof, and Satin Proof coins. All three coins show identical damage to the last ray on the right, and both Proof coins show damage to the second long ray. The defect on the circulation coin is not as obvious.

Ray damage on 1921 high-relief circulation-strike and Proof coins. Left to right: details of circulation, Sandblast Proof, and Satin Proof coins.

The 1921 reverses also have four rays below the word ONE to the left of the eagle, and seven rays between the eagle's tail and the rock. Most rays have rounded tips. The last A in AMERICA has a pointed top, while the other A has a flat, angled top.

1922—High-Relief Circulation (Discovered in 2007)

Obverse. The same obverse was used on the 1922 high-relief Proofs, discussed shortly.

Reverse. This is the same reverse as used for 1921 production. Only one example is known and this piece was likely one that escaped from the short production run identified by Robert W. Julian. The variety was identified by David W. Lange in 2007.

1922—High-Relief Proof

Obverse. The overall style is consistent with the 1921 original, although it incorporates several improvements, including sharper modeling of the letters and date. This revised design has the point of the neck overlaying part of the 9 in the date. This is similar to the 1922 medium-relief variety.

Reverse. The overall style is consistent with the original and incorporates noticeable improvement to the sharpness and consistency of lettering. This revised model has ray *D* above ONE lengthened, a ray added below the eagle's tail (producing eight rays between the tail and the rock—one more than on the 1921 models), a tiny cut in the eagle's wing at ray *C*, and a defect in the field between the olive branch and the eagle's leg slightly above the right talon.

These coins and 1922 medium-relief coins, discussed later, are the only ones that share the obverse and reverse diagnostic points just mentioned. Even though there are extensive differences, the common diagnostic points suggest a common origin for the two varieties.

1922—Experimental Medium Relief (Discovered in 2001)

Overall impression is of a sharper, more detailed design, yet not as subtle and expressive as the 1921 design. This medium-relief obverse design has a sloppy, rushed look to it that is incompatible with de Francisci's style.

Some have suggested that the discovery coin is simply a 1922 Proof that was spent and damaged while in circulation, or deliberately re-tooled. The image below, a detail of the date, overlays the 1922 experimental coin (medium gray) with the 1922 high-relief Proof. Notice that the position of the date relative to the rim differs; also note the angled base on the 1. There are many other major differences in the positions of the elements that refute any claim that this coin is merely a circulated Proof.

Superimposing an image of the 1922 experimental-relief Peace dollar over an image of a 1922 high-relief Proof demonstrates that the former is not merely a worn version of the latter.

Obverse. This obverse is possibly based on the high-relief 1922 Sandblast Proof but with considerable reworking; it may have been made from a completely new hub. The relief of the portrait has been reduced and its outline recut. Lettering is lower in relief and flattened. Many details were added or strengthened in the hair, and the date was completely reworked. In most cases, the reworking is to the detriment of the design. The treatment of Liberty's nose, mouth, and chin is awkward, and the date is particularly sloppy, with numerals crooked and clumsily sculpted. The S in TRVST is narrow and distorted. This reduced-relief version retains the peculiarity of having the point of the neck overlie part of the 9, although it appears to have been recut. This is the only direct connection between the Proof and medium-relief obverses, and is consistent with Fraser's January 29 comments.

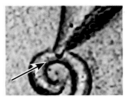 

Left: detail of a 1922 high-relief Proof, where the point of the bust lies over the top of the 9. Right: the same area on the 1922 experimental-relief obverse.

Reverse. Visible near the eagle's talon is a defect that links this coin directly to the 1922 high-relief Proof variety. The other diagnostic details mentioned for the 1922 Sandblast Proof reverse are also present.

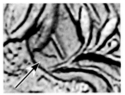 

Details of the eagle-claw area of a 1922 high-relief Proof (left) and the 1922 experimental-relief obverse. When superimposed, they are virtually indistinguishable.

The eagle's relief appears slightly lower than on the Proof, and the tail feathers near the rim appear bolder; the lettering is slightly shallower and flatter. When images of the Proof and medium-relief reverse are superimposed, there is virtually no difference. The olive branch has the same arrangement of branches and leaves as on all 1921 and 1922 high-relief Proofs.

1922—Low-Relief Trial Strike and Proof

The relief is substantially lower than on any of the preceding varieties. Proof coins are sharper and more detailed than the trial strikes but appear to be from the same master hubs.

The low-relief Proofs (left) and trial strikes (right) show depressed areas (indicated by arrows) in the field parallel to many of the obverse rays.

Obverse. This resembles the "original" 1921 design, although made from a new model. The lettering and numerals are clear and well-defined, with little tendency to flatness; the upper surfaces are gently rounded. Some of the long rays have depressed areas parallel to the rays that create the appearance of greater relief. Much of this engraving appears to have been polished off the master die before the Proof die was made. This produced the ghost rays next to some of the long rays and also resulted in thinner, more delicate rays and lettering. The rim is well defined.

It is believed that after the low-relief obverse hub was created, the area parallel to the rays was cut below the field in an attempt to give greater definition to the rays. When the Proof dies were made from the low-relief hubs, most of this touch-up work was polished off the obverse die. The remnants are faint, ghostly outlines to some of the Proof-coin rays. This polishing also accounts for the somewhat thinner rays on the Proofs than on the trial strikes. This version may have been used on some 1922-D and 1922-S coins.

Reverse. The lettering is slightly rounded on the upper surface. There are two hills in the mountains to the right of PEACE; the olive branch is not connected to the eagle's talon; the C and A of AMERICA are very close. All low-relief coins have the same arrangement of olive branches and leaves, which differs from the high-relief varieties. The rim is well defined. Used on Philadelphia trial strikes and on some 1922-D and 1922-S coins.[1]

1922—LOW-RELIEF CIRCULATION

The relief is similar to the trial strikes, though not as well defined. The lettering is broad and flat and in the same positions as on the trial-strike and Proof coins; this is also true for the reverse, where the rays are nearly identical.

Obverse. The lettering and numerals are poorly defined, with a tendency to flatness. LI–TY and 1 are often flattened on the portion closest to the rim; the upper surfaces usually appear nearly flat. The rays are broader than on the earlier coins; some of the long rays have flattened tips near the rim.

Reverse. The lettering is poorly defined and less sharp than on the trial-strike variety; the upper surfaces are flat. There are three hills in the mountains to the right of PEACE; the olive branch is connected to the eagle's talon; the C and A of AMERICA are well separated.

The illustration superimposes the circulation variety over the Sandblast Proof. The light gray areas next to the narrow rays show where material exists on the circulation variety but not on the Proofs. The distance between the centers of adjacent rays remains the same.

An image of the low-relief circulation strike superimposed over the Sandblast Proof. The arrows point to areas of the rays that are present on the circulation strike but not the Proof.

When the four versions of 1922 low-relief coins are compared, any difference in position of the design elements is trivial. The only substantive differences between the Proof and circulation coins are the width of the lettering, and the length and number of hills along the reverse rim.

Conclusions

The following conclusions are based on the foregoing observations.

1921 PEACE DOLLARS, HIGH RELIEF

The same pair of master dies was used to produce all Proof and production dies. Differences are attributable to die preparation, striking pressure, planchet dimensions, and other factors normally encountered in a production environment. For this year there is only one variety.

1922 PEACE DOLLARS, HIGH AND MEDIUM RELIEF

Both sides of the high-relief Proofs were probably made by reworking the lettering and making other modifications to the 1921 design. However, none of the 1921 coins the author examined share diagnostic details with the 1922 varieties, and the conclusion is that the 1922 coins came from new, extensively recut hubs.

Although differing considerably in visual appearance, the high- and medium-relief varieties probably originated with the 1922 high-relief Proof models. The obverses have only the overlapped 9 in common, although this is not identical on the two varieties examined. The Proof reverses share identical diagnostic elements, notably the defect near the eagle's talon, that are not present on any other Peace dollars. A unique coin, combining the 1922 high-relief obverse and 1921 reverse, is known and appears to have been struck on a production press rather than a medal press. This coin likely preceded the medium-relief reverse.

When the decision was made to lower the design's relief, the 1922 Proof obverse may have been used as the basis for rework to create the medium-relief die. The reverse of the Proof was used with only minor changes. Linkage between the 1922 high-relief Proof coin and the medium-relief experimental coin establishes that the Philadelphia Mint produced the discovery coin. Its complete lack of Proof characteristics further supports the contention that it was one of the 3,200 Peace dollars (intended to test new dies prior to production) produced and rejected by Fraser in the later part of January 1922. Several variations on this design were possibly tried and discarded during January. The coin illustrated herein is the only example known to have survived.

1922 PEACE DOLLARS, LOW RELIEF

De Francisci's final 1921 obverse and modified reverse models do not exactly match the 1922 coins, although the reverse rays are closer to the original than on the 1921 coins. New models were made; these were placed in the Janvier reducing machine, and under the sculptor's supervision, the relief was reduced. The same pair of new low-relief hubs was used to produce dies for Proof and trial-strike varieties. The term "trial strike" can only be applied to the Philadelphia Mint coins of this variety: many, even most, were probably made before the design was approved. After acceptance of the new hub on February 14, many of the dies were mint-marked and sent to the Denver and San Francisco branch mints. In the context of branch-mint production, these are no longer considered trial strikes, but simply another variety.

Later, a second pair of hubs was produced and became the basis for the rest of the 1922 circulation coins. Other differences resulted from die preparation, striking pressure, planchet dimensions, and other factors normally encountered in a production environment. Differences in lettering and ray style between the Proof and circulation varieties are attributable to retouching and polishing of Proof dies.

The trial-strike obverse or reverse (IV-C) may exist combined with dies from the second set of low-relief hubs (V-C2) for the Philadelphia, Denver, and San Francisco mints.

VARIETY NUMBERING

To better differentiate the origins of the varieties, the following table groups the coins by date, design, and variety based on my examination. The numbering system is adapted from Breen's *Complete Encyclopedia of U.S. and Colonial Coins*, Van Allen and Mallis's variety-numbering system (VAM), and Q. David Bowers's *Silver Dollars and Trade Dollars of the*

United States. A roman numeral is used to designate the obverse die and an alphabetic character is used for the reverse die.

Date	Obverse	Reverse	VAM	Comment
1921	I	A	I-A	High-relief Sandblast Proof.
1921	I	A	I-A	High-relief Satin Proof.
1921	I	A	I-A	High-relief circulation strike. All 1921.
1922	II	A	N/A	High-relief Circulation trial strikes (condemned).
1922	II	B	IA-AA	High-relief Sandblast Proof.
1922	II	B	IA-AA	High-relief Satin Proof (?).
1922	III	B2	N/A	Medium-relief experimental (condemned).

Modified II-B designs (one known):

Date	Obverse	Reverse	VAM	Comment
1922	IV	C	II-B1	Low-relief trial strikes (placed in circulation). Some 1922, 22-D, 22-S.
1922	IV	C	II-B1	Low-relief Sandblast Proof.
1922	IV	C	II-B1	Low-relief Satin Proof.
1922	V	C2	II-B2	Low-relief circulation strikes. Most 1922, 22-D, 22-S, 1923–28.

If we extend this numbering to the balance of the Peace dollar series, the results are as follows:

VI	C2	III-B2	1934, 34-D, 34-S, 1935, some 35-S.
VI	D	III-C	Some 1935-S.

Thus, there are five distinct varieties and 10 versions of 1921 and 1922 Peace dollars: 1921 (three versions); 1922 high relief (two versions); 1922 medium relief (one version); 1922 low-relief Proof and trial strikes (three versions); and 1922 low-relief circulation (one version).

For the convenience of readers, the following obverse and reverse descriptions have been adapted from the list in Bowers and are presented for consistency with prior literature.[2]

Obverse I. High-relief type of 1921, Proofs and circulation coins. The head and features are in higher relief than on later years; the obverse field is noticeably concave, the reverse field only slightly concave. The rays on Liberty's tiara are thicker and lack the short rays between the first four long rays; the headband differs from later years, especially to the right of the wave of hair crossing the band. (VAM I.)

Obverse II. High relief, similar to 1921 but used only on the 1922 high-relief Proofs. This die is not identical to 1921; this has short rays added between long rays at the front of the tiara. The motto and lettering are strengthened and better proportioned. (Not in VAM; Bowers calls this "IA.")

Obverse III. Medium-relief intermediate between 1921 and later 1922 low-relief coins; the field is less concave. This die is more detailed than the previous, but crudely cut, dies; the date is crooked, the motto not straight; the style of lettering is closer to 1922 high-relief Proofs. Certified by NGC in August 2001. (Not in VAM or Bowers.)

Obverse IV. Low-relief hub from new model prepared under de Francisci's and Fraser's supervision. The field is nearly flat; the edges of the lettering are sharper and the letters better formed than in the following dies; the first hair curl above headband is centered between the rays. (Not in VAM or Bowers.)

Obverse V. Low relief used from 1922 through 1928. This die has similar relief as IV, but the lettering is not as sharp; the lettering tends to be poorly brought up, with the surfaces near the rim blending into the field. The first hair curl above the headband is to the right, between rays; other details are as on IV. (VAM II.)

Obverse VI. Similar to Obverse V, but there is thinner lettering in the motto; the tail of the R in TRVST is straighter than on the preceding; the headband is more prominent behind the wave of hair. This was used only in 1934 and 1935. (VAM III.)

Reverse A. High-relief type of 1921 Proof and circulation coins. The eagle and other features are in slightly higher relief than in the following years, but not as high as the corresponding obverse; the field is only slightly concave. The olive branch is configured with the split close to the eagle; there are four rays below ONE and seven rays below the tail; there is a defect in the last two long rays near the right rim. (VAM A.)

Reverse B. High-relief type of 1922 Proofs only. This die is similar to the previous one, but the lettering is more consistent and better defined;

all of the A's are of the same style; there are four rays below ONE and eight rays below the tail; there is no defect in the long rays near the right rim; there is a defect in the field very close to the eagle's talon and the branch. (Not in VAM; Bowers calls this "AA.")

Reverse B2. Medium-relief intermediate between 1921/22 high relief and 1922 low relief. This die is similar to B, above, but the letters are flatter on the top and somewhat broader; the die has the same ray configuration as Reverse B and also shares the defect near the talon. (Not in VAM or Bowers.)

Reverse C. Low-relief, early circulation design from new model. The lettering is flat and poorly defined; the olive branch does not touch the eagle's talon; there are two hills to the right of the eagle; the leg of the R in DOLLAR is short and touches the nearest ray; there are three rays below ONE and six rays below the tail. (VAM B1.)

Reverse C2. Low-relief, normal circulation design. The lettering is flat and poorly defined; the olive branch touches the eagle's talon; there are three hills to the right of the eagle; the leg of the R in DOLLAR is longer and extends beyond the ray; there are three rays below ONE and six rays below the tail. (VAM B2.)

Reverse D. Similar to Reverse C, but this die has four rays below ONE and seven rays below the tail, as found on the 1921 reverse. (VAM C)

ORDER OF PRODUCTION

With the information collected from available specimens, we can make a reasonable guess at the order in which the various models and working dies were produced. We do not know the order in which the coins themselves were struck.

> 1921 high-relief Sandblast and Satin Proof versions, high-relief circulation version
>
> 1922 high-relief obverse, 1921 reverse for circulation; most melted
>
> 1922 high-relief Sandblast and Satin (?) Proof versions; most melted
>
> 1922 medium-relief experimental version; most melted
>
> 1922 low-relief Sandblast and Satin Proof versions, trial strikes

Early Peace Dollar Hub Relationships

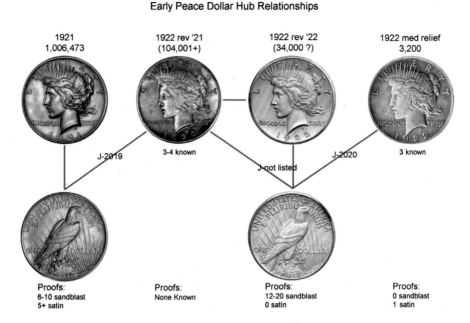

| 1921
1,006,473 | 1922 rev '21
(104,001+) | 1922 rev '22
(34,000 ?) | 1922 med relief
3,200 |

J-2019   3-4 known   J-2020   3 known

J-not listed

| Proofs:
6-10 sandblast
5+ satin | Proofs:
None Known | Proofs:
12-20 sandblast
0 satin | Proofs:
0 sandblast
1 satin |

This diagram presents a visual representation of the relationships between production, pattern, and trial pieces for early Peace dollars.

1922 Low-Relief Circulation Version

This production sequence is further supported by the Mint's need to strike silver dollars at a substantial rate. The failure of the 1922 high- and medium-relief redesigns by Morgan had cost the Mint nearly a month—time when the coining staff was largely idle and silver was piled up in the vaults. For all of a numismatist's musing about the beauties of a coin design or its merit, the Mint was (and is) a factory for the production of huge numbers of stamped metal objects. Every coined silver dollar meant that a dollar in paper Silver Certificates could be issued, and getting the paper money into circulation was one of the Treasury's priorities.

PRODUCTION QUANTITIES

No records have been located that state the number of Sandblast or Satin Proofs made of any variety. Likewise, little information is available on the number of 1922 high-relief coins made and later melted. The following table summarizes estimated mintage.

Date	Variety	Quantity
1921	High relief, circulation*	1,006,473
1921	High relief, Proof	5+
1922	High relief, circulation	32,401±
1922	High relief, Proof	5+
1922	Medium relief, circulation	3,200
1922	Medium relief, Proof	2+
1922	Low relief, circulation	51,737,000
1922	Low relief, Proof	5+

* Net, including 505 assay pieces. "Proofs" are counted in the respective circulation quantities.

1922 MEDIUM- AND HIGH-RELIEF TRIAL PIECES

Until publication of *Renaissance of American Coinage 1916–1921* in 2005, collectors were unaware of the existence of trial pieces for the low-relief 1922 Peace dollar. Although I touched on trial pieces earlier in this chapter, it might be helpful to review the subject in more detail. According to Philadelphia Mint engraver Charles Barber, writing to superintendent John Landis on May 14, 1910: "A *trial* piece is made from dies for coin to be issued, in order to prove the correctness of the die, that is, to test whether the dies fully answer the mechanical requirements of coinage."[3]

Barber's definition identifies several important characteristics of a trial piece. First, the design has been accepted; second, it is planned to use this design from these dies for circulation; third, the pieces are struck to make sure the dies perform as expected under normal operating conditions; fourth, the test is of mechanical production, not aesthetics; and fifth, the work occurs prior to the initiation of production. This type of test requires the use of standard coinage presses and the making of thousands or hundreds of thousands of pieces. Just as with any manufacturing company that wants to be sure everything is ready for mass production, the Mint wanted to be sure the dies were ready to be placed in daily use before making hundreds of working dies and sending them to the branch mints.

Mint archives include several references to trial pieces being struck for coins other than the Peace dollar. In most instances, we have no way to determine whether the test was successful since documents rarely describe the coins. Presumably, these pre-production coins were approved and then released along with other coins, indistinguishable from one another.

It should be clear that a trial piece is not a pattern or experimental coin. It is not intended to break new ground for a design, alloy, or production method. It is a simple, large-scale test of dies to verify readiness for production.

The 1921 high-relief version did not fully strike up under normal production conditions. At first Morgan resorted to increased pressure and frequent die replacement to produce acceptable coins. After the first day of production, he cut pressure back to normal range and allowed dies to remain in use for a longer time. Nearly all of the 1921-dated coins show incomplete striking, although high relief still produced an impressive coin.

During most of January 1922, Morgan struggled with improving the striking of the new Peace dollar. He first attempted to improve the high-relief obverse and for 1922 created a new hub and master die. Paired with a 1921 reverse, he struck approximately 32,401 trial pieces on a production press before January 19. The results were no better than in 1921, and Morgan next attempted to alter the reverse.

A small number of pattern samples of this new high-relief 1922 obverse / modified reverse pairing were struck on a medal press, but it appears no extensive trials were undertaken. Failure of the high-relief trial production (with 1921 reverse) probably doomed this version. Finally, Morgan went back to the obverse and attempted to reduce the relief and add detail to Liberty's hair. This medium-relief version was paired with the revised reverse and 3,200 trial pieces were struck before the dies failed.

After a month of failure and frustration, sculptor Anthony de Francisci was called in and asked to make a pair of new, low-relief models for the Peace dollar. When de Francisci completed his work, James Earle Fraser from the Commission of Fine Arts supervised trial striking of the coins. According to documents in the Treasury Department, 100,000 trial pieces per day were struck on February 13 and 14.[4] After examining the new low-relief coins, Fraser gave his reluctant approval on February 14:

> To avoid delay will accept new dollar under protest. Hair over ear not raised to level of strand on each side as we desired. Cheek bone good. Lettering good. Hair must be raised over ear on new dies being made. Coins already struck can be put out.[5]

It should be noted that Fraser not only approved normal production of the coins, but he specifically stated that coins already struck could be released. Thus, 200,000 trial pieces were released along with other Peace dollars. All low-relief trial pieces were struck at the Philadelphia Mint.[6]

After receiving Fraser's approval, the Mint began distribution of working dies to Denver and San Francisco, where production began on February 21 in Denver and 23 in San Francisco. They continued to use the same hubs Fraser had accepted until approximately mid-March, when new hubs were made. These had slightly softer lettering on the obverse, and the olive branch was now connected to the eagle's talon. All three mints used their stock of available dies until they needed replacement. Consequently, the trial pieces struck at Philadelphia on February 13 and 14 are identical to several hundred thousand circulation coins made during the next few weeks. All pieces from Denver and San Francisco that use the trial reverse, with the detached olive branch, are normal circulation coins and *not trial pieces*.

There is no detailed description of the trial pieces, so how can they be identified?

Fortunately, Morgan made a small quantity of Sandblast Proofs with the low-relief design. These were intended for examination by the director and other Mint officials, and were likely produced before Fraser approved the design. Some were kept by recipients, and others were returned to Philadelphia. One of these was sold to collector Andrew Swasey on March 1, 1922, for face value.[7] (Swasey had been on the 1922 Assay Commission that met at the Philadelphia Mint in February.) Examination of Swasey's coin, and all other known low-relief Proofs, shows a distinctive identifier on the reverse: the olive branch does not touch the eagle. This information, combined with Fraser's comments and past actions of the Mint in making trial production pieces of Peace dollar versions, suggests that low-relief Proofs, trial pieces, and early production coins were made from the same hubs.

Trial production coins are very seldom identified in numismatic literature. Does that make these coins hidden rarities? The short answer is "No." A log book of silver coins received for assay from the Philadelphia Mint in February 1922 exists. Deliveries 1 and 2 appear to coincide with the trial period and account for 200,000 coins. (This is consistent with the Treasury Department's separate production journal.) Deliveries 3 through 15 cover February 15 through 28 and account for an additional 2,150,000 pieces. With these being struck from the original detached-olive-branch hubs, and with more coins made until the new hub was utilized in mid-March, at minimum 2,350,000 of the trial variety were struck. This is approximately 5 percent of the 1922-P mintage and could be as much as 10 percent, depending on how long the older dies were in use.

Given the ready availability of "trial-variety" coins from Denver and San Francisco, it is likely that detached-olive-branch pieces account for a much greater percentage of branch-mint production. If the same number of dies were shipped to the branch mints, each could have struck 15 to 20 percent of their 1922 dollars from the trial-variety reverse dies.

While the trial strikes are an important variety and have notable historical value, they are probably not destined to soar in price.

RAYMOND T. BAKER FAMILY COINS

In August 2014 Stack's Bowers Galleries auctioned a small but remarkable group of pattern and experimental Peace dollars. All of the coins originated with the family of former Mint director Raymond T. Baker (March 1917 to March 1922), and the group included materials that greatly improved our understanding of these coins.[8]

Among the coins was a 1921 early production coin that had been sandblasted and antiqued in the manner usually applied to medals. This treatment gave the coin the appearance of a small medal and enhanced the overall artistic impression of the design. A 1922 High Relief trial production coin treated in the same manner—which is also distinguished by the fact that it was made on a toggle-type production press—was sold in the Goldberg Coins and Collectibles auction of June 2014.[9] These two coins were mentioned in a letter dated January 8, 1922, from Philadelphia Mint Superintendent Freas Styer to Mint Director Baker. Other 1921 and 1922 High Relief examples of sandblasting and antiquing might exist, possibly mis-described as "Proof." Also included was a medal-press Proof striking of the 1922 Medium Relief design with a satin—not sandblast—surface (below, right).

The Baker 1921 Peace dollar
obverse with an antiqued finish.

The Baker 1922 Peace dollar
obverse with a satin finish.

The most interesting Baker Estate coin was a 1922 toggle-press example from the 3,200 trial pieces made of the Medium Relief Peace dollar. As noted previously, Mint documents state that the number "3200" was written on the last coin struck before the trial dies broke. Amazingly, this piece was among the Baker coins and is shown below. Notice the typical lack of central detail affecting nearly all toggle-press production coins.

The final Medium Relief Peace dollar stuck in a trial of
3,200 pieces, taken from Baker's collection.

The Baker Estate also included two 2x2-inch coin envelopes that provide insights on early 1922 trial manufacture.

The envelope shown at the top of the next page contained a sample from the trial production on a standard toggle press of 1922 High Relief dollars using the original 1921 reverse. The envelope shows that at least 104,001 trial pieces were struck from this design combination. At present only four are known. This coin was sandblasted and antiqued in a manner similar to some 1921 and 1922, High Relief / Reverse of 1922, High Relief pieces noted above. The coin realized $102,813, although the authentication and description of the coin as a "Proof" were faulty.

1922 High Relief, Reverse of 1921, trial piece.

The envelope containing the trial piece.

The other envelope contained a Sandblast Proof 1922 High Relief coin with the second reverse—the first of those struck with that new design combination. Given the language on the envelope, it seems likely that 20 Proofs were made. All of the pieces currently known were sandblasted at the Mint. This coin sold for $458,500 in June 2014.

The envelope containing
the Sandblast Proof.

1922 High Relief Sandblast Proof.

PROOF-COIN DIAGNOSTICS

The decision to call a particular Peace dollar specimen a "Proof" has often depended on subtle diagnostic marks such as die polishing lines, or "years of experience," or thinly disguised guesswork. Auction catalogs over recent decades contain numerous optimistic references to "possible 1921 Proof" accompanied by illustrations of coins that clearly are not Proofs. After reviewing the various Proof and circulation varieties, I suspect that genuine Proof coins can be discerned according to the following diagnostic features. These features have been used to evaluate several Proof and alleged Proof coins and appear to be reliable.

Most Proof coins have a partial knife rim due to a mismatch between design relief and planchet milling (upsetting of the rim). All Proof specimens were struck on a medal press and with higher-than-normal pressure. Be cautious, though—Proof dies were used to make circulation coins in addition to the Proofs. This is very likely for 1921 due to the problems with short die life and the need to produce new coins as quickly as possible. Be wary of any coin that matches Proof diagnostics, yet lacks exceptional sharpness and sandblast or satin surfaces. Careful third-party authentication is recommended for any Peace dollar described as a "Proof."

1921 HIGH-RELIEF PROOFS

Obverse. All have two roughly parallel lines within the truncation of the bust beginning just right of the 9 in the date. There are also two small lumps within these lines. The circulation strikes have remnants of these lines and lumps, but also have many extra tool marks, as if someone attempted to remove the two original lines from the master die or hub after the Proofs were made. See 1921 VAM-3 (in chapter 9) for photographs of tool marks.

1922 HIGH-RELIEF PROOFS

Obverse. All have the point of the bust sharply overlaying the 9 in the date.

Reverse. All have a small defect in the area between the eagle's talon and leg and the olive branch; the rays are rounded.

1922 MEDIUM-RELIEF PROOFS

Obverse. All have the point of the bust sharply overlaying the 9 in the date with recutting evident. The hair is extensively detailed, and the face distorted.

Reverse. All have a small defect in the area between the eagle's talon and leg and the olive branch; the rays are rounded. (At least one specimen was sent to the director's office and is presently unaccounted for.)

1922 LOW-RELIEF PROOFS

All low-relief Proof coins came from the same hubs as the trial strikes and share the same diagnostic marks. Any coin purported to be a Proof but missing these marks should be accepted only with great skepticism.

Obverse. All have ghost rays at the sides of many of the tiara's rays; these are less pronounced than on the trial strikes. The rays are also thinner than on any of the trial or circulation pieces; upper surfaces of the rays are rounded rather than flattened, as on the trial strikes. The ray tips are pointed.

Reverse. The rays are broad and flat at the base and become narrow and rounded toward the tip; olive branch does not touch eagle's claw.

A very well struck trial coin could mimic a Proof, provided it had flawless surfaces, very sharp features, indistinct cutting parallel to the rays, and complete sandblast or satin finish.

Note. No Proofs are known of the normal circulation-hub designs with connected olive branch and very flat lettering. It is possible, however, that they exist and remain hidden and unidentified in old collections. Characteristics of these Proofs might include a satin or sandblast surface matching the 1921 and 1922 genuine Proofs; a partial fin rim; exceptionally sharp details on the eagle; and a sharp, square corner between field and rim.

How Peace Dollar Proofs Were Made

Decades of speculation have thoroughly confused the process used to produce Proof specimens by the Philadelphia Mint during the early 20th century. Original documents help to shed light on how Proofs were made and, more importantly, why they were produced in very small quantities.

There is no record of any special examples of Peace dollars being struck for coin collectors. That some coins found their way into collectors' hands says more about the collecting psyche than actual distribution of the coins. All of the 1921 and 1922 Satin and Sandblast Proof pieces were prepared for examination by Mint Bureau and Treasury Department officials. A few were used within the Philadelphia Mint by the engraver to verify quality of the dies, but most specimens were shipped to the director's office in Washington, D.C. From there, pieces were distributed to the secretary of the Treasury, the Mint director, and often one or more assistant Treasury secretaries as evidence of the coin design's quality. In their day, Satin and Sandblast Proofs were nothing more than production examples intended to show the coin, at its best, to government officials. That they differed somewhat from regular production coins did not seem to be of importance: the officials were, nearly always, not coin collectors.

Until the mid-20th century, little attention was paid to tracking each of these examples. Sometimes the director's office sent cash or a check to the Philadelphia Mint so the cash account could be balanced. Other times, coins of the same metal and face value were returned, and on other occasions, pattern, experimental, and Proof examples were retained by the director for several years before they were discovered in an old office safe. Further, the sale of pattern and experimental pieces at face value was openly encouraged by President Roosevelt following introduction of the new gold designs in 1907. For several Mint officials, including Mary O'Reilley and Fred Chaffin during the Peace dollar introduction, these production examples were inexpensive personal mementos of the new design. There is no mention in any document of any Mint or Treasury official obtaining special examples of the Peace dollar for personal gain.

It is from the director's office and other officials that collectors obtained examples of Satin and Sandblast Proofs for their collections. So far as has been determined, only one collector, Ambrose Swasey, recorded his acquisition of a Proof Peace dollar.

Satin and Sandblast Peace Dollars

Before 1907, all Proof coins—gold, silver, copper-nickel, and bronze—were made with polished fields and sometimes a dull, unpolished portrait and lettering. In 1907, the Saint-Gaudens designs were adopted for the eagle and double eagle. Due to die curvature and texture of the field (or "ground," as Mint engravers called it), polishing the dies to make brilliant Proofs was not practical. A similar situation occurred in 1908 with the Pratt-designed half and quarter eagles. To provide special coins for collectors, the Philadelphia Mint produced Sandblast (also called "dull" by Mint staff) Proof coins for all four gold denominations in 1908. The next year the Mint tried a different variation on Proof gold and this resulted in the Satin Proof (inaccurately called a "Roman" Proof).

To create a Satin Proof in either gold or silver, the Mint started with a pair of new dies and clean planchets selected for absence of nicks and scrapes. The dies were installed in a high-tonnage hydraulic medal press, and the coins were struck using approximately 150 tons of pressure. The resultant Proof coin had sharply defined square rims, full details, and smooth fields free of the luster collectors associate with normal-production coins made from used dies.

To create a Sandblast Proof coin, the Satin Proof was lightly sandblasted. Each coin was treated individually, so no two Sandblast Proofs are identical. The Mint engravers felt that a sandblasted coin showed the design (and their engraving skill) in its best possible form. To help understand the differences between Satin and Sandblast Proof coins, the following illustrates each, along with a short description of how the pieces were manufactured.[10]

Satin Proof, Gold

The so-called Roman Proof, minted in 1909 and 1910, has lustrous, non-mirror surfaces, lacking the mint frost commonly seen on normal circulation strikes. These were produced on a hydraulic press from new, carefully impressed dies. Hubs were lightly buffed before annealing to remove stray burrs left from cutting the metal on the reducing lathe. Planchets were not polished, although they were selected for smooth surfaces. They received no post-strike treatment. These were easily confused with early circulation strikes that were made the same way but on normal coining presses. Standard gold "Proof coins" were sold to collectors in 1909 and 1910.

The surface is easily marred on these coins. There is also minimal visual distinction between these and ordinary circulation strikes. "Roman Proofs" are analogous to the Satin Proofs of later years.

Sandblast Proof, Gold

These pieces are characterized by dull, non-reflective surfaces. Proofs were struck on a hydraulic press from new, carefully impressed dies. Dies and planchets were not polished, although the planchets were selected for smooth surfaces. After striking, the coins were lightly sandblasted in a manner similar to medals. Standard gold Proof coins were sold to collectors in 1908 and from 1911 to 1915. These are correctly called Sandblast Proofs, since this describes how the pieces were made. The surface is very delicate and easily marred.

Sandblasting tends to exaggerate the color of the gold, particularly the greenish specimens (their green tint caused by excess silver in the alloy).

Satin Proof, Silver

Satin Proofs are characterized by smooth, fine-grained, non-reflective surfaces with little "mint bloom" and only slight luster. These were struck on a hydraulic press from new, carefully impressed dies. Hubs were not buffed, which resulted in very fine texture. Dies were not treated, nor were planchets polished, although they were usually selected for smooth surfaces. They received no post-strike treatment. The process was analogous to creating "Roman" Proofs as seen on gold coins in 1909 and 1910.

This style is seen on 1921 and 1922 Peace dollars and the occasional later Saint-Gaudens gold coins, as well as some commemorative half dollars from the 1920s and 1930s. This surface was called "bright," in contrast to "sandblast," by Mint personnel in 1922. These are easily confused with first strikes from new dies, since this is essentially what a Satin Proof is, except for the greater detail and square rims imparted by the hydraulic press. This was not a standard Mint Proof surface until late 1980s, when the U.S. Mint started calling them "Matte Proof." The surface is easily marred.

Sandblast Proof, Silver

Sandblast Proofs are characterized by dull, non-reflective surfaces. These were struck on a hydraulic press from new, carefully impressed dies. Dies and planchets were not polished, although planchets were selected for smooth surfaces. After striking, the coins were lightly sandblasted in a manner similar to medals. This process was used on 1921 and 1922 Peace dollar Proofs and on some commemorative halves.

These are correctly called Sandblast Proofs, since this describes how the pieces were made. The surface is very delicate and easily marred.

Sandblasting tends to give silver a gray, pewter-like color.

As noted by Philadelphia Mint superintendent John Landis in September 1910, a Sandblast Proof could be made by sand-blasting a satin piece.

Except for Sandblast Proofs, any excess pieces were usually put into circulation.

1921 Proof—High Relief

Proof Mintage: Satin 3–4
Sandblast 5–8

The first 1921 Peace dollars were struck for circulation at the Philadelphia Mint on December 28 at 8:30 a.m. Satin and Sandblast examples were evidently made and sent to Washington for review by acting Mint Director O'Reilley and Assistant Secretary Gilbert. These were probably made between December 26 and 29, since after the 29th Morgan was busy making new, sharper hubs for 1922.

All obverses have two roughly parallel lines within the truncation of the bust beginning just right of the 9 in the date. There are also two small lumps within these lines. The circulation strikes have remnants of these lines and lumps, but also have many extra tool marks as if someone attempted to remove the two original lines from the master die or hub after the Proofs were made.

Relative Rarity

Within the series of Proof Peace dollars, the 1922 is the second most commonly encountered. Although the estimated mintage is slightly greater than that of 1921, the 1922 Proofs have consistently appeared with less frequency at auction during the past 20 years. Specimens reported by the major third-party grading services cluster in the PF-63 to PF-65 range.

Within the series of Proof Peace dollars, the 1921 is the most commonly encountered. Although the estimated mintage is slightly less than that of 1922, the 1921 Proofs have consistently appeared with greater frequency at auction during the past 20 years. Specimens reported by the major third-party grading services cluster in the PF-63 to PF-65 range.

Relative Rarity Within the 24-Coin Series

PF-63	PF-64	PF-65	PF-66	PF-60–PF-70
1/24	1/24	4/24	8/24	1/24

Varieties

No varieties other than Satin and Sandblast have been identified.

Collecting Advice

Collectors should insist on authentication by one of the major grading services of any Proof Peace dollar. Examples accompanied by old letters of authenticity should be examined with great skepticism.

Valuations Note

A *genuine* 1921 Sandblast or Satin Proof, high relief, would be valued at about $50,000 to $75,000 if graded at PF-65.

1922 CIRCULATION—HIGH-RELIEF TRIAL

Mintage: ±32,401

High-relief 1922 Peace dollars were probably struck at the Philadelphia Mint between January 3 and 19, 1922. Examples were sent to Mint headquarters on several occasions. These trial pieces are consistent with research by Robert W. Julian in the 1970s as discussed elsewhere in this book and in more detail in Bowers's *Encyclopedia*.

In early 2007, a 1922 high-relief Peace dollar was identified by numismatist David W. Lange that combined the 1922 high-relief obverse with the 1921 reverse. Although the coin (illustrated above) was determined to be genuine and graded Very Fine, it has several characteristics that differ from previously known high-relief specimens. (Compare it with the 1922 high-relief Proof.)

First, the strike is shallow, unlike the full-rounded 1922 high-relief Proofs struck on a medal press. In this regard it more closely resembles an ordinary 1921 production coin. Second, the reverse die does not match that used on any 1922 high-relief Proof or on the only known 1922 medium-relief example. The reverse is, in fact, that of 1921. Taken together, these anomalies suggest that the coin was struck on a production press from a 1922 high-relief obverse and a 1921 high-relief reverse. This is what might be expected if the Philadelphia Mint were making a test run of the redesigned obverse. If this is correct, it also indicates that 1922 high-relief Proofs were struck after these trial pieces were made and a new reverse hub had been completed. Sequentially, this scenario is consistent with hub linkage between the 1922 high-relief Proofs and the medium-relief specimen, and supports the order of production noted in the preceding table.

Planning for use of the high-relief design was far enough along that working dies were distributed to the branch mints. An invoice dated February 27, 1922, to the San Francisco Mint from the director's office states that 10 pairs of dollar dies were shipped to San Francisco on January 6 and returned on January 12. Presumably, Denver received similar quantities of dies. Production was not authorized and no "D" or "S" high-relief coins are known to have been struck.

Relative Rarity

Only one coin pairing the 1922 high-relief obverse and 1921 reverse has been located, therefore the term "rarity" is meaningless. The coin was found in an otherwise nondescript batch of circulated Peace dollars, which suggests that others might exist. This coin was featured in Stack's Americana Sale of January 15 and 16, 2008, lot 8545, where it was incorrectly attributed as a "1922 high relief satin proof (NCS), 'improperly cleaned.' Our grade proof 60." The coin did not meet reserve on an opening bid of $30,000.

Collecting Advice

Any alleged 1922 high-relief Peace dollar must be authenticated.

Valuations Note

Although some 30,000-plus pieces were struck, all but this example are presumed to have been melted. It is not possible to assign a dollar value to this unique piece.

1922 PATTERN PROOF—HIGH RELIEF

Proof Mintage: Satin Unknown
Sandblast 5–10

High-relief 1922 Proof Peace dollars were struck at the Philadelphia Mint, most likely between January 3 and 19, 1922. This was during or just after 1922 high-relief trial production and after Morgan had revised the reverse, but before completion of the medium-relief obverse. Examples were sent to Mint headquarters on several occasions.

Although one example of a 1922 high-relief obverse and 1921 reverse is known, it is likely that all of the 34,000 production trial strikes identified by Robert W. Julian were from this initial pairing of dies. Later, Morgan reworked the reverse hub and created the version used for these Proofs and all known medium-relief pieces.

To many, this version is the most pleasing and attractive of all Peace dollar variations. Design and lettering are well defined with a boldness lacking in later, low-relief pieces.

All obverses have the point of the bust sharply overlaying the 9 in the date. The reverses all have a small defect in the area between the eagle's talon and leg and the olive branch; the rays are rounded.

Relative Rarity

Within the series of Proof Peace dollars, the 1922 is the second most commonly encountered. Although the estimated mintage is slightly greater than that of 1921, the 1922 Proofs have consistently appeared with less frequency at auction during the past 20 years. Specimens reported by the major third-party grading services cluster in the PF-63 to PF-65 range.

Relative Rarity Within the 24-Coin Series

PF-63	PF-64	PF-65	PF-66	PF-60–PF-70
1/24	1/24	4/24	8/24	1/24

Varieties

No varieties other than Sandblast Proofs have been identified. Satin-surface pieces are mentioned in historical documentation but have not been located.

The edge collar used was somewhat different than that used on production coins, generally lacking the fine, vertical line inside the groove between reeds.

Collecting Advice

Collectors should insist on authentication by one of the major grading services of any Proof Peace dollar. Examples accompanied by old letters of authenticity should be examined with great skepticism as the variety was unknown to most collectors until publicized by Walter Breen in 1959.

Valuations Note

A genuine 1922 Sandblast Proof, high relief, would be valued up to $125,000 or so if graded at PF-65.

A close-up of the edge collar used on pattern Peace dollars.

1922 PATTERN—MEDIUM RELIEF

Mintage: Trial Strikes 3,200
Satin 1
Sandblast 1

In August 2001, NGC authenticated a 1922 Peace dollar that differs from both the 1921 and 1922 designs. This design seems to be intermediate between the high relief of 1921 and the low relief of February 1922, and is referred to as "experimental" or "medium relief." Thus, it would seem that Morgan's final modification for 1922 was a medium-relief design that was even less successful than that of the 1921 or 1922 high-relief coins. All of the 3,200 trial strikes held at the Philadelphia Mint were melted.

Mint documents indicate that three specimens of this design were sent to the director's office in Washington, D.C. The coins included a Sandblast Proof and a Satin Proof made on a medal press, and a normal coin made on a production press.

One specimen—we don't know which—was sent to sculptor James Earle Fraser for evaluation. Fraser rejected the modified design. The fate of the other two specimens sent to Washington is not known, but they might have been purchased by Mint staff as souvenirs much as occurred with "Proof" versions of the other three varieties. At least one specimen was held in the personal collection of Raymond T. Baker (see p. 160.)

The only known example was found in a bag of circulated Peace dollars. It is listed in the book *United States Pattern Coins*, by J. Hewitt Judd, as Judd-2020.

Valuations Note

Although 3,200 examples of this pattern design were struck, all but this example are presumed to have been melted. It is not possible to assign a dollar value to this unique piece.

1922 PROOF—LOW RELIEF

Proof Mintage: Satin 2–4
Sandblast 3–6

Proof 1922 low-relief Peace dollars were likely struck at the Philadelphia Mint between February 6 and 14, 1922. The only dateable example was sold for face value to collector Andrew Swasey on March 1, 1922.

Although Proofs show maximum detail, it is evident that de Francisci's lettering is soft and poorly defined. Compared with Morgan's interpretation (1922 high-relief, discussed earlier), the low-relief coin, particularly the reverse, is a poor imitation. Considering the reputation of the sculptor and James E. Fraser, who approved the work, it is odd that they would agree to such a bland and uninteresting version.

Varieties

All known examples are from a reverse die with the olive branch disconnected from the eagle's talon. This characteristic is shared by the Philadelphia trial strikes and presumably the early production from Denver and San Francisco. This was corrected later in production by manually adding a small line connecting stem and talon. Eventually, a new hub was made.

A close-up of the reverse, showing the branch disconnected from the talon.

In addition, these two photos show portions of the edge of a 1922 high-relief Sandblast Proof (left), and a similar edge section of a 1922 low-relief Sandblast Proof. Notice that the 1922 low-relief coin has a prominent line running through the cut adjacent to each reed. The high-relief specimen shows little of this machining line. Edge collars similar to that shown on the low-relief example were used on Peace dollars through 1935. New edge dies were prepared in 1964 for use with the planned resumption of Peace dollar coinage.

Valuations Note

A genuine 1922 Sandblast Proof, low relief, would be valued at about $50,000 to $75,000 if graded at PF-65.

Edge details of two 1922 Sandblast Proofs, one in high relief (left) and one in low relief. The low-relief Proof has a thin line running lengthwise along the top edge of each reed; the high-relief does not.

1922 TRIAL STRIKES—LOW RELIEF

Mintage: 200,000 (plus 5% to 10%
of total circulation mintage)

Trial pieces of 1922 low-relief Peace dollars were struck at the Philadelphia Mint between February 12 and 14, 1922. The only dateable example was sold for face value to collector Andrew Swasey on March 1, 1922.

These are true production trials intended to test the suitability of the dies. About 200,000 were struck on February 12 and 13.

The trial-strike coins are not considered to be particularly rare, however they are the only U.S. coins identified as likely trial strikes that ever entered circulation. These coins were probably released with the first batch of 1922 dollars sent to Federal Reserve and commercial banks. As such, it is likely that most went directly into circulation, with some saved for their curiosity value as souvenirs of the new design.

Because the same hubs were used after the coin was accepted, the available quantity is much greater than those struck only on February 12 and 13.

Valuations Note

The 1922 low-relief trial strikes are readily available and represent approximately 10 percent of the total Philadelphia Mint production for the year. A reasonable price for one graded MS-65 would be $150 to $250.

Shown here are a 1922 low-relief coin from the first, or trial, hubs (left) and a 1922 low-relief Sandblast Proof struck in early February. Minor differences are due to production variations between circulation and Proof coins.

PEACE DOLLAR VARIETIES BY DATE AND MINT

In this chapter collectors will find detailed information on every date and mintmark combination in the Peace dollar series. Also included are descriptions and photos of the most significant die varieties as of the publication of this book. Together, this represents the most complete collection of knowledge on the Peace dollar ever assembled.

SPECIFICATIONS OF THE PEACE DOLLAR

All dates and mints, including 1964-D trial pieces, conform to these specifications:

Designer: Anthony de Francisci, professional sculptor, New York City.

Diameter: 1.5 inches (38.1 millimeters).

Composition: 90 percent fine silver, 10 percent copper.

Weight: 412.5 grains (26.73 grams); net weight of pure silver is 0.77344 troy ounces.

Thickness: 0.113 inches (2.86 millimeters; thickness not a legally defined value for Peace dollars).

Tolerance: In 1908 the diametric tolerance for U.S. coins was established at ±0.0025 inches. The thickness tolerance, measured at the rim, was defined as ±0.020 inches per pile of 20 coins (or an average of ±0.001 inches per coin).

Mintmarks: The mintmark "D" for Denver, Colorado, or "S" for San Francisco, California, is located on the reverse near the rim, just above the eagle's tail feathers. Coins struck at the Philadelphia Mint have no mintmark. From 1922 through part of 1934, the mintmarks were small. At the end of 1934 and throughout 1935, large mintmarks were used.

1921-P

Mintage: 1,006,473

Whitman Coin Guide (WCG™)

VF-20	EF-40	AU-50	MS-60	MS-63	MS-64	MS-65	MS-66	MS-67
$110	$140	$150	$275	$450	$850	$2,100	$6,500	$55,000

The first 1921 Peace dollars were struck at the Philadelphia Mint on December 28 at 8:30 a.m. The designer, Anthony de Francisci, was present, along with Mint engraver George T. Morgan and Philadelphia Mint superintendent Freas Styer. The first production coin was reserved for President Warren G. Harding and sent to the White House later that day. Coins were struck daily through the normal 1:00 p.m. closing of the mint on Saturday, December 31. No coins dated 1921 were struck in 1922.

Public distribution began on January 4, 1922, in New York City. Long lines formed at the New York sub-Treasury, forcing Treasury officials to limit citizens to one coin each. As with all new coin issues, the novelty quickly wore off and the coins soon became a glut in local bank vaults. An audit of Philadelphia Mint vaults in June 1936 showed there were still 154,800 1921 Peace dollars sitting in storage along with nearly 150 million other silver dollars.

These were only the third circulation-issue U.S. coins struck in high relief. (The first two were Saint-Gaudens's $20 double eagle with MCMVII date and his 1907 $10 eagle with knife rim and periods. Both of these were struck in very limited quantities on orders from President Roosevelt.) High relief proved difficult for the Philadelphia Mint, as it took tremendous pressure to properly strike the coin and bring out all the details. The die life was very short and the Mint soon resorted to reduced striking pressure to compensate. This, of course, resulted in many of the coins being struck very weakly. This is most evident on the obverse by a flat spot and/or lack of hair detail near Liberty's ear, and on the reverse by a lack of feather detail on the eagle's breast.

There is high demand for this issue, as it is the first year for the series, and also due to the much sought-after high-relief design. Many seek it as the representative coin of the Peace dollar series when building type sets. A large percentage of the issue was stored in government vaults for many years and many coins acquired bagmarks from being shifted from one location to another. These are readily available in circulated and Uncirculated conditions, although well-struck, fully lustrous pieces are uncommon and command a significant premium.

Unlike most other issues in the series, these coins are typically colored a deep slate gray. David W. Lange believes these are coins that remained in Mint vaults through the end of the 1930s. Other specimens have a more typical golden patina covering the surfaces.

1921 Dollar Categories

1921 Peace dollars fall into two broad categories: (1) coins struck from relatively fresh dies and made during the first day or two of production, and (2) coins struck from overused dies during the latter part of production. Pieces from the first group often have smooth surfaces with limited luster, generally lacking the "cartwheel effect" preferred by collectors. Surfaces are similar to Satin Proof coins, although other aspects do not match Proofs. They are generally well struck, with AU-58 specimens exhibiting more detail and definition than MS-65 pieces from later dies. These include the coins first released in New York and others made on December 28 and possibly early on the 29th. After finding die life was poor, George Morgan ordered that dies be run longer and at lower pressure in the presses, and this resulted in most of the second group of coins having better luster, but less sharpness and detail. Most of the weakly struck pieces were likely minted on December 30 and 31.

According to Treasury Department records, production was clearly divided into two parts:[1]

December 28, 1921	200,000
December 29, 1921	103
December 30, 1921	656,370
December 31, 1921	150,000
Total	*1,006,473*

The annual Assay Commission reserved 505 pieces. The quantity actually destroyed during commission work is unclear, but likely it was fewer than 100 specimens. The balance was placed into circulation.

Fully struck examples are very elusive and will show detail similar to Satin or Sandblast Proof specimens. Ordinary specimens will have varying amounts of detail in the hair over Liberty's ear and the feathers above the eagle's right leg. There are an unusual number of well-struck pieces in About Uncirculated condition, which may be the remnants of the first release of coins. In addition to being well struck (although not full strikes), these pieces commonly exhibit smooth fields and suppressed luster consistent with early strikes from new dies. Many of these AU's may have acquired their wear as pocket pieces and souvenirs.

Two very interesting specimens are held by the Smithsonian American Art Museum in Washington, D.C. These were part of de Francisci's display board of sample medallic designs, and donated to the museum by his widow. To show both sides of the coin, a brass rod was soldered to the obverse of one specimen and the reverse of the other. The sides that faced out likely tarnished quickly in the New York City atmosphere. They appear to have been cleaned with abrasive multiple times and are badly damaged. However, the side with the mounting rod, except for the splash of solder near the center, is virtually as-struck. Both pieces exhibit well-struck details and smooth, nearly luster-free surfaces. These may give collectors a good idea of what the initial group of Peace dollars looked like. These pieces probably came from the batch of 50 purchased by de Francisci and shipped to him on January 3, so they likely came from the earliest production dies. I believe, having personally examined the pieces, that had they remained in original condition, they would probably rank among the finest known 1921 examples. Strike and surfaces are exceptional and they could pass for Satin Proofs if they had other characteristics of coins struck on a medal press.

No dies dated 1921 were distributed to the Denver or San Francisco mints.

Relative Rarity

Within the Peace dollar series, 1921 is one of the more common issues in Uncirculated condition, as shown here:

Relative Rarity Within the 24-coin Series

MS-63	MS-64	MS-65	MS-66	MS-60–MS-70
20/24	20/24	20/24	18/24	20/24

Significant Examples

The finest known examples of the 1921 issue are graded MS-67, and at this writing only a dozen have been so certified by the major grading companies. One of the most famous specimens is from the Jack Lee I & II collections, and is graded MS-67 by PCGS. It is a blast-white coin that is very well struck and has only a few trivial contact marks. The example illustrated is from the Heritage Signature and Platinum Night Auction #414 held on August 13, 2006 (lot 5400). Although the coin is about typical for the strike, the surfaces are exceptionally free of marks. This piece realized $51,750, including buyer's fee.

Varieties

There are approximately two dozen die varieties documented. The following are of special interest to collectors.

OBVERSE RIM DIE BREAK   VAM N/A

A prominent die break is on the obverse, its right rim extending from the Y downward to opposite the right-most strand of hair.

VF-20	EF-40	AU-50	MS-60	MS-63	MS-64	MS-65
$150	$185	$200	$365	$750	$1,200	$3,500

Rays on Top of LL   VAM 3 I 1 Ac

Reverse Ac—Two rays strengthened by an engraver in vicinity of LL in DOLLAR. This resulted in a ray over the horizontal bar of the left L and over the lower-left tip on the right L instead of the usual letters-over-rays. (The master die has evidence of an engraver's touchup, with five engraving lines on the top tail feather, short engraving lines on the lower serifs of the E in ONE and LLAR in DOLLAR; top serifs of UNITE ST-TE -F AMERI, E U-I-U, and LLA; and long curved engraving line on the top right of the D in UNITED.) This variety accounts for approximately 2 percent of 1921 Peace dollars.

VF-20	EF-40	AU-50	MS-60	MS-63	MS-64	MS-65
$165	$180	$225	$315	$500	$900	$2,500

Polishing Lines   VAM 1H I 1 Aa

Obverse I 1—Fine polishing lines around OD WE, across the neck, and in the left and right fields. *Die markers*—Numerous tight elliptical polishing lines below the jaw and just below the bottom of the hair bun. Die used for Satin Proofs and circulation strikes.

 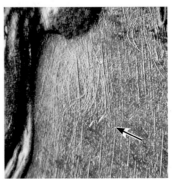

Reverse Aa—Fine polishing lines above and below ONE, around the eagle's feet, through S OF AM, and below the last A in AMERICA. *Die markers*—Numerous horizontal die polishing lines between the last S in STATES and O in OF, single light polishing line at bottom inside of R in AMERICA. Die chip at the top end of the fourth ray below the eagle's tail feathers. Die used for Satin Proofs and circulation strikes.

VF-20	EF-40	AU-50	MS-60	MS-63	MS-64	MS-65
$150	$185	$200	$365	$550	$1,000	$3,250

Collecting Advice

The 1921 is second only to the 1934-S in importance in a Peace dollar collection, and therefore demands a very strong example. Even though it is effectively a common date because of the number of samples in existence, the uniqueness of this first-year issue places it almost in the key-date category. Prices are commensurate with the popularity of this issue, in spite of the relatively large supply.

Look for a specimen that has as strong a strike as possible, which will be difficult due to the reasons stated earlier. A coin with a good strike will set the entire collection off. Specimens in MS-65 should be the minimum for a nice set, as coins in MS-64 or lower are likely to have a very weak strike and/or excessive marks. If you can afford the MS-66 level, by all means, find one. The requirements for an above-average strike at the MS-66 and higher levels will result in a coin that is a very attractive example of this first-year issue. Note that most grading services ignore strike when assigning a grade to this coin. Therefore, look for the best-struck example among any group of coins with the same numerical grade.

Many of these coins have unsightly toning, so avoid those. Some are available with attractive toning, and these are of interest to some collectors. Avoid raw coins that are toned, as it is difficult to identify *artificial* toning, and there are several "coin doctors" in existence who attempt to modify coins to specifically produce toning.

For the first Peace dollars, the combination of high relief and hurried production led to many 1921 coins being poorly struck. The figure on the following page illustrates several commonly encountered differences in striking quality. Although coins from 1922 through 1935 also show divergence in striking quality, the differences are much less pronounced than for 1921.

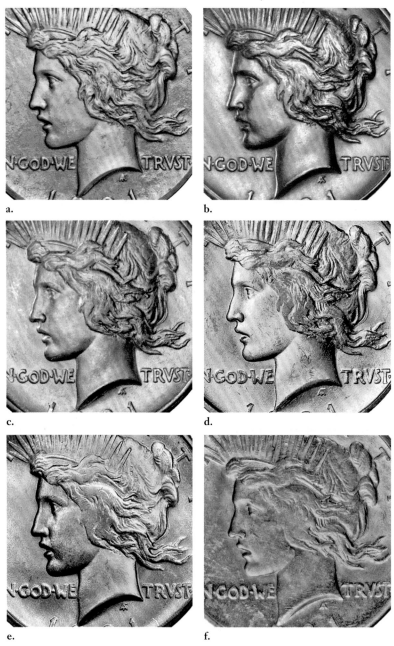

a.   b.

c.   d.

e.   f.

Differences in striking quality: (a) original bronze model; (b) very well-struck circulation coin; (c) above-average strike; (d) typical strike; (e) below-average strike; (f) weak strike. Compare the detail of the hair next to Liberty's cheek and over her ear. An average to above-average strike must have the two locks of hair at Liberty's cheek separate and distinct. No Peace dollars, including the Proofs, maintain the full detail of the artist's original.

Close examination of the original model reveals a wealth of fine detail in the hair, particularly adjacent to Liberty's cheek and forehead. By the time the Mint had completed hubs and dies, the most delicate details had apparently faded from the dies. Sandblast Proofs, struck on a high-pressure medal press, do not match the bronze cast in detail. For most collectors, the simplest criterion for identifying a 1921 coin with an acceptable strike (average or above), is to look for complete separation of the hair curls immediately to the right of Liberty's cheek below the eye. Coins with better-delineated features will have these two curls clearly separated and might show some rounding to the hair. Below-average strikes will have the two curls blended together, but there will be a small separation between the curls and the cheek. A weakly struck coin will not only have the two curls blended together, but they will merge into the cheek and parts of the hair leaving a flat, almost feature-less area at the design's center. Major grading services pay little attention to strike, so collectors can sometimes pick up a bargain by looking beyond the numbers on a plastic slab. (The best-struck coin in the illustration on the opposite page is actually an About Uncirculated piece that has been cleaned.)

Most 1921 Peace dollars on the market will show average to below-average strikes.

There are also a significant quantity of 1921 coins that are well struck at the center but have weak dates and/or peripheral features. This was evidently caused by the dies not being perfectly parallel.

1922-P

Mintage: 51,737,000

Whitman Coin Guide (WCG™)

VF-20	EF-40	AU-50	MS-60	MS-63	MS-64	MS-65	MS-66	MS-67
$25	$28	$30	$32	$40	$60	$125	$600	$9,000

The high-relief design of 1921 was difficult to produce and exhibited very poor die life. After several failed experiments with modifying the original design, Mint Director Baker ordered that a low-relief version be produced. Sculptor Anthony de Francisci quickly created new models with reduced relief, which would be more suitable for large-scale production. The 1922 low-relief Peace dollars were struck from two different pairs of hubs. The first pair was produced in early February from de Francisci's low-relief models and was used for Philadelphia pre-production trial strikes. Production figures suggest at least 200,000 pieces can be considered trial pieces, although later coins struck from the same hubs cannot be differentiated from these trial strikes.

February 13, 1922	100,000
February 14, 1922	100,000
February 15, 1922	150,000

Once these were approved for use by James E. Fraser on February 14, 1922, the same hubs produced working dies for all three mints. The first obverse hubs had sharper lettering than later versions, with the sides of characters nearly perpendicular to the fields. The reverse hub is distinguished by the olive branch being disconnected from the eagle's right talon. These hubs were also used for the low-relief Proof specimens.

The second hubs were made in March and had obverse lettering somewhat less prominent, with the lettering's sides more angled than the earlier version. The reverse had the olive branch connected to the talon by a short, hand-engraved piece of stem. Later in the year, this was smoothed so that the engraving was less noticeable. Most 1922 coins were struck from these second hubs.

Although trial-strike coins can be easily identified by the disconnected olive branch, continued use of the same hubs for at least a month resulted in hundreds of thousands, or even millions, of identical pieces being struck. Collector Barry Lovvorn and I estimate that approximately 10 percent of the Philadelphia Mint dollars are from the first hubs. As one of the very few documented production trial designs available to collectors, these pieces are a distinctive part of a Peace dollar collection. They are, however, common enough to be available to any collector with a little patience.

The Mint was authorized to strike as many coins as possible to convert the Pittman silver back into coins; accordingly, more Peace dollars were minted by Philadelphia that year than in any other single issue year/mint. Initial Philadelphia production of low-relief coins was 150,000 per day, but by August this had increased to 300,000 per day—an output often greater than that of the other two mints combined.

A great many 1922-P coins were released into circulation, but millions were also held back in Treasury vaults for decades, leaving many for collectors to pursue. Over the years, as bagged coins were shifted from one vault to another, many coins acquired numerous bagmarks and scrapes.

This issue is notable for containing what appear to be water spots on the coins. These were likely imparted onto the coins by improper washing of the planchets. As with other issues in the series, coins are typically found with a light golden patina covering the surfaces.

Relative Rarity

Within the entire series, the 1922 is the second most common issue in Uncirculated condition, as shown here, with only the 1923 issue more abundant in MS-60 and higher.

Relative Rarity Within the 24-coin Series

MS-63	MS-64	MS-65	MS-66	MS-60–MS-70
23/24	23/24	23/24	22/24	23/24

Significant Examples

A well-known example of 1922-P came from the Jack Lee II collection and was graded MS-67 by PCGS (shown). It also has blinding luster, and there are no visible marks on the coin. It has traded several times in the recent past, but always seems to end up in one of the most significant Peace dollar collections.

Varieties

As would be expected with a large issue, many varieties have been identified. The detached olive branch variety from the first hubs and 13 more from the VAM Top 50 are shown here.

For 1922 and 1923, there are a great many coins that have thin or hairline die cracks across the neck and through Liberty's hair. In general, these are not individually attributed as VAM die varieties until the fine crack has enlarged into a noticeable break.

DETACHED OLIVE BRANCH   VAM N/A

Reverse B—The olive branch is completely detached from the eagle's talon. This is a characteristic of the first hub for 1922. Trial strikes were made from this hub at the Philadelphia Mint. Approximately 10 percent of the 1922 Philadelphia mintage might be from this hub.

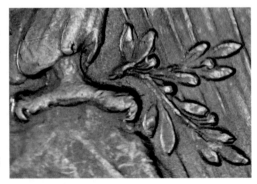

VF-20	EF-40	AU-50	MS-60	MS-63	MS-64	MS-65
$60	$95	$110	$135	$365	—	—

Die Gouge in Rays   VAM 1A II 1 B¹A

Obverse II 1—There is a horizontal die gouge in the rays below B in LIBERTY.

VF-20	EF-40	AU-50	MS-60	MS-63	MS-64	MS-65
$30	$35	$38	$40	$50	$80	$170

Reverse Field Die Break   VAM 1F II 1 B¹A

Reverse B¹a—There is a die break in the field above DOLLAR, causing a diagonal sliver of raised metal.

VF-20	EF-40	AU-50	MS-60	MS-63	MS-64	MS-65
$100	$200	$400	$800	$2,500	—	—

Earring Die Break   VAM 2A II 1 B²A

Obverse II 1—Note the earring die break in late die state, causing a shaft of metal from the ear down to the neck.

VF-20	EF-40	AU-50	MS-60	MS-63	MS-64	MS-65
$80	$160	$290	$350	$2,300	—	—

EXTRA-HAIR DIE BREAK   VAM 2C II 1 B²A

Obverse II 1—A pair of die breaks is visible in the back of Liberty's hair. Shaped like a backward C, these breaks are fairly large and raised well above the hair.

VF-20	EF-40	AU-50	MS-60	MS-63	MS-64	MS-65
$40	$60	$90	$180	$385	—	—

REVERSE WING DIE BREAK   VAM 2E II 1 B²A

Reverse B²a—There is a die break on the left side of the eagle's wing, showing as a tear drop.

VF-20	EF-40	AU-50	MS-60	MS-63	MS-64	MS-65
$60	$90	$110	$155	$385	$675	—

"HAIRPIN" DIE GOUGE IN RAYS   VAM 2F II 1 B²A

Obverse II 1—There is a horizontal die gouge in the rays below E in LIBERTY.

VF-20	EF-40	AU-50	MS-60	MS-63	MS-64	MS-65
$35	$38	$41	$65	$125	$250	—

DOUBLED MOTTO   VAM 4 II 2 B²A

Obverse II 2—Note the slightly doubled bottom of WE TR, the designer's monogram, the date digits, and the lower hair strands.

VF-20	EF-40	AU-50	MS-60	MS-63	MS-64	MS-65
$35	$38	$41	$65	$135	$275	—

SCAR CHEEK   VAM 5A II 1 B²C

Obverse II 1—There are a vertical die break and a large die chip just behind Liberty's mouth.

VF-20	EF-40	AU-50	MS-60	MS-63	MS-64	MS-65
$48	$75	$190	$400	$650	—	—

DOUBLED LEAVES   VAM 6 II 1 B²D

Reverse B²d—Note the doubled bottom of the middle olive leaves, left side of the top, and lower olive leaves; left side of the rays below DOL, the base of DOLLAR, below the middle and right talon, the back of the leg feathers, and the base of E in E PLURIBUS UNUM.

VF-20	EF-40	AU-50	MS-60	MS-63	MS-64	MS-65
$40	$50	$60	$115	$235	$400	—

DOUBLED WING   VAM 7

Reverse B²e—The edge of the wing is doubled.

VF-20	EF-40	AU-50	MS-60	MS-63	MS-64	MS-65
$35	$38	$41	$85	$165	$325	—

Doubled Tiara   VAM 8 II 3 B²A

Obverse II 3—Note the doubled die in the 9:00 direction. Rays of light in the tiara are doubled on the left side. The nose, lips, and chin are slightly doubled. L in LIBERTY is doubled towards the rim. N GOD WE, T in TRVST, and the designer's initials are doubled on the left side.

VF-20	EF-40	AU-50	MS-60	MS-63	MS-64	MS-65
$38	$41	$50	$65	$150	$225	—

Mustache   VAM 12A II 1 B²H

Obverse II 1—There is a die break from the nose to the end of the upper lip of Liberty's head.

VF-20	EF-40	AU-50	MS-60	MS-63	MS-64	MS-65
$45	$70	$90	$200	$500	$975	—

Collecting Advice

The 1922-P is one of the common dates for the series, and many quality samples in MS-65 and higher grades exist. The grade of MS-66 should be the target for the collector, and because of the great numbers in existence, a technically superior coin should be selected. Choose a sample with an outstanding strike, great luster, and no distracting marks (particularly on Liberty's face and neck). Avoid coins with water spots, as they can be unattractive to many collectors and therefore difficult to resell.

1922-D

Mintage: 15,063,000

Whitman Coin Guide (WCG™)

VF-20	EF-40	AU-50	MS-60	MS-63	MS-64	MS-65	MS-66	MS-67
$28	$30	$33	$50	$85	$150	$625	$2,200	$30,000

Denver Mint silver dollars during the first two years of issue, 1922 and 1923, are usually well struck. The mile-high mint's technique focused mainly on increasing the striking pressure, which resulted not only in short die life, but also in many of the dies cracking. (Note the long, thin crack across Liberty's neck in the image.) Often, operators would not realize the dies had cracked and would continue to produce coins long after they should have. These die cracks were then transferred to the planchet in the striking process, leaving their images on the finished coins. These mostly appear as concentric lines beginning around the base of Liberty's neck, and extending clockwise up through the motto into the field to the left of Liberty's face.

As a result of excessive use of the dies, the surface of some coins also displayed an "orange peel" effect.

Examples exist from both the first and second pair of hubs. Approximately the first 15 to 20 percent of coins were struck using the original low-relief hub, with the remainder struck from a new hub introduced in March. (High-relief 1922 dies were shipped in January but never used.)

Production began on February 20 but rarely exceeded 25,000 pieces per day until August, when the daily average was 200,000 dollars.

February 20, 1922	25,000
February 22, 1922	25,000
February 23, 1922	25,000

1922-D coins do not suffer from water marks to the extent of 1922-P specimens.

Relative Rarity

The 1922-D is the most common of the issues produced in Denver, with many nice coins to choose from in Uncirculated condition. More Peace dollars were minted by Denver in 1922 than the rest of the Denver issues combined. Gems are easy to find, with many nice examples available. This issue should be considered a common date in the series, although that was not always the case. For a long time, Gems (MS-65 and better) were considered quite rare. With the discovery of several large hoards and subsequent release of those previously unknown coins, many nice examples became available to collectors.

Relative Rarity Within the 24-coin Series

MS-63	MS-64	MS-65	MS-66	MS-60–MS-70
17/24	18/24	19/24	20/24	18/24

Significant Examples

The finest known examples of the 1922-D issue are graded MS-67, and at this writing fewer than twenty have been so certified by the major grading companies. One of the more prominent examples was part of the Robert Moreno Collection, and was graded MS-67* by NGC (the * denotes superior eye appeal and is given to a very few coins from each issue). It has an interesting toning streak across the obverse, and is technically superior with a strong strike and virtually no visible marks.

Varieties

There are dozens of die varieties documented for this issue, including the first hub. The most popular varieties are described here.

DETACHED OLIVE BRANCH   VAM N/A

Reverse B—The olive branch is completely detached from the eagle's talon. This is a characteristic of the first hub for 1922. Trial strikes were made from this hub at the Philadelphia Mint. Approximately 15 to 20 percent of the 1922 Denver mintage might be from this hub.

VF-20	EF-40	AU-50	MS-60	MS-63	MS-64	MS-65
$45	$50	$55	$95	$200	$500	$875

DOUBLED OLIVE BRANCH   VAM 3 III 1 B²c

Reverse B²c—Doubled lower reverse. The olive branch and leaves are doubled to the left.

VF-20	EF-40	AU-50	MS-60	MS-63	MS-64	MS-65
$45	$55	$65	$145	$345	$920	—

DOUBLED MONOGRAM   VAM 4 II 2 B²c

Obverse II 2—De Francisci's monogram, TRVST, and the date are doubled towards the rim, with slight doubling along the bottom of the neck and the end of the hair.

 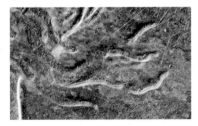

Reverse B²c—Note the doubled bottom edge of the right leaves, left edge of the eagle's left leg feathers, and rays below the leg feathers.

VF-20	EF-40	AU-50	MS-60	MS-63	MS-64	MS-65
$50	$60	$80	$150	$360	—	—

TRIPLED REVERSE   VAM 7 II 1 B²ᴅ

Obverse II 1—There is a small diagonal die gouge in front of the tiara and a short one at the back of the hair.

Reverse B²d—Note the tripled lower edge of the olive leaves, the eagle's right talon, and the back of the rear leg feathers. Also note the doubled lower edge of the olive branch, DO in DOLLAR, and the eagle's middle talon.

VF-20	EF-40	AU-50	MS-60	MS-63	MS-64	MS-65
$42	$48	$60	$150	$360	—	—

Collecting Advice

The coin selected for the 1922-D slot in any collection should be an excellent example, graded at least MS-65, and ideally MS-66. Whether a coin has a die-crack impression should not be a major determinant, but more of a personal preference. Some collectors find these impressions interesting, and seek them out. Others consider them flaws in the coins and avoid them. As always, look for a coin with few marks on the face and neck, and one that has a terrific strike. There are numerous coins available that are struck very well, and because of that, a good collection should have a coin that is highly detailed.

1922-S

Mintage: 17,475,000

Whitman Coin Guide (WCG™)

VF-20	EF-40	AU-50	MS-60	MS-63	MS-64	MS-65	MS-66	MS-67
$28	$30	$33	$50	$95	$300	$2,400	$20,000	—

The first Peace dollar struck at San Francisco presented challenges for the mint by the bay. The mint management was interested in extending the life of the dies, and therefore reduced striking the pressure to prolong the life. This resulted in most coins being weakly struck, a characteristic that plagued the San Francisco Mint during the entire Peace dollar run. Overall, this particular issue is a poor one.

Examples exist from both the first and second pair of hubs. (High-relief 1922 dies were shipped in January but never used.)

Production began on February 22 with 60,000 pieces struck the first day; on the 23rd, 100,000 pieces were coined. Average production was initially 150,000 per day and remained relatively constant for the balance of the year.

The total mintage was high, but there was not a great amount of coins withheld from circulation, making the Uncirculated population remain very low on a percentage basis. Bagmarks for those coins that remained uncirculated are also a factor for this coin.

As with other issues in the series, 1922-S dollars are typically found with a golden patina covering the surfaces.

Relative Rarity

The 1922-S, along with the 1923-S, is often regarded as the most common San Francisco Mint issue in the Peace dollar series. But while examples are readily available in MS-62 to MS-64 grades, Gems are rare due to strike and surface-preservation problems. Within the entire series, the 1922-S is one of the more common issues in Uncirculated condition, as shown here.

Relative Rarity Within the 24-coin Series

MS-63	MS-64	MS-65	MS-66	MS-60–MS-70
15/24	14/24	10/24	9/24	14/24

Significant Examples

The finest known examples of the 1922-S are graded MS-66, and at this writing fewer than two dozen have been certified in this condition by the major grading companies. One of the higher-quality coins was part of the Robert Moreno Collection and is graded MS-66 by NGC. It has a much better than average strike for this issue, and possesses good luster. It has some very colorful rim toning, which adds character to the coin.

Varieties

There are several dozen minor die varieties known, in addition to pieces struck from the initial hub. The most popular varieties are shown here.

DETACHED OLIVE BRANCH   VAM N/A

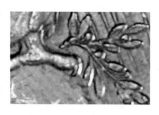

Reverse B—The olive branch is completely detached from the eagle's talon. This is a characteristic of the first hub for 1922. Trial strikes were made from this hub at the Philadelphia Mint. Approximately 30 percent of the 1922 San Francisco mintage might be from this hub.

VF-20	EF-40	AU-50	MS-60	MS-63	MS-64	MS-65
$42	$48	$60	$150	$215	$490	—

TRIPLED REVERSE   VAM 3 II 1 B²B

Reverse B²b—Note the tripled front edge of the eagle's right wing; the doubled top of the eagle's head, top inside of the upper beak, throat, and right edge of the neck feathers; the tripled rays below, through, and above ONE; the doubled back of the leg feathers; the slightly doubled right side of the rays through DOLLAR; the slightly tripled lower olive leaves; and the doubled top olive leaf on the left side.

VF-20	EF-40	AU-50	MS-60	MS-63	MS-64	MS-65
$34	$40	$50	$95	$150	$560	—

DIE FILE LINES ON REVERSE, EXTRA RAY   VAM 10 II 1 B²F

Reverse B²f—The rays in the die-clash area to the right of the olive leaves were strengthened, with two rays now extending down over the middle mountain. Further attempts to remove the clash marks left heavy die file lines at the tops of the eagle's left and right shoulder, above the end of the left wing, around the lower olive leaves, and around DOLLA. (Note: This variety was formerly VAM 2o; this number has been incorporated into VAM 10.)

Collecting Advice

The 1922-S is difficult to find in MS-65 and higher, particularly with a combination of good strike, strong luster, and minimal marks. Because the general quality of this issue is low, finding a coin with those three attributes will be a long and tedious search, and will also involve a high price tag. Therefore, seek a coin in MS-64 condition that has as strong a strike as can be found.

1923-P

Mintage: 30,800,000

Whitman Coin Guide (WCG™)

VF-20	EF-40	AU-50	MS-60	MS-63	MS-64	MS-65	MS-66	MS-67
$25	$28	$30	$32	$40	$60	$125	$550	$4,000

Although the 1923-P dollar does not have the largest mintage in the Peace dollar series, it is considered the most common. Many 1922 dollars were placed in circulation, but by 1923 commerce was saturated with the new coins. Large quantities of 1923-P dollars survived in Mint bags, untouched for decades. Overall, it is among the highest-quality issues in the series, with good strikes and strong luster. Like the 1922 issue from Philadelphia, many examples exhibit water spots, some of which are very obvious and render those coins difficult to sell.

The mint in Philadelphia was still experimenting with dies, trying to maximize die life by repairing rather than replacing them. Much effort was spent trying to fix chips and other imperfections, resulting in many different varieties for the specialty collector to pursue.

Relative Rarity

The 1923-P is the most common Peace dollar in Uncirculated condition, as shown here. About 60 percent more of the 1923-P issue have been graded by the major third-party services at this writing than of the second most common issue (1922-P).

Relative Rarity Within the 24-coin Series

MS-63	MS-64	MS-65	MS-66	MS-60–MS-70
24/24	24/24	24/24	24/24	24/24

Significant Examples

The finest known examples of the 1923-P are graded MS-67, and at this writing approximately 100 have been certified at this level by the major grading companies. One of the most famous specimens is from the Jack Lee I & II collections, and is graded MS-67 by PCGS. It is a blast-white coin that is very well struck and has only a few trivial contact marks. The luster

from this coin is truly blinding. It has traded several times in the recent past, and always seems to end up in one of the most significant Peace dollar collections.

Varieties

There are several dozen die varieties listed in detailed variety guides and Web sites. The nine most significant are described here.

For 1922 and 1923 there are a great many coins that have hairline die cracks across the neck and through Liberty's hair. In general, these are not individually attributed as VAM die varieties until the fine crack has enlarged into a noticeable break.

WHISKER JAW VAM 1A II 1 B²A

Obverse II 1—There is an extra sliver of metal from the jaw to the neck due to a die break.

VF-20	EF-40	AU-50	MS-60	MS-63	MS-64	MS-65
$43	$50	$80	$125	$265	$550	—

EXTRA HAIR VAM 1B II 1 B²A

Obverse II 1—There is a sliver of metal at the back of the hair due to a die break. Several variations of this type of die break exist with the metal positioned at various places on Liberty's hair.

VF-20	EF-40	AU-50	MS-60	MS-63	MS-64	MS-65
$50	$80	$125	$200	$400	$600	—

DIE BREAK REAR OF TIARA RAYS; VAM 1C II 1 B²A TAIL ON O

Obverse II 1—There is a short, thin diagonal die break to the right of the last ray in the tiara.

Reverse B²a—Note the die break from the lower part of O in DOL-LAR extending diagonally down to the left.

VF-20	EF-40	AU-50	MS-60	MS-63	MS-64	MS-65
$140	$175	$275	$650	$1,800	—	—

WHISKER CHEEK VAM 1D II 1 B²A

Obverse II 1—The sliver of metal on the cheek is due to a die break.

VF-20	EF-40	AU-50	MS-60	MS-63	MS-64	MS-65
$47	$80	$165	$250	$475	$875	—

DIE BREAK ON EAGLE'S BACK VAM 1E II 1 B²A

Reverse B²a—There is a die break from the top left of the eagle's wing down across the back to the middle of the right wing.

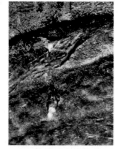

VF-20	EF-40	AU-50	MS-60	MS-63	MS-64	MS-65
$150	$250	$450	$1,250	—	—	—

CHIN BAR VAM 1F II 1 B²A

Obverse II 1—The chin bar variety is the result of a die gouge that runs from Liberty's chin just to the right of the letter D in GOD, all the way down to the 1 in 1923. See 1924 VAM 1A for a similar variety.

VF-20	EF-40	AU-50	MS-60	MS-63	MS-64	MS-65
$43	$53	$65	$90	$125	$185	$375

BAR WING VAM 1O II 1 B²A

Reverse B²a—A die break is at the top of the eagle's right wing, below a vertical die clash mark showing as a crescent.

VF-20	EF-40	AU-50	MS-60	MS-63	MS-64	MS-65
$70	$88	$140	$160	$275	$575	—

DOUBLED RAYS VAM 2 II 4 B²A

Obverse II 4—The rays of light in the tiara are doubled on the left side, with those in the rear having the strongest doubling. Tops of TR in TRVST, the lower back hair curl, the rear of the neck, and the right side of the designer's initials are slightly doubled.

VF-20	EF-40	AU-50	MS-60	MS-63	MS-64	MS-65
$43	$50	$58	$75	$160	$375	—

DOUBLED LOWER REVERSE   VAM 3 II 1 B²B

Reverse B²b—Note the doubled lower reverse, including the olive leaves, rays, and back of the feathers on the legs.

VF-20	EF-40	AU-50	MS-60	MS-63	MS-64	MS-65
$43	$50	$60	$80	$170	$390	—

Collecting Advice

The 1923-P is among the most common of Peace dollars and the collector should strive to make this coin the most technically perfect one in the set. There are many, many fine examples because of the volume of coins that have been graded to date. The MS-66 level should be the goal, although there are many MS-65 coins in existence. Regardless of the choice, the coin should have a very detailed strike, with little or no marks on the devices, and terrific luster. Don't settle for an average example of this one.

1923-D

Mintage: 6,811,000

Whitman Coin Guide (WCG™)

VF-20	EF-40	AU-50	MS-60	MS-63	MS-64	MS-65	MS-66	MS-67
$28	$30	$40	$70	$160	$375	$1,300	$4,750	—

In common with other Denver Mint silver dollars, this issue is typically very well struck. Like the 1922-D, die cracks are common, likely due to above-normal striking pressure. Excess force caused the dies to crack, and the cracks were either not noticed or not considered significant by Mint employees, resulting in many coins showing these impressions.

Most coins in this issue possess good luster, although some have a very dull appearance even without toning present. Even though there was a large quantity minted, a proportionately small percentage of coins survived in Gem condition because of excessive bagmarks. Even those that have received an MS-65 or better grade will likely have some marks that are noticeable, and at times even distracting.

Relative Rarity

Within the entire series, the 1923-D is in the top third of the scarcest Uncirculated issues in the series. Note, however, that Gems are more readily available.

Relative Rarity Within the 24-coin Series

MS-63	MS-64	MS-65	MS-66	MS-60–MS-70
6/24	6/24	11/24	13/24	7/24

Significant Examples

The finest known examples of the 1923-D issue are graded MS-66, and at this writing approximately 100 have been so certified by the major grading companies. One of the best known specimens is graded MS-66 by PCGS. It is a blast-white coin that is very well struck and has only a few trivial contact marks. The luster from this coin is truly blinding.

Varieties

There are many 1923-D die varieties known, most having to do with one or more die breaks. The only variety from this issue among the Top 50 Peace VAMs is described here.

Doubled Reverse   VAM 2 II 1 B²b

Reverse B²b—Note the slightly doubled top of the eagle's head, mouth, beak, and shoulder; and the slightly doubled top olive leaf, doubled branches, and bottom olive leaves on the left side. The back leg feathers are doubled on the left side, as are the rays through ONE.

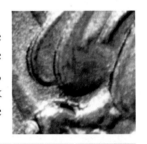

VF-20	EF-40	AU-50	MS-60	MS-63	MS-64	MS-65
$65	$95	$200	$550	$1,000	—	—

Die Break Left of Y #3,   VAM 1AH2 II 1 B²a
Die Break Above IN

Obverse II 1—A die crack runs from the neck, over through IN, and up to the L in LIBERTY, with a connecting radial die crack above IN creating a displaced field break above IN.

Collecting Advice

Many fine examples of the 1923-D exist for reasonable cost at MS-64 and, with the typical strong strike, will make a fine example for a good date or type collection. However, MS-65 coins are plentiful enough that they are within the budget of most collectors and are an ideal candidate for a nice collection. Avoid any coin that is weakly struck, as they are in the minority for this issue, and resale will be difficult in competition with so many well-struck examples. Also avoid any coin with the previously mentioned lackluster finish; find an example with good luster. Avoid examples with unsightly toning or marks on the face and neck.

1923-S

Mintage: 19,020,000

Whitman Coin Guide (WCG™)

VF-20	EF-40	AU-50	MS-60	MS-63	MS-64	MS-65	MS-66	MS-67
$28	$30	$36	$55	$90	$450	$6,000	$30,000	$60,000

Similar to the 1922 issue from San Francisco, this one is typically very softly struck. Because of the large mintage, the striking force was reduced even further to extend the life of the dies, at the expense of well-formed coins.

Many were released into circulation, and those that weren't are covered with bagmarks. A good many have lackluster surfaces, without much reflectivity. For all these reasons, it ranks as one of the poorest issues in the entire Peace dollar series. In spite of the large mintage, finding quality Uncirculated examples is very difficult.

Those Uncirculated examples that exist are mostly in the MS-63 or 64 category, as not many had sufficient strike or few enough marks to make it to the Gem level. Even some that are graded MS-65 are questionable and could be argued back into the MS-64 range.

Relative Rarity

The 1923-S presents something of a dichotomy when discussing rarity in Uncirculated state. In the lower grades of MS-63/MS-64, it is very common and easily had; in Gem and better, it is *extremely* rare.

Relative Rarity Within the 24-coin Series

MS-63	MS-64	MS-65	MS-66	MS-60–MS-70
18/24	15/24	5/24	4/24	15/24

Significant Examples

There are a handful of 1923-S dollars graded MS-66, but a single coin received the Superb Gem rating of MS-67 by PCGS, and it is formerly from the Jack Lee collection. This coin is one of the more famous Peace dollars, because the overall quality of this issue was so poor, and a scant few made it to MS-66. It is truly an oddity, in that somehow it managed both to be struck well and to survive without bagmarks.

Varieties

There are dozens of 1923-S die varieties documented, most involving die cracks and doubling. The only one listed in the Peace VAM Top 50 is described here.

PITTED REVERSE   VAM 1C II 1 B²A

Reverse B²a—There are raised dots below and above the N in ONE, curving left to the rim due to a damaged or deteriorating die.

VF-20	EF-40	AU-50	MS-60	MS-63	MS-64	MS-65
$55	$65	$125	$250	$450	$975	—

Collecting Advice

It will be challenging to find a nice 1923-S that is well struck, has good luster, and bears few marks. One with all three of those attributes will be very expensive, so choose which two are most important and go from there. This is a coin that collectors typically allow to be less than ideal, because of the general quality of this issue. An MS-64 example will be adequate for most collectors, and it is not worth spending much time searching for a high-end coin, because they are very rare. With an unlimited budget, by all means, seek out an MS-65 coin, but be prepared for a considerable outlay and a long search.

1924-P
Mintage: 11,811,00

Whitman Coin Guide (WCG™)

VF-20	EF-40	AU-50	MS-60	MS-63	MS-64	MS-65	MS-66	MS-67
$25	$28	$30	$32	$40	$60	$125	$650	$6,750

The 1924-P issue is typical of coins produced in Philadelphia, with good strikes and many with attractive luster. There is a wide variance in luster, however; some coins have a dull, non-reflective finish that leaves them looking bland. This variance is likely due to overuse of the dies—they become pitted and worn as more coins are struck, resulting in a rough, uneven finish.

There were many coins released into circulation, but enough were held back to make this issue a common date for the series. As with other issues in the series, 1924-P dollars are typically found with a golden patina covering the surfaces.

According to numismatist David W. Lange, the entire motto is retouched on the 1924 dollars. This has been known for some time, but I have been unable to identify the discoverer.

Relative Rarity

Within the entire series, the 1924 is one of the common dates in Uncirculated condition, as shown here.

Relative Rarity Within the 24-coin Series

MS-63	MS-64	MS-65	MS-66	MS-60–MS-70
21/24	21/24	21/24	21/24	21/24

Significant Examples

The finest known examples of the 1924 issue are graded MS-68, and at this writing, one each exists from NGC and PCGS. The PCGS coin carries the Jack Lee II pedigree and has the most intense luster I have ever seen in a Peace dollar. The luster scintillates and races around each side in an unbroken sheet of original silver. As can be imagined, there are no

visible marks anywhere on this coin. It is also one of the most outstanding Peace dollars of any date that a collector could ever encounter.

Varieties

There are a few dozen die varieties known, but the four most popular are illustrated here.

BAR D VAM 1A II 1 B²A

Obverse II 1—Note the vertical bar of metal from the left side of the D in the motto down to the rim. See 1923-P for a similar die gouge.

VF-20	EF-40	AU-50	MS-60	MS-63	MS-64	MS-65
$50	$60	$70	$155	$260	$425	$650

DOUBLED REVERSE VAM 2 II 1 B²I

Reverse B²i—The rays above ONE and the eagle's back and rear feathers of the leg are doubled.

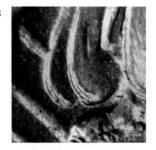

VF-20	EF-40	AU-50	MS-60	MS-63	MS-64	MS-65
$45	$55	$63	$110	$225	$375	$600

Wing Break   VAM 5A II 3 B²a

Reverse B²a—There is a large circular die break in the center of the wing.

VF-20	EF-40	AU-50	MS-60	MS-63	MS-64	MS-65
$55	$85	$130	$200	$475	—	—

Breaks in Hair   VAM 8A II 1 B²a

Obverse II 1—Two vertical die breaks at back of hair.

VF-20	EF-40	AU-50	MS-60	MS-63	MS-64	MS-65
$50	$85	$115	$160	$335	$700	—

Collecting Advice

The 1924-P is a common date, and therefore the collector should strive for a technically sound example, ideally in MS-66. There are many quality coins available at this lofty grade, and if money is an issue, a very nice coin can also be found in MS-65 for a very reasonable price. To be technically sound, the coin should have a strong strike with few visible marks and should have good, smooth, reflective luster. Avoid coins that look dull, as they are not popular with most dealers and collectors, making resale difficult.

1924-S

Mintage: 1,728,000

Whitman Coin Guide (WCG™)

VF-20	EF-40	AU-50	MS-60	MS-63	MS-64	MS-65	MS-66	MS-67
$28	$40	$60	$220	$500	$1,300	$8,500	$43,500	—

The 1924 issue from San Francisco is typical of this mint's offerings, in that it is usually poorly struck. Compounded with the low mintage in this year, high-quality coins that are well struck are extremely rare. Luster also usually appears dull on this issue, making it very tough to find an attractive coin.

Quite a few coins were released into circulation and the issue is readily available in circulated conditions. Most Uncirculated examples, even ones from hoards or in the Treasury's releases of the early 1960s, are heavily bag marked. Finding Gem samples of this issue is difficult indeed, and attractive Gems even more so. Overall, this is one of the poorer issues in the series.

Relative Rarity

Within the entire series, the 1924-S is a very rare issue in Uncirculated condition, as shown here, with only two other issues being rarer within the collectible set of 24 coins.

Relative Rarity Within the 24-coin Series

MS-63	MS-64	MS-65	MS-66	MS-60–MS-70
4/24	4/24	4/24	5/24	2/24

Significant Examples

The finest known examples of the 1924-S issue are graded MS-66, and at this writing only a handful have been so certified by the major grading companies. They are very rarely traded and difficult to locate, existing solely in the finest collections. Shown is a very nice example in MS-65 with some toning that is unique, especially for a Peace dollar.

Varieties

There are seven varieties documented, but only one is listed in the Top 50 Peace VAMs.

DOUBLED REVERSE   VAM 3 II 1 B²C

Reverse B²c—The bottom edges of the top stems and leaves in the olives sprig are doubled. The bottom of the D in DOLLAR, left edge of the leg feathers, left edges of the first three rays above ONE, and left edge of the top ray above the back of the leg feathers are doubled.

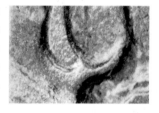

VF-20	EF-40	AU-50	MS-60	MS-63	MS-64	MS-65
$45	$65	$150	$325	$725	$1,550	—

Collecting Advice

The 1924-S is very tough to find in attractive Mint State. Finding one with a good strike, in any grade, is extremely difficult. An MS-64 coin is within the reach of most collectors, and is the grade most should strive for. Seek an example with good luster; if you can find one with an average or better than average strike, stop looking. Gems are very rare, and attractive ones are very expensive. The price of Gems varies greatly, because of differences in strikes and the variation in luster.

1925-P

Mintage: 10,198,000

Whitman Coin Guide (WCG™)

VF-20	EF-40	AU-50	MS-60	MS-63	MS-64	MS-65	MS-66	MS-67
$25	$28	$30	$32	$40	$60	$125	$600	$4,000

The 1925-P issue, along with the 1922, 1923, and 1924 issues also from Philadelphia, is considered a common date in the series. Even though some issues have far higher mintages, many of these coins survived untouched for decades, locked away in Treasury vaults. According to David W. Lange, few were released until the mid-1940s, and they were priced like a key date at that time. Dealers quickly acquired the few specimens that were issued until it later became evident that the coin was not scarce, and consequently the price fell. Coupled with the high quality of production, there remain today thousands of fine Uncirculated examples. Oddly, this is the scarcest coin of the series in well-circulated conditions.

Most were formed boldly with good strikes. Luster is usually very good, but many, if not most, of the issue are covered in a thin layer of light gold toning on both obverse and reverse. Coins that are brilliant have likely been dipped to remove the gold toning.

Relative Rarity

The 1925-P is one of the most common dates in the Peace dollar series relative to the entire set of 24 coins.

Relative Rarity Within the 24-coin Series

MS-63	MS-64	MS-65	MS-66	MS-60–MS-70
22/24	22/24	22/24	23/24	22/24

Significant Examples

There are two 1925-P coins graded MS-68, one by NGC and one by PCGS. The PCGS sample carries a pedigree to the Jack Lee collection, and sold at auction on August 12, 2011, for $89,125.

Varieties

There are approximately two dozen die varieties documented, with only three listed among the Top 50 Peace VAMs.

Tiara Gouge   VAM 1A II 1 B²A

Obverse II 1—There is a horizontal die gouge in the rays well below the B in LIBERTY.

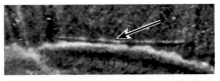

VF-20	EF-40	AU-50	MS-60	MS-63	MS-64	MS-65
$43	$48	$63	$80	$100	$175	$325

Doubled Rays   VAM 3 II 1 B²C

Reverse B²c—The rays above DOLL are doubled on the right side. D in DOLLAR and the right wing are slightly doubled on the upper right side. The two top olive leaves are slightly doubled on the right side.

VF-20	EF-40	AU-50	MS-60	MS-63	MS-64	MS-65
$40	$55	$70	$95	$140	$245	$450

MISSING RAY VAM 5 II 1 B²A

Reverse B²a—The center of the die is over-polished, resulting in the top ray missing under the eagle's tail feathers and some rays shortened away from the lower wing edge.

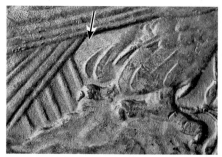

VF-20	EF-40	AU-50	MS-60	MS-63	MS-64	MS-65
$43	$48	$65	$85	$145	$250	$400

Collecting Advice

Collectors should strive for an excellent example of the common 1925 issue from Philadelphia. Many high-quality examples exist that possess good strikes, high luster, and few marks. The MS-66 grade is within reach of most collectors. With several thousand having been graded at this level, a little patience can result in locating some very nice coins. Focus on coins with better than average strikes and good luster. Avoid those with unsightly toning or marks on the face and neck.

1925-S

Mintage: 1,610,000

Whitman Coin Guide (WCG™)

VF-20	EF-40	AU-50	MS-60	MS-63	MS-64	MS-65	MS-66	MS-67
$28	$32	$45	$100	$280	$900	$27,500	—	—

As with several other issues from San Francisco, this one is very tough to find in really nice Uncirculated condition. A low mintage, combined with being the most poorly struck Peace dollar, ensures that quality coins are few and far between. This is a very poorly struck issue in the series, and along with the 1928-S, is perhaps the most difficult coin to find in high grades.

This is a key date in the series and for good reason. There are very few graded as MS-65, and many of those have to be considered marginal due to softness of strike.

Relative Rarity

Within the series, the 1925-S is one of the key dates. There are very few graded as MS-65, and many of those have to be considered marginal due to softness of strike. Gem examples are extremely rare, and are valued accordingly. This is the only issue that has no examples graded higher than MS-65, and only the 1928-S is rarer at the MS-65 level.

Relative Rarity Within the 24-coin Series

MS-63	MS-64	MS-65	MS-66	MS-60–MS-70
16/24	13/24	2/24	1/24	13/24

Significant Examples

The finest known examples of the 1925-S dollar are graded MS-65 and at this writing, just under 100 have been so certified by the major grading companies. One of the most famous specimens carries the Jack Lee pedigree and has a strike deserving of the Gem category. The coin shown is as good as the 1925-S gets!

Varieties

There are a dozen die varieties documented, but only two of them are part of the Top 50 Peace VAM list.

DOUBLED OLIVE BRANCHES   VAM 2 II 1 B²B

Reverse B²b—Note the doubled olive branches and leaves on the left side, rear feathers of the eagle's legs, and the rays below the olive branches, behind the legs, and above and below ONE on the left side.

VF-20	EF-40	AU-50	MS-60	MS-63	MS-64	MS-65
$45	$50	$75	$145	$360	$925	—

DOUBLED WING   VAM 3 II 1 B²C

Reverse B²c—Doubled outside edge of eagle's right wing, from shoulder down to right talon; bottoms of eagle's right leg feathers; and bottom edges of top olive leaves.

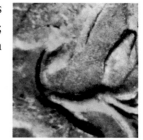

VF-20	EF-40	AU-50	MS-60	MS-63	MS-64	MS-65
$45	$55	$85	$155	$375	$975	—

Collecting Advice

A 1925-S dollar will be very hard to find with limited surface abrasions and well-struck designs. Only a handful of collectors are willing to pay the high price necessary to secure an example graded MS-65. With no coins graded higher, upgrading is difficult. At the MS-64 level, several thousand coins are known to exist, but many of them are poorly struck, which is the reason there are so few Gems available. Select a coin with excellent luster and few marks as a trade-off for not having a well-struck coin.

1926-P

Mintage: 1,939,000

Whitman Coin Guide (WCG™)

VF-20	EF-40	AU-50	MS-60	MS-63	MS-64	MS-65	MS-66	MS-67
$28	$32	$37	$52	$110	$140	$600	$2,100	—

This issue is characterized by a satiny finish, usually with good luster. Many coins were struck well in this issue, and what usually limits the grade are bagmarks and/or poor luster. It is one of the better mintages in the series, and is also a better date than the earlier Philadelphia-minted coins because of the fairly low population. In spite of the low mintage, Uncirculated examples are fairly common, and there are many quality Gems to be had.

Many coins can be found with a golden patina covering the surfaces, similar to the 1925 issue from Philadelphia.

All 1926 Peace dollars were produced from a master die that had the word GOD manually retouched. The word GOD shows slightly irregular recutting of all letters, particularly the O. The workmanship is completely different than on the balance of the coin.

The motto IN GOD WE TRUST became progressively weaker in 1924 and 1925. By the time it was necessary to produce 1926 master dies, the word IN was very weak and it is possible that the word GOD was also very weak. At that time, the fall of 1925, it is possible that John R. Sinnock tried to correct the problem by using fine engraving tools to recut and strengthen the motto. He might have begun with the middle word simply because it was convenient. After retouching was complete on one word, no further work appears to have been done. IN and WE are flat, almost blending into the field, giving added prominence to the single altered word. There are no records indicating why this was done or if it was a change ordered by Mint Director Robert J. Grant or something done ad hoc by Sinnock. (All lettering on Peace dollars has poorly defined vertical edges and easily blur, into the fields. This contributes to the coins' dull, poorly defined appearance.)

This curious "alteration" was first identified by David W. Lange in 1999, in a *Numismatic News* article. Lange speculated there might be some connection with the Scopes Evolution Trial *(Tennessee v. John Scopes)* held July 10 through 21, 1925, in Dayton, Tennessee.

Relative Rarity

Within the entire series, the 1926 is fairly common in Uncirculated condition, as shown here.

Relative Rarity Within the 24-coin Series

MS-63	MS-64	MS-65	MS-66	MS-60–MS-70
19/24	19/24	18/24	16/24	19/24

Significant Examples

There is a single 1926-P coin that has been graded MS-67, by NGC. It was part of the Robert Moreno Collection for some time before being sold at auction. It is a blast-white coin that is very well struck and has only a few trivial contact marks. The luster from this coin is spectacular.

Varieties

There are nine die varieties documented at this writing, but only one of them is listed in the Top 50 Peace VAMs.

Strong Motto   VAM N/A

The word GOD in the obverse motto is much more prominent than the other words. It appears to have been manually cut into the master die.

VF-20	EF-40	AU-50	MS-60	MS-63	MS-64	MS-65
$55	$60	$65	$80	$150	$225	$550

DOUBLED OLIVE BRANCHES   VAM 2 II 1 B²B

Reverse B²b—Note the doubled olive branches and leaves on the left side, the rear feathers of the eagle's legs, and the rays below ONE on the left side.

VF-20	EF-40	AU-50	MS-60	MS-63	MS-64	MS-65
$38	$40	$47	$65	$110	$160	$500

Collecting Advice

The 1926-P should be easy to find in MS-65 grade. Look for a well-struck version, with good luster. With more than 200 MS-66 coins available, that level is within reach of most collectors as well. Avoid those with dull luster, unsightly toning, or marks on the face and neck.

1926-D

Mintage: 2,348,700

Whitman Coin Guide (WCG™)

VF-20	EF-40	AU-50	MS-60	MS-63	MS-64	MS-65	MS-66	MS-67
$28	$32	$44	$85	$230	$410	$1,000	$2,500	$30,000

The 1926 issue from Denver is one of the best in the entire series, with strong strikes and great luster. Unlike the earlier Denver coins, this one is mostly free from die-crack impressions. There are many high-quality coins around, and only a few have unsightly toning or dull luster. Many are bag marked; however, enough survived to make this a very good issue on the whole.

Manual strengthening of the word GOD is a feature of all 1926 silver dollars, regardless of mint, and, as with other issues in the series, coins are typically found with a golden patina covering the surfaces.

Relative Rarity

Within the entire series, the 1926-D is one of the more common issues in Uncirculated condition, as shown here.

Relative Rarity Within the 24-coin Series

MS-63	MS-64	MS-65	MS-66	MS-60–MS-70
3/24	8/24	16/24	19/24	8/24

Significant Examples

The finest known examples of the 1926-D graded MS-67, and at this writing about a dozen have been so certified by the major grading companies. One of the most famous specimens is from the Jack Lee I & II collections, and is graded MS-67 by PCGS.

Varieties

Four notable die varieties have been identified in addition to the motto common to all 1926 dollars. See 1926-P for discussion of the obverse motto.

DIE BREAKS, LOWER MIDDLE OF HAIR   VAM 1B II 1 B²N

Obverse II 1—Note the vertical V-shaped die crack in the lower middle of the hair, with breaks on the top segment of the V.

VF-20	EF-40	AU-50	MS-60	MS-63	MS-64	MS-65
$45	$48	$50	$110	$190	$425	$950

DOUBLED 26   VAM 3 II 2 B²A

Obverse II 2—The 26 in the date are slightly doubled, with the 2 doubled at the top inside of the upper loop and the 6 doubled on the right side of the top curved bar. Note the slightly doubled designer's monogram toward the date and TRV on the right side.

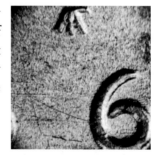

VF-20	EF-40	AU-50	MS-60	MS-63	MS-64	MS-65
$50	$53	$55	$110	$190	$450	$975

Collecting Advice

The 1926-D is easy to find in MS-65, and that is what the collector should strive to obtain. It should be a technically excellent example, because of the number of high-quality examples in existence. Finding one with good luster should not be a problem, and almost all are very well struck. Avoid any coin from this issue that is not well struck, as it will be in the minority and hard to resell. As with all other issues, also make sure the devices are free from distracting marks, especially on the face and neck of Miss Liberty.

1926-S

Mintage: 6,980,000

Whitman Coin Guide (WCG™)

VF-20	EF-40	AU-50	MS-60	MS-63	MS-64	MS-65	MS-66	MS-67
$28	$32	$38	$60	$120	$300	$1,100	$4,850	$32,000

The 1926 issue from San Francisco is one of the better-looking coins sporting an S mintmark in the entire Peace dollar series. The strikes were generally as good as those produced in Denver and Philadelphia and were especially strong considering where the coins were minted. There are some very lustrous examples in existence, with a plentiful supply of Gems. Many high-quality coins were introduced as a part of the Redfield hoard disbursement.

This issue is one of the more under-appreciated ones in the series, and will certainly be more sought-after as its overall quality becomes more widely recognized.

Relative Rarity

Within the entire series, the 1926-S is one of the more common issues in Uncirculated condition, as shown here.

Relative Rarity Within the 24-coin Series

MS-63	MS-64	MS-65	MS-66	MS-60–MS-70
12/24	16/24	14/24	12/24	16/24

Significant Examples

There are two 1926-S dollars graded MS-67, both by PCGS. These are recently graded coins, and not much is known about them. There are

also approximately 100 coins in the MS-66 NGC and PCGS populations, with the most famous coin formerly part of the Jack Lee Collection. This coin is well struck, with few marks. The luster is good, and the coin has some interesting toning on the obverse, proving that it is original and has not been dipped.

Varieties

There are approximately a dozen varieties documented, three of them significant enough to have made the Top 50 Peace VAM list. See 1926-P for discussion of the obverse motto.

DOT ON REVERSE   VAM 4 II 1 B²D

Reverse B²d—There is a small circular raised dot on the field between the lower left olive leaf and the mound. Two tiny dots are below OF in STATES OF. A large dot is below, between the lower left olive leaf and the mound.

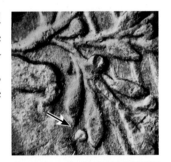

VF-20	EF-40	AU-50	MS-60	MS-63	MS-64	MS-65
$42	$45	$55	$90	$200	$360	—

DOT AND DIE FILE LINES ON REVERSE.   VAM 4A II 1 B²D

Reverse B²d—There are heavy die file lines in the field on the right side of the eagle and to the left of the middle of the eagle's left wing; these were from an effort to remove clash marks.

VF-20	EF-40	AU-50	MS-60	MS-63	MS-64	MS-65
$47	$50	$60	$95	$210	$385	—

Doubled Lower Reverse   VAM 5 II 1 B²ᴇ

Reverse B²e—Note the doubled right side of DO in DOLLAR, the right edge of the top two olive leaves, the right edge and bottom edge of the eagle's leg feathers, the middle of the bottom edges of the eagle's right wing, and the top right of the rays from the leg to DOLL.

VF-20	EF-40	AU-50	MS-60	MS-63	MS-64	MS-65
$42	$45	$50	$80	$185	$350	—

Collecting Advice

A nice-looking 1926-S is easily obtainable in MS-65, and that grade should be the goal of most collectors. Since most are well struck, ensure that the coin selected is too. Poorly struck samples will be hard to resell. Also make sure that the coin has plenty of luster and no significant marks. Especially avoid a coin that does not have plenty of eye appeal, since this is one of the better issues in the series.

1927-P

Mintage: 848,000

Whitman Coin Guide (WCG™)

VF-20	EF-40	AU-50	MS-60	MS-63	MS-64	MS-65	MS-66	MS-67
$39	$42	$50	$85	$200	$625	$2,900	$23,000	—

The 1927 issue from Philadelphia is a good one, with strong strikes and above-average luster. Many coins have very bright fields, some almost prooflike. In spite of the low mintage (only the 1928-P has a lower total mintage), a fair amount of Uncirculated examples have survived.

While once thought to be relatively common in Gem condition, it has now emerged as very elusive at the MS-65 grade. Fortunately, because of the overall high quality of coins that comprise this issue, MS-64 grades are usually very nice coins.

Relative Rarity

The 1927 issue is the rarest Philadelphia-minted coin in Uncirculated condition, although the 1928 is often given this honor because of its very low total mintage. Coins in MS-63 are fairly common, but in MS-64 and higher, this coin is one of the rarer issues in the series.

Relative Rarity Within the 24-coin Series

MS-63	MS-64	MS-65	MS-66	MS-60–MS-70
13/24	9/24	9/24	6/24	11/24

Significant Examples

The finest known examples of the 1927-P issue are graded MS-66, and at this writing fewer than a dozen have been so certified by the major grading companies. One of the most famous specimens is from the Jack Lee I & II collections and was graded by PCGS. It is a blast-white coin that is very well struck and has only a few trivial contact marks. Another (shown) is from the Robert Moreno Collection, graded by NGC, and is technically a very nice coin with some interesting color and toning.

Varieties

Two varieties are documented; one is discussed here.

DOUBLED MOTTO   VAM 2 II 2 B²A

Obverse II 2—The designer's monogram is doubled to the lower right, OD WE is doubled on the right side, and TRVS is slightly doubled on the right side. Note the doubled hair, back of the eye, and left side of the lower rays between B and E.

VF-20	EF-40	AU-50	MS-60	MS-63	MS-64	MS-65
$45	$50	$70	$100	$250	$625	$2,600

Collecting Advice

The 1927-P can be found in MS-64 very handily, and is priced within the reach of most collectors. However, it is not well known that in MS-64 and higher, it is in the top seven for rarity in the entire series. This issue is much undervalued in these grades, although still expensive in MS-65 and higher. Make sure to purchase only a strongly struck specimen, as this issue is known for that. Avoid pieces with unsightly toning or marks on the face and neck.

1927-D

Mintage: 1,268,900

Whitman Coin Guide (WCG™)

VF-20	EF-40	AU-50	MS-60	MS-63	MS-64	MS-65	MS-66	MS-67
$39	$45	$75	$180	$400	$1,050	$4,750	$25,000	—

Similar to the 1926 issue from Denver, the 1927-D is a good-looking coin. Strong strikes are common and few coins show evidence of die cracks. Most have strong luster. Many were released into circulation, making Uncirculated specimens difficult to find.

Marks on the coin are usually what limit the grade for this issue, as those that were left in bags must have been moved around without much care. Some of the marks can be very deep and in very noticeable spots, so be choosy about where you're willing to accept marks.

Relative Rarity

Within the Peace dollar series, the 1927-D is the second rarest overall in Uncirculated condition, next to the 1934-S. This is not widely known, as some of the San Francisco issues such as the 1924-S and 1925-S are generally thought be rarer due to dealer promotion.

Relative Rarity Within the 24-coin Series

MS-63	MS-64	MS-65	MS-66	MS-60–MS-70
5/24	2/24	6/24	7/24	3/24

Significant Examples

The finest known examples of the 1927-D issue are graded MS-66, and at this writing just over a dozen have been so certified by NGC and PCGS. One of the more noteworthy examples belonged to the Robert Moreno collection. It is a completely untoned coin that is very well struck and has no mentionable marks.

Varieties

There are three die varieties documented, but none of the doubled dies are easy to spot.

DOUBLED OBVERSE   VAM 2 II 2 B²A

Obverse II 2—Note the slightly doubled bottom left sides of the front rays. WE TR of the motto and the designer's initials are doubled on the right side.

VF-20	EF-40	AU-50	MS-60	MS-63	MS-64	MS-65
$48	$52	$90	$195	$465	$1,050	$4,950

DOUBLED LEFT OBVERSE   VAM 3 II 3 B²A

Obverse II 3—GOD WE and the designer's initials are doubled towards the date. LIB

and the front rays of the tiara over to the B are doubled on the left side.

VF-20	EF-40	AU-50	MS-60	MS-63	MS-64	MS-65
$48	$52	$100	$210	$475	$1,150	$5,000

Doubled Left Obverse   VAM 3A II 3 B²A

Obverse II 3—There is a striated diagonal die gouge in the rays below E in LIBERTY. (Former VAM 1A)

VF-20	EF-40	AU-50	MS-60	MS-63	MS-64	MS-65
$48	$52	$100	$210	$475	$1,150	$5,000

Collecting Advice

The 1927-D is very scarce in Uncirculated condition, but prices at the MS-63 and 64 levels do not yet reflect the scarcity as of this writing and should be good investments. The MS-64 coin of course will be a more technically superior specimen, and is not much more expensive. This should be the level that most collectors seek. The quality of coins in this issue should result in a nice MS-64 coin. The MS-65 coins from this issue are exceptional and, unfortunately, priced accordingly. There is a quantum leap in price to get to the Gem level, but if one can afford it, this is the place to make extra investment because of the quality of the issue and its scarcity.

1927-S

Mintage: 866,000

Whitman Coin Guide (WCG™)

VF-20	EF-40	AU-50	MS-60	MS-63	MS-64	MS-65	MS-66	MS-67
$39	$45	$75	$200	$600	$1,300	$9,750	$45,000	—

The 1927 issue from the San Francisco Mint was a very poor one, characterized by weak strikes. Coupled with the low mintage, Uncirculated examples are rare, and high-quality coins are even rarer. Luster is average for these coins, but a few are known to be very reflective.

The Redfield hoard contained several bags of this issue, and many were of high quality. Prior to that, the 1927-S was a very rare coin to be had, and even with the Redfield coins added to the population, it still remains one of the rarest in Uncirculated condition.

Relative Rarity

Within the entire series, the 1927-S is one of the rarer issues in Uncirculated condition, as shown here.

Relative Rarity Within the 24-coin Series

MS-63	MS-64	MS-65	MS-66	MS-60–MS-70
8/24	7/24	3/24	3/24	6/24

Significant Examples

The finest known examples of the 1927-S issue are graded MS-66, and at this writing only three have been so certified by the major grading companies. One of the most famous specimens is from the Jack Lee I & II collections, and is graded MS-66 by PCGS. It is a blast-white coin that is very well struck and has only a few trivial contact marks, and its luster is truly blinding. The coin pictured here is one of the nicest MS-65 specimens.

Varieties

There are 10 die varieties documented. The most significant are illustrated below.

Rim Cud Right Reverse   VAM 1A II 1 B²A

Reverse B²a—There is a small rim cud just below A in AMERICA.

VF-20	EF-40	AU-50	MS-60	MS-63	MS-64	MS-65
$50	$55	$90	$200	$475	$1,175	—

Die File Lines Reverse   VAM 1B II 1 B²A

Reverse B²a—Extensive die-file and polishing lines reveal an attempt to remove clash marks.

VF-20	EF-40	AU-50	MS-60	MS-63	MS-64	MS-65
$45	$50	$80	$185	$475	$1,175	—

Die File Lines Obverse   VAM 1C II 1 B²A

Obverse II 1—There are die file and polishing lines all over the fields.

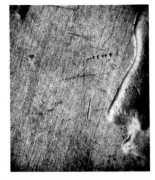

VF-20	EF-40	AU-50	MS-60	MS-63	MS-64	MS-65
$45	$50	$80	$185	$475	$1,175	—

Die File Lines Top and Right Obverse   VAM 1D II 1 B²A

Obverse II 1—Die file lines at the top and to the right of the hair bun reveal efforts to remove clash marks.

VF-20	EF-40	AU-50	MS-60	MS-63	MS-64	MS-65
$50	$55	$90	$200	$475	$1,175	—

Die File Lines Around Liberty Head   VAM 1E II 1 B²A

Obverse II 1—Heavy die file lines reveal efforts to remove clash marks at Liberty's head below the chin, back of the neck, back of the hair bun, next to the forehead and nose, and around ERT.

VF-20	EF-40	AU-50	MS-60	MS-63	MS-64	MS-65
$50	$55	$90	$200	$475	$1,175	—

DIE FILE LINES REVERSE   VAM 1F II 1 B²A
Reverse B²a—Strong die polishing around the eagle reveal efforts to remove the effects of clashed dies.

VF-20	EF-40	AU-50	MS-60	MS-63	MS-64	MS-65
$50	$55	$100	$205	$500	$1,350	—

DOUBLED LEAVES   VAM 3 II 1 B²C
Reverse B²c—Note the doubled bottom edges of the upper olive leaves and slightly doubled rear edge of the leg feathers.

VF-20	EF-40	AU-50	MS-60	MS-63	MS-64	MS-65
$50	$55	$195	$260	$575	$1,300	—

DOUBLED LEAVES #2   VAM 5 II 1 B²E
Reverse B²e—The reverse is slightly doubled at the bottom edge of the upper, lower middle olive leaves, the lower branch, the upper leaves of the lower sprig, and the back of the two rear leg feathers. Doubling is not as strong as that of VAM 3.

VF-20	EF-40	AU-50	MS-60	MS-63	MS-64	MS-65
$50	$55	$140	$190	$475	$1,200	—

Collecting Advice

The 1927-S can be found in MS-64, but because of the poor strikes, an MS-63 sample will be an acceptable specimen. There will not be an appreciable difference in quality between the two, and the upper end of the MS-64 coins have recently been running up in price as collectors have discovered their true rarity and overall poor quality. To find a coin with few marks and a good strike is going to take a long time and require a significant expenditure, so the collector may have to choose between the two options.

1928-P

Mintage: 360,649

Whitman Coin Guide (WCG™)

VF-20	EF-40	AU-50	MS-60	MS-63	MS-64	MS-65	MS-66	MS-67
$300	$340	$375	$500	$850	$1,250	$4,500	$25,000	—

This issue has the lowest mintage in the entire series, and next to the 1934-S has the fewest coins available in Uncirculated condition. It is considered one of the key dates and brings a significant price even in circulated conditions. Coins produced in 1928 in the Philadelphia Mint were struck softly compared to the other issues from this mint, and luster is also average. Many of these are heavily toned an unattractive gold. Finding one that is white usually means it has been dipped.

In spite of the overall average quality of this issue, it is collected heavily and sought after widely. There is a single collector who has amassed a significant portion of the MS-64 coins graded by PCGS as of this writing. Many coins were held out of circulation, but in spite of this, many specimens contain numerous bagmarks.

David W. Lange notes that the entire motto was reinforced on the master die for that year, and the change affects all coins from both the Philadelphia and San Francisco mints.

All 1928-P silver dollars were struck between April 13 and 20. The last Peace dollars produced under provisions of the Pittman Act were struck at the Philadelphia Mint on April 20, 1928, when 15,649 pieces were coined—exactly enough to complete replacement of the dollars melted in 1918 and 1919.[2]

When Peace dollar production ended in 1928 the U.S. Mint had struck a total of 270,232,722 silver dollars from metal purchased under the Pittman Act. Of this, Peace dollars accounted for 183,502,722 coins; the other 86,730,000 were Morgan-design dollars dated 1921. With all of the coins melted between 1918 and 1919 replaced, there was no need to coin more standard silver dollars and production ceased. Philadelphia Mint engraver John Sinnock coated the hubs and unused reverse dies with oil or perhaps bees wax to protect them from rust and packed them in storage boxes. It would be six years—near the end of a devastating financial depression—before more silver dollars would be needed.

The 1928-P dollar is usually well struck, but many coins have light golden toning.

Relative Rarity

Within the entire series, the 1928-P is usually noted as the rarest in circulated condition because of the low mintage, although this distinction actually belongs to the 1925-P issue. 1928-P is not necessarily rare in Uncirculated condition, as shown here; however, the low total mintage results in very high prices for any coin of this issue, regardless of grade. (This is similar to the situation for 1909-S V.D.B. cents and several other popular, high-priced, but not particularly difficult to locate coins.)

Relative Rarity Within the 24-coin Series

MS-63	MS-64	MS-65	MS-66	MS-60–MS-70
11/24	10/24	8/24	8/24	10/24

Significant Examples

The finest known examples of the 1928-P are graded MS-66, and at this writing just over a dozen have been so certified by the major grading companies. These specimens are rarely seen; the last was publicly sold through Heritage Auctions in 2002. Note the gold color of the coin, and also the strength of the strike.

Varieties

There is one notable variety documented.

Doubled Tiara Rays and **IBER**   VAM 2 II 2 B²A

Obverse II 2—Note the doubled short rays in the tiara, from fourth to eighth. There is slight doubling on the long rays from the front to E in LIBERTY. I in LIBERTY is doubled on the lower left side, B at the right inside of the lower loop, E at the top of the middle and lower crossbar, and R at the right inside of the loop.

VF-20	EF-40	AU-50	MS-60	MS-63	MS-64	MS-65
$400	$450	$500	$700	$950	$1,450	$4,650

Collecting Advice

The 1928-P coin should be readily found in attractive condition in MS-64, and within the price range of most collectors. There is little difference in price from MS-63 to MS-64, but making the jump to MS-65, and especially MS-66, is very costly. There are many coins that are borderline MS-64/MS-65, but cannot make the leap due to softness of strike. These are very worthwhile findings for this issue because of the low mintage and overall scarcity, while a coin like this would not be valuable in one of the common issues. Avoid coins with unsightly toning or marks on the face and neck. Many will be found with golden toning; whether to collect one of these is a personal choice.

If buying uncertified coins, be very careful of counterfeits. Some have been made from 1923 issues, by turning the 3 into an 8. Also watch for sliders: coins that are AU at best but are being sold as Uncirculated.

1928-S

Mintage: 1,632,000

Whitman Coin Guide (WCG™)

VF-20	EF-40	AU-50	MS-60	MS-63	MS-64	MS-65	MS-66	MS-67
$39	$48	$65	$200	$475	$1,100	$20,000	—	—

The 1928 issue from San Francisco was another poorly produced one, with notoriously weak strikes. Luster on the coin is good, but because of the insufficient strikes, Gems are difficult to find. Many MS-65 graded pieces have marginal strikes, achieving the MS-65 technical grade simply due to a lack of marks and abrasion.

Once thought to be relatively common due to the mintage, especially compared to the 1928 issue from Philadelphia, it has now rightfully taken its place as the rarest Peace dollar issue in Gem condition. Many were released into circulation, with precious few left untouched.

This final group of silver dollars struck at San Francisco under authority of the Pittman Act was made from January 16 through February 29, 1928. Average production was approximately 42,000 pieces per working day.[3]

Relative Rarity

Within the series, in Uncirculated condition the 1928-S is near the midpoint in market prevalence, but it is the rarest in Gem condition.

Relative Rarity Within the 24-coin Series

MS-63	MS-64	MS-65	MS-66	MS-60–MS-70
10/24	11/24	1/24	2/24	9/24

Significant Examples

There are two examples of the 1928-S graded MS-66, one from each of the two major grading companies at this writing. Shown is an MS-65 specimen formerly in the Robert Moreno Collection. This coin is truly beautiful, with incredible luster and a very good strike. The only visible flaws are on the reverse.

Varieties

There are 11 major die varieties documented, with VAM 3 the only one on the Top 50 list. Several are shown here.

DOUBLED MOTTO STRONG LOWER RIGHT, MEDIUM-HIGH S   VAM 3 II 2 B²b

Obverse II 2—Note the doubled OD WE TR on the lower right, the back of the bun, the back of the hair, the back of the neck, the designer's initials, and the right side of the rear tiara rays. *Die marker*—Doubled right side of rear rays.

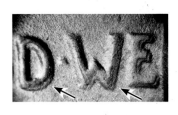

Reverse B²b—Small S mintmark set medium high. *Die marker*—Faint double curved lines on the third from bottom ray below the tail feathers.

VF-20	EF-40	AU-50	MS-60	MS-63	MS-64	MS-65
$48	$55	$95	$220	$485	$1,700	—

DOUBLED TRV, NOSE, AND LIPS, VAM 4 II 3 B²B MEDIUM-HIGH S

Obverse II 3—Note the doubled designer's initials and TRV on the right side; and slightly doubled D WE on the bottom right side and at the back of the neck; doubled nose and lips; and slightly doubled front rays on the left side.

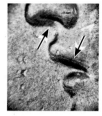

VF-20	EF-40	AU-50	MS-60	MS-63	MS-64	MS-65
$48	$55	$95	$220	$485	$1,700	—

DOUBLED MOTTO TO RIGHT, VAM 7 II 5 B²B MEDIUM-HIGH S

Obverse II 5—Note the doubled D WE TR to the right, the back of the hair bun, the back of the hair, the back of the neck, and the designer's initials. *Die marker*—Faint diagonal polishing line below the front tiara band.

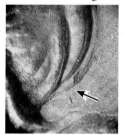 

VF-20	EF-40	AU-50	MS-60	MS-63	MS-64	MS-65
$45	$55	$95	$220	$600	$1,700	—

Collecting Advice

The 1928-S dollar is readily available in MS-63 and MS-64. Because of the lack of MS-65 coins, MS-64 values are inflated. Many of these are near-Gems, lacking only a reasonable strike to make the next grade. Look for a solid MS-63 or MS-64 coin; do not take one at the lower end of those grades, as there is a great variety within these ranges. In fact, there is a greater difference in the range of these two grades than for any other coin in the series. Focus on coins with better than average strikes and good luster.

1934-P
Mintage: 954,057

Whitman Coin Guide (WCG™)

VF-20	EF-40	AU-50	MS-60	MS-63	MS-64	MS-65	MS-66	MS-67
$44	$45	$50	$115	$225	$375	$750	$3,000	$27,000

It had been six years since the last Peace dollars were struck. Although there was no commercial reason for producing more of the unwanted coins, the Treasury Department was looking for ways to increase the money supply. One method was to issue more Silver Certificates and back them with standard silver dollars and bullion in the Treasury's vaults. (Silver bullion was worth less than half the face value of a paper Silver Certificate or silver dollar coin.) In December 1933, the Treasury announced that it would buy domestically produced silver at a price substantially greater than the commercial market value in order to support the domestic price of silver. This produced a relatively modest inflow of approximately 1.5 million ounces of fine silver per month. Some of this silver was used to strike standard dollars in 1934 and 1935. Large quantities of subsidiary silver coins were also struck from this and other silver purchased beginning in 1934.

Only a handful of the Peace dollar issues were minted in numbers less than one million, and although the 1934 dollar from Philadelphia is one of them, it is not a particularly rare or sought-after coin. While it is considered a better date, it is generally not considered a key date.

Overall, it is a very nice issue, with solid strikes and good luster. Many exist in Gem and better condition. This issue is sure to be more widely collected in the future, and is a bargain at current price levels.

There were many coins held out of circulation, which explains why Uncirculated specimens exist in considerable quantity. But in spite of good availability, many coins from this issue contain numerous bagmarks.

Silver dollars dated 1934 and 1935 were authorized by the Silver Purchase Act of June 19, 1934, and feature a new obverse master hub, possibly from de Francisci's 1922 low-relief models.

Relative Rarity

Within the entire series, the 1934 has average availability in Uncirculated condition, as shown here. Although a better date, coins are plentiful at MS-65 and better.

Relative Rarity Within the 24-coin Series

MS-63	MS-64	MS-65	MS-66	MS-60–MS-70
9/24	12/24	13/24	14/24	12/24

Significant Examples

The finest known examples of the 1934 issue from Philadelphia are graded MS-67, and at this writing fewer than a dozen have been certified by the major grading companies. One of the best examples was sold by Heritage Auction Galleries in 2006, from the Belle Glade collection. This coin has a few marks that probably should have kept it from reaching the MS-67 level, but the luster is so strong and blinding that this feature alone almost warrants the grade. It is so bright that it is an extremely difficult coin to photograph. The strike is completely full, with incredible amounts of hair detail.

Varieties

There is only one notable die variety that has been identified.

Collecting Advice

The 1934-P issue can be easily found in very nice MS-64 condition. Most collectors should strive for a MS-65 specimen, which is within the reach of many serious collectors. This is another coin of very good overall quality, and the specimen sought should be a technically superior coin. Make sure the coin selected has a completely full strike, and it should also have very strong luster.

1934-D

Mintage: 1,569,500

Whitman Coin Guide (WCG™)

VF-20	EF-40	AU-50	MS-60	MS-63	MS-64	MS-65	MS-66	MS-67
$44	$45	$50	$150	$375	$600	$2,100	$4,900	$37,500

This last issue in the Peace dollar series from Denver is, by and large, a good one. Strikes are generally strong, with few die crack impressions, and many coins have very nice coruscating luster. There are some truly outstanding specimens available in the Superb Gem category.

This issue also contains some of the more interesting die varieties, including a nearly complete doubling of the entire obverse. There are also two different-sized mintmarks, which appear in a variety of locations, providing further interest.

Relative Rarity

Within the entire series, the 1934-D is one of the rarer issues in Uncirculated condition, as shown here, although several of the other Denver issues are scarcer in MS-65 and MS-66. An interesting fact to note is the surprising rarity in MS-64.

Relative Rarity Within the 24-coin Series

MS-63	MS-64	MS-65	MS-66	MS-60–MS-70
7/24	3/24	12/24	11/24	5/24

Significant Examples

The finest known examples of the 1934-D issue are graded MS-67, and at this writing just a handful have been so certified by the major grading companies. One of these precious few came from the Robert Moreno collection and traded hands recently. It is a blast-white coin with terrific luster and nearly flawless devices and fields. It is certainly among the finest of all Peace dollars in existence, regardless of issue or grade.

Varieties

There are 12 notable varieties currently documented, of which VAM 3 and 4 are on the Top 50 Peace dollar list.

LARGE D, DIE GOUGE BELOW G   VAM 2A III 1 B²B

Obverse III 1—There is a shallow vertical die gouge below G in GOD.

VF-20	EF-40	AU-50	MS-60	MS-63	MS-64	MS-65
$45	$50	$105	$200	$575	$800	$1,800

DOUBLED OBVERSE   VAM 3 III 2 B²B

Obverse III 2—Note the doubled forehead, eyelids, nose, lips, and chin on Liberty's head. The motto letters and date digits are doubled slightly on the right side, with WE having large shifts. The rays of light in the tiara from midway between B and E to the back are doubled on the left side, with the last three having very distinct, separate images.

Reverse B²b—Large II D mintmark, filled.

VF-20	EF-40	AU-50	MS-60	MS-63	MS-64	MS-65
$45	$50	$105	$200	$575	$800	$1,800

Doubled Obverse, Small D VAM 4 III 2 B²A

Obverse III 2—Same as VAM 3.

Reverse B²a—Small D mintmark, not filled. The image to the left shows the small D mintmark that is not filled; compare to the filled mintmark of VAM 3 to the right.

VF-20	EF-40	AU-50	MS-60	MS-63	MS-64	MS-65
$115	$185	$375	$750	$1,650	—	—

Doubled Right Obverse VAM 10 III 3 B²B

Obverse III 3—Note the slightly doubled designer's initials, TRV on the right side, and back edge of the lower hair.

VF-20	EF-40	AU-50	MS-60	MS-63	MS-64	MS-65
$53	$60	$110	$200	$625	$800	$1,700

Collecting Advice

In spite of its relative rarity in MS-64, the 1934-D is easily located in that grade, and most collectors will be happy with the quality of such a specimen from this issue. It will likely have a solid strike with good luster. Of course, the serious collector will want a Gem, and that level is priced within the reach of most. Ignore coins with poor strikes, as they are in the minority and difficult to resell at a later time. As always, avoid those with unsightly toning or marks on the face and neck.

1934-S

Total Mintage: 1,011,000

Whitman Coin Guide (WCG™)

VF-20	EF-40	AU-50	MS-60	MS-63	MS-64	MS-65	MS-66	MS-67
$80	$175	$500	$2,500	$4,400	$7,000	$9,000	$27,500	—

The San Francisco Mint received orders to strike dollar coins on October 26, and completed all of its silver dollars on and after November 1. The 1934-S has long been regarded as the key to the Peace dollar series. In addition to having one of the smaller mintages, many of these coins were released into circulation, making Uncirculated examples fairly rare. Population reports from the major third-party grading companies show that of all 24 individual Peace dollar issues, the 1934-S has the smallest population of coins in MS-60 and higher.

Contributing to this scarcity is the fact that, during the 1930s and 1940s, this issue was thought by collectors to be very common because five other issues were produced in smaller numbers. Therefore, no significant hoards of 1934-S coins were established. The misconception is no longer held, and today the 1934-S is sought by many. Quality Uncirculated examples sell for more than any other circulation-strike Peace dollar issue.

Typical 1934-S coins are covered with a golden patina; some are light and attractive, but many are dark and unsightly. Luster on the coin can be very strong, but many have surfaces that are hidden by the patina. As with all coins struck in the San Francisco Mint, this issue usually exhibits flatness in Liberty's hair just above her ear, and also lacks detail in the feathers on the eagle's breast on the reverse.

Relative Rarity

Within the entire series, the 1934-S is the rarest issue in Uncirculated condition, as shown here, although several of the other San Francisco issues are scarcer in MS-65 and MS-66.

Relative Rarity Within the 24-coin Series

MS-63	MS-64	MS-65	MS-66	MS-60–MS-70
1/24	1/24	7/24	10/24	1/24

Significant Examples

The finest known examples of the 1934-S dollars are graded MS-66, and at this writing, a little more than three dozen have been so certified by the major grading companies. One of the most famous specimens is from the Jack Lee I & II collections, and is graded MS-66 by PCGS. It is a blast-white coin that is very well struck and has only a few trivial contact marks.

Varieties

There are three varieties documented, of which VAM 3 is on the Top 50 Peace dollar list.

DOUBLED RAYS   VAM 3 III 2 B²A

Obverse III 2—The rays in Liberty's tiara between E and R in LIBERTY are doubled and tripled on the right sides. A couple top hair locks are also slightly doubled on bottom.

VF-20	EF-40	AU-50	MS-60	MS-63	MS-64	MS-65
$105	$235	$575	$2,500	$3,500	$4,750	$8,250

Collecting Advice

The 1934-S should form the cornerstone of a Peace dollar collection. If there is one coin that should warrant a premium outlay of funds, this is it. Examine many examples before purchasing one. Specimens in MS-64 should be the minimum for a nice set, as that level of quality sells for roughly the same price as an MS-62 or 63 coin. If you can afford the MS-65 level, by all means, buy it; it is likely that any quality coins in MS-64+ will appreciate or at least maintain their value due to the demand and the relatively small supply. Focus on coins with better than average strikes and good luster. Avoid those with unsightly toning or marks on the face and neck.

If buying uncertified coins, be very careful of counterfeits and sliders (coins being passed off as Uncirculated which are really AU). Because of the generally high prices and high demand associated with this issue, there is considerable incentive for unscrupulous sellers to take advantage of collectors.

1935-P

Mintage: 1,576,000

Whitman Coin Guide (WCG™)

VF-20	EF-40	AU-50	MS-60	MS-63	MS-64	MS-65	MS-66	MS-67
$44	$45	$50	$85	$125	$275	$800	$2,500	$20,000

Even with its relatively small mintage, the 1935 issue from Philadelphia is considered a fairly common date. Much of the stock was held in Treasury vaults for years, never seeing circulation. Many high-quality coins therefore survived in nice condition.

As Peace dollars from Philadelphia go, this issue was not particularly well struck compared to issues like the 1926-P, but very nice coins can be found through diligent searching. Luster on the coin varies significantly; some specimens are very bright, while others appear dull and flat.

As with other issues in the series, coins may be found with a golden patina covering the surfaces.

The Treasury Department had been trying to get rid of the standard silver dollar since 1873. It succeeded in 1873, again in 1904, and again in 1928, but in each case success was short-lived and the pesky, large coin kept returning to life despite being buried in dank vaults for decades. When the last 1935 Peace dollar clanked into the receiving bin, officials must have felt that this, at last, marked the final rest of the standard silver dollar. A generation later, the silver dollar coin arose once again, then quickly vanished amid escalating silver prices and a coin shortage.

Relative Rarity

Within the entire series, the 1935-P is one of the more common issues in Uncirculated condition, as shown here.

Relative Rarity Within the 24-coin Series

MS-63	MS-64	MS-65	MS-66	MS-60–MS-70
14/24	17/24	17/24	17/24	17/24

Significant Examples

The finest known examples of the 1935-P issue are graded MS-67, and at this writing only a handful have been so certified by the major grading companies. All of the specimens that have been graded at this lofty level were awarded that distinction by NGC. One of these examples (shown) was sold at auction several years ago, and that particular coin is blast-white, very well struck, and has only a few trivial contact marks. This example is one of the very best Peace dollars in existence.

Varieties

There are four varieties documented, of which three are discussed below.

DIE SCRATCHES RIGHT REVERSE   VAM 1A III 1 B²A

Reverse B²a—There are thin, horizontal die scratches above the middle olive leaves, in the rays above R in DOLLAR, and across the ray below the eagle's right shoulder.

VF-20	EF-40	AU-50	MS-60	MS-63	MS-64	MS-65
$68	$90	$110	$190	$210	$500	$1,420

DIE SCRATCH TOP RAY   VAM 1C III 1 B²A

Reverse B²a—Note the thin horizontal die scratch through the top of the ray to the right of the eagle's neck.

VF-20	EF-40	AU-50	MS-60	MS-63	MS-64	MS-65
$68	$90	$110	$190	$210	$500	$1,420

Die File Lines Lower Obverse   VAM 1D III 1 B²a

Obverse III 1—There are heavy die file lines in the lower field, at the left field, and around IBER.

Reverse B²a—A thin horizontal die scratch is to the right of the middle olive leaves.

VF-20	EF-40	AU-50	MS-60	MS-63	MS-64	MS-65
$68	$90	$110	$190	$210	$500	$1,420

Collecting Advice

The 1935-P is readily available in MS-64, and serious collectors will also be able to afford MS-65 due to the quantity of coins available. This issue has the most noticeable variation in both strike and luster of all the Peace dollar series, so be very selective when seeking a coin to fill this slot. Look particularly at the strike; many are mediocre, but there are also some coins that are very well defined. Seek out well-struck examples, as they will always command a premium and will be easier to resell in the future. Avoid coins with a dull finish.

1935-S

Mintage: 1,964,000

Whitman Coin Guide (WCG™)

VF-20	EF-40	AU-50	MS-60	MS-63	MS-64	MS-65	MS-66	MS-67
$44	$50	$88	$275	$500	$675	$1,500	$4,000	$40,000

The last of the Peace dollars struck in San Francisco, this is one of the better ones from the mint by the bay. Unlike most other "S" dollars, this one is typically struck very well. There are a few exceptions that were softly struck, but the percentage is small compared to issues such as the 1925-S, which is usually found weakly struck.

According to San Francisco Mint records, the last 1935-S dollars were shipped from the mint on June 9, 1939. However, many coins must have been stored at Reserve Banks because few 1935-S coins seem to have entered circulation. Unlike other issues, bagmarks are not excessive.

A design change was made to the reverse that affects approximately half the issue. A fourth ray was added below the word ONE on the lower left, and a seventh ray was added below the eagle's tail. The ray is of a different shape than the others and slightly crooked. The designs are designated as either 3-rays or 4-rays and seem to be of equal availability.

According to David W. Lange, the extra ray appears to have been manually cut into the die, much as the word GOD was mysteriously enhanced on 1926 coins. No explanation has been identified for why engraver John Sinnock added the ray.

Relative Rarity

Within the Peace dollar series, 1935-S is one of the scarcer issues in Uncirculated condition, as shown here. This is not widely recognized; 1935-S coins trade for moderate values compared to some of the key dates such as 1934-S. Interestingly, MS-65 samples appear to be more abundant than nice MS-63 and 64 grades.

Relative Rarity Within the 24-coin Series

MS-63	MS-64	MS-65	MS-66	MS-60–MS-70
2/24	5/24	15/24	15/24	4/24

Significant Examples

The finest known examples of the 1935-S issue are graded MS-67, and at this writing fewer than a dozen have been so certified by the major grading companies. One of the best specimens is formerly of the Robert Moreno Collection, and is graded MS-67 by NGC. It is a blast-white coin that is very well struck and has only a few trivial contact marks. This coin has very strong luster with no toning.

Varieties

There are six principle die varieties documented, one of which is in the Top 50 Peace dollar list.

S Leaning Left   VAM 2 II 1 B²b
Reverse B²b—Small S mintmark leaning left.

VF-20	EF-40	AU-50	MS-60	MS-63	MS-64	MS-65
$50	$65	$115	$320	$550	$800	$1,800

EXTRA RAY   VAM 3 III 1 CA

Reverse Ca—Normal C type reverse with small S mintmark. There is an added fourth ray below ONE and an added seventh ray below the eagle's tail.

VF-20	EF-40	AU-50	MS-60	MS-63	MS-64	MS-65
$70	$100	$165	$320	$600	$1,000	$2,150

DOUBLED LOWER REVERSE   VAM 4 III 1 CB

Reverse Cb—Note the slightly doubled bottom edges of the top right leaves and top two olives in the olive sprig, the bottom edge of the left and right claws of the eagle's right foot, and the lower left edge of the left leg feathers.

VF-20	EF-40	AU-50	MS-60	MS-63	MS-64	MS-65
$70	$100	$165	$320	$600	$1,000	$2,150

HORIZONTAL DIE GOUGE   VAM 5A III 2 B²C
BELOW OLIVE LEAVES

Reverse B²c—Note the slightly doubled bottom edges of the top right leaves and top two olives in the olive sprig, the bottom edge of the left and right claws of the eagle's right foot, and the lower left edge of the left leg feathers.

VF-20	EF-40	AU-50	MS-60	MS-63	MS-64	MS-65
$50	$65	$115	$320	$550	$800	$1,800

DOUBLED LOWER LEFT REVERSE RAYS   VAM 6 III 1 Cc

Reverse Cc—Note the slightly doubled four rays below ONE and the last left ray below the tail feathers on the left side.

VF-20	EF-40	AU-50	MS-60	MS-63	MS-64	MS-65
$70	$100	$165	$320	$600	$1,000	$2,150

Collecting Advice

The coin chosen for this final spot in your collection should be an excellent example, ideally in MS-65. Because nice examples are relatively common at this level, it will not be much more expensive than an MS-64 coin. Make absolutely sure that this one has a terrific strike, as specimens that are poorly struck are in the minority and will be hard to resell later. Also look for coins with strong luster. Since this issue is typically higher quality than most others, do not settle for an average coin simply because it was a bargain. Choose a high-quality MS-64 coin over an average MS-65 specimen. Avoid pieces with unsightly toning or marks on the face and neck.

The Extra Ray variety commands no premium, and therefore should not be a determining factor in the purchase. It may be of interest to have one of each variety because of the obvious difference between the two.

1964-D

Mintage: 322,394 (estimated)

A low resolution photo of the obverse die was recently discovered, but it lacks sufficient detail for more than general confirmation of the 1964 design. It is shown reversed for visibility.
Photographs of genuine coins are unknown.

Trial production of Peace dollars was begun on May 13, 1965, at the Denver Mint annex—a converted trolley car building. The trial ended May 24, 1965.

With all trial-production 1964-D Peace dollars melted, the end finally had come for the standard silver dollar. Dollar-size base-metal tokens bearing the unflattering portrait of former President Dwight D. Eisenhower served casinos and assorted one-armed bandits, with a few debased silver versions sold to coin collectors. Small-diameter versions with new designs were tried for a few years beginning in 1979 and again in 2000, and yet again starting in 2007, but none have caught the interest or imagination of collectors like the old silver dollars.

Appendix

BIOGRAPHIES OF
KEY PARTICIPANTS

This section includes a short biography for each of the principal characters in the Peace dollar story. Sources of information follow each biography. Readers who want more information should consult the reference section of their local library or appropriate online resources.

ANTHONY DE FRANCISCI

If you look in almost any reference on American sculpture, you will find the names of Augustus Saint-Gaudens, Hermon A. MacNeil, Adolph A. Weinman, and others well known to numismatists. By comparison, Anthony de Francisci was not well known in his time and, except for the Peace dollar and perhaps the Maine Centennial half dollar, he remains a little-known artist today; most art references omit him entirely.

Anthony de Francisci was born on July 13, 1887, in Palermo, Italy. He studied at the Palermo Institute of Fine Art and later went to Rome for further study. He came to the United States in 1903 and became a U.S. citizen in 1913. He studied at Cooper Union and then the National Academy of Design. James Earle Fraser was his teacher at the Art Students' League. Later, he worked as an assistant to several sculptors, including MacNeil, Weinman, and Fraser. In 1915, Columbia University hired him as an instructor. He opened his own studio in New York two years later. Anthony and Maria Teresa Cafarelli were married in 1920 after an extensive courtship. The couple had one child, a daughter they named Gilda, born in July of 1924.

In 1920, de Francisci was commissioned to created models for the Maine Centennial half dollar from drawings supplied to him. The design was dictated to the sculptor and he had little artistic freedom. He also participated in design competitions for the Verdun City medal and several other military and award medals. He was invited to participate in the Peace dollar competition of 1921, a few months after the Verdun competition, which was also organized by the Commission of Fine Arts.

His other numismatic works were medals, mostly for the U.S. military. Among them were the Reserve Officers Training Corps medal, the Naval Defense pin, and the Badge of Service (Honorable Discharge). The Badge of Service was a gold-plated brass emblem, the result of General Orders No. 13, June 2, 1925. Any veteran with an honorable discharge could wear the Badge of Service. In 1943, the design was modified slightly and the general orders

Top left, Anthony de Francisci self-portrait medal, 1948. Above, Maria Teresa Cafarelli de Francisci portrait bas-relief, 1923. Bottom left, Gilda de Francisci portrait bas-relief, 1931.

allowed it to be worn by any veteran of World War II. To millions of men and women, it was known as the "Ruptured Duck." This same design also served as the lapel decoration for the World War II Victory Medal and was used on a postage stamp.

De Francisci also created the congressional gold medal awarded to General John J. Pershing, commander of the American forces in World War I. The American Institute of Mining Engineers commissioned the sculptor for the medal they awarded to Herbert Hoover, who began his professional life as an engineer. In 1944, de Francisci assisted Max Kalish in creating a series of sculptures of the Roosevelt cabinet. The Smith-sonian American Art Museum in Washington, D.C., has more than 100 of his works, but they are rarely displayed. Several more can be found at Brookgreen Gardens in South Carolina. His most public sculpture, *Independence Flagstaff*, at Union Square in New York City, shows allegorical figures of Good and Evil during the struggle for independence.

He served for many years as an instructor of sculpture at Columbia University. His final medallic work was the official medal for the 1964 New York World's Fair. Anthony de Francisci died on October 10, 1964, at the age of 77. His wife survived him by almost three decades, passing on October 20, 1990, at the age of 91.

Sources:

- Archives of American Art. *Anthony De Francisci, papers.* Biographical information prepared by the sculptor.
- Marotta, Michael E. "The Peace Dollar." *The Numismatist,* June 1998.
- Howe, Marvie. Obituary "Teresa DeFrancisci: Miss Liberty model for coin, dies at [91]." *New York Times,* October 21, 1990, p. 1.

RAYMOND T. BAKER

Raymond T. Baker (1878–1935) was born in Reno, Nevada. He was influential in banking and was often identified with the development of mining in Nevada. He was a friend of Utah mining millionaire Sam Newhouse and was a politically well-connected Democrat. Ray Baker was one of the best-known people in southern Nevada. He spent some time helping his brother, Cleve, in a successful campaign for attorney general of the state and was rewarded by appointment as warden of the state prison. After the death of his brother, Baker left the prison job and took an active part in the campaign of Key Pittman. Pittman defeated state senator W.A. Massey in a special election for the United States Senate in 1912.

Baker followed Pittman to Washington and was connected with committees of which Pittman was chairman. (The senator later co-authored the Pittman Act of 1918, which caused millions of silver dollars to be melted.) Baker was a good friend of Joseph P. Tumulty, the very influential private secretary of President Woodrow Wilson. Baker was also private secretary of Ambassador George T. Marye at Petrograd (now St. Petersburg), Russia, from October 1915 to March 1916. He returned to Washington, D.C., shortly after the 1916 presidential campaign. Political connections lead to his appointment by President Wilson to succeed Fredrich Johann Hugo von Engelken as director of the Mint, in which office he served from March 15, 1917, to March 6, 1922. Baker also helped Senator Pittman draft the Silver Purchase Act of 1918.

In June 1918, Baker married Margaret Emerson McKim Vanderbilt (widow of Alfred Gwynne Vanderbilt, who went down with the *Lusitania* in 1915). This added to Baker's social status and the couple was much in demand at Washington social events. They had one daughter, Gloria, born on June 6, 1920. The Bakers later divorced and Margaret married Charles Minot Amory. Raymond married Delphine Dodge Cromwell and the couple had a daughter, Anna May. Raymond died on April 28, 1935, of heart disease.

A WW II Liberty ship (#2236) was named after Baker in 1944. He was the first of three Nevadans to hold the post of Mint director. His Nevadan successors include Eva Adams and Henrietta Holsman Fore.

CHARLES MOORE

Charles Moore (1855–1942) was born in Ypsilanti, Michigan. He graduated from Harvard in 1878, and while there developed an appreciation of art from his teacher, Charles Eliot Norton. Upon graduation, Moore entered the field of journalism and became a reporter for the *Detroit Evening Journal*. Around 1889, he was sent to Washington as a correspondent for Detroit newspapers, and in that capacity he met Senator James McMillan of Michigan. The following year Moore became the senator's political secretary, and when McMillan became chairman of the Senate Committee on the District of Columbia, Charles Moore

Portrait medal of Charles Moore honoring his 25th anniversary on the Commission of Fine Arts.

became his clerk. Later he was appointed secretary to the Senate Park Commission and edited the report submitted to the Senate.

He returned to Detroit in 1902 to become secretary to the Security Trust Company there. It was at this time that his friendship with Charles L. Freer developed. Freer was managing director of the Michigan Car Company and had acquired a notable collection of Oriental art, numbering more than 8,000 pieces. Moore convinced Freer to donate his collection to the Smithsonian Institution, which became the basis for the Freer Gallery of Art in Washington, D.C.

He was a member of the National Commission of Fine Arts from its inception in 1910 and was chairman of the commission from 1915 to 1937. He acted as chief of the division of manuscripts of the Library of Congress (1918–1927) and authored several books. He was also on the board of overseers of Harvard University. Charles Moore died on September 25, 1942, at Gig Harbor, Washington.

Sources:

- Kohler, Sue. *The Commission of Fine Arts, A Brief History 1910– 1995.*
- *Charles Moore papers.* Library of Congress, Manuscript Division.
- *Adolph A. Weinman papers.* Smithsonian Institution Archives of American Art. Unsigned manuscript biography and appreciation of Moore.

James Earle Fraser

James Earle Fraser was born in Winona, Minnesota, on November 4, 1876, to Thomas Alexander and Caroline West Fraser. His father was a mechanical engineer employed by the Chicago-Milwaukee Railroad. During construction of the railroad from Mason City, Iowa, into the Black Hills, South Dakota, the family moved to the Dakota Territory. During their first year in the territory, the Frasers lived in a boxcar. Native Americans were frequent visitors to the Frasers' camp.

At night, James Fraser recalled, "We were surrounded by packs of wolves. Their mournful howling caused my spine to tingle and impressed upon me the lonely vastness of the West." At the age of eight, James Earle started carving things out of stone from a nearby quarry and wanted to attend an art school. His father wanted him to be an engineer, but he received such praise from railroad officials about his art that he finally relented. At the age of 15, James Earle was sent to study at the Art Institute of Chicago. Before he was 17, a model of one of his most celebrated works was completed. His *End of the Trail* statue, showing a weary Indian slumped down over his rack-ribbed horse, has been copied (some say "pirated") around the world. It is often regarded as the best-known sculpture in America.

After graduating from the Art Institute of Chicago, Fraser traveled to France, where he studied under the French sculptor Jean Alexander Falguiere, attended École des Beaux Arts, the Julian Academy, and the Colarossi. Young Fraser exhibited his model *End of the Trail* in Paris in 1898, which won him the $1,000 prize sponsored by the American Art Association. It also attracted the attention of the world-renowned artist, Augustus Saint-Gaudens, who asked him to become his assistant. This initial contact led to a strong friendship, and Fraser became Saint-Gaudens's disciple.

The artist's four years with Augustus Saint-Gaudens shaped his future; from Saint-Gaudens he gained inspiration and developed techniques and working habits that were to dignify his contributions. Saint-Gaudens gave his young protégé an important break when he recommended that Fraser do the bust of President Theodore Roosevelt. The great artist complained that he was too ill to comply with the president's request that he do the portrait.

From this time forward, James Earle Fraser was never without commissions. After Saint-Gaudens's death in 1907, Fraser took up residency in New York and established a studio in picturesque MacDougal Alley in Greenwich Village. From 1906 through 1911, he was instructor in sculpture at the Art Students' League in New York City. He was one of the first to make artistically fashionable what was once a block of famous old carriage houses of New York aristocrats. Among the group of artists and writers who came here, several were to grow into national prominence, principally Robert Henri, Gertrude Vanderbilt Whitney, Daniel Chester French, Anthony de Francisci, George Deforest Brush, Ernest Lawson, James Huneker, and the poet Edwin Arlington Robinson.

Apart from many large-scale works, Fraser was known as a gifted designer of medals. These included medals to honor Saint-Gaudens and Thomas Edison; the E.H. Harriman Safety Medal; the Medal of Award by the Academy of Arts and Letters; the Award Medal of the American Institute of Graphic Arts; the

American Committee for Relief of Devastated France medal; the Yale University Howland Memorial Medal; the Theodore Roosevelt Memorial Association Medal of Honor; and the Melville Medal for the American Society of Mechanical Engineers. Fraser further distinguished his career by designing two important military medals: the Victory Medal of World War I and the Navy Cross.

To most coin collectors, Fraser is best known for his Buffalo nickel design (1913) and his collaboration with his wife, Laura Gardin Fraser, on the Oregon Trail commemorative half dollar. As a member of the Commission of Fine Arts from 1920 to 1925, Fraser was dedicated to promoting the highest standards of quality for U.S. coinage, and he had significant influence over the designs of many commemorative coins.

Sources:

- Excerpted from a brief biography by Dean Krakel, managing director of the National Cowboy Hall of Fame and Western Heritage Center, Oklahoma City, Oklahoma.
- *The Columbia Electronic Encyclopedia.* Columbia University Press.
- *The Columbia Encyclopedia,* sixth edition. Columbia University Press.
- *Infoplease Dictionary.* Family Education Network.
- *Random House Webster's Unabridged Dictionary.* Random House, Inc.

GEORGE T. MORGAN

George T. Morgan was born in Birmingham, England, in 1845. He attended the Birmingham Art School, and won a scholarship to the South Kensington Art School. He worked for many years as an assistant under the Wyons at the British Royal Mint. Morgan was brought to the Philadelphia Mint in 1876 as a "special engraver," reporting directly to Mint Director Henry R. Linderman. The father-and-son team of William and Charles Barber, also from England, were engraver and assistant engraver, respectively, at the time. Although Morgan's design was selected for the new standard silver dollar in 1878, he was relegated to the assistant's position from 1880 until Charles Barber's death in 1917. Only then, at the age of 72, was Morgan able to assume the position of engraver.

During his career he designed many medals and insignia and collaborated in several commemorative coin designs. Other than supervising the creation of dies and production of Proof coins, Morgan's creative involvement with the Peace dollar was limited to an unsolicited entry in the design competition, the high-relief designs of 1922, and the experimental medium-relief version coins of January 1922. Morgan died on January 4, 1925, at his home in Germantown, Pennsylvania. He was 79.

Sources:

- DeLorey, Thomas K. "George T. Morgan Remembered," *COINage,* September, 1996. National Archives and Records Administration, record group 104. Correspondence between Morgan and Linderman.

NOTES

CHAPTER 1

1. The troy ounce is commonly used to measure the weight of precious metals. One troy ounce equals 31.1035 grams.
2. *Annual Report of the Director of the Mint*, 1928, pp. 5–7.
3. As late as November 6, 1920, old silver dollars numbering 111,168 were melted at the Denver Mint to supply metal for subsidiary coinage. Philadelphia Mint usage was 1.8 million ounces of fine silver per month. (*U.S. Mint*. NARA-CP, op. cit. Entry 235, vol. 433. Letter dated November 6, 1920, to Secretary of the Treasury Houston from acting Mint director Mary M. O'Reilly.)
4. *Federal Reserve Bulletin*, December 1, 1917, "Christmas Gifts," p. 931, and "War Savings Certificates as Christmas Gifts," p. 951.
5. "War Stamps Liked in District as Gifts," *Washington Post*, December 20, 1917, p. 11.
6. "Gold Coin Gifts Hard to Get," *Washington Post*, December 22, 1917, p. 6.
7. "Gold for Christmas Presents Once More," *New York Times*, December 17, 1922, p. 104.

CHAPTER 2

1. In 1906 Saint-Gaudens had suggested adding the words *Law* or *Justice* to the double eagle. This was rejected because it would have required Congressional approval.

CHAPTER 4

1. *U.S. Mint*. NARA-CP, record group 104, entry 330 (NN3-104-00-001) Central Files, box 23, folder 1. Memorandum dated February 28, 1963, to Wallace from Adams, p. 1, 2–4.
2. *U.S. Mint*. NARA-CP, op cit. Memorandum dated February 28, 1963, to Wallace from Adams, p. 3.
3. *U.S. Mint*. NARA-CP, op cit. Quoted in a background paper ND (Sept. 1964) prepared for Secretary Dillon.
4. *U.S. Mint*. NARA-CP, op cit. Letter dated September 27, 1963, to Denver Mint Superintendent Miller from Frederick W. Tate, deputy director of the Mint.
5. *U.S. Mint*. NARA-CP, op cit. Memorandum dated July 31, 1963, to Wallace from Adams.
6. *U.S. Mint*. NARA-CP, op cit. Memorandum dated July 31, 1963, to Wallace from Adams. Oddly, there was no mention of consulting the Commission of Fine Arts, the government commission with responsibility for coin and medal designs.
7. *U.S. Mint*. NARA-CP, op cit. Memorandum dated September 9, 1963, to Dillon from Wallace.
8. *U.S. Mint*. NARA-CP, op cit. Manuscript note dated September 23, 1963, initialed by Roosa. The "new notes" were Federal Reserve notes being prepared for issuance in denominations of $1, $5, and $10. These did not require backing by silver and were intended to replace silver certificates.
9. *U.S. Mint*. NARA-CP, op cit. Internal Treasury memorandum dated September 19, 1963. No signature.
10. *U.S. Mint*. NARA-CP, op cit. Internal Treasury memorandum dated September 19, 1963. No signature.

11. *U.S. Mint.* NARA-CP, op cit. Memorandum dated September 23, 1963, to Dillon from Wallace.

12. *U.S. Mint.* NARA-CP, op cit. Letter dated September 27, 1963, to Miller from Tate, p. 1.

13. A "finger" is a short metal rod that pushes planchets into place and pushes coins away from the dies.

14. *U.S. Mint.* NARA-CP, op cit. Letter dated October 15, 1963, to Miller from Walter J. Judge.

15. *U.S. Mint.* NARA-CP, op cit. Letter dated October 23, 1963, to Miller from Judge.

16. *U.S. Mint.* NARA-CP, op cit. Letter dated November 6, 1963, to Wallace from Adams. An accompanying table shows silver purchased from fiscal year 1935 through 1963 and the profit already taken on the metal.

17. *U.S. Mint.* NARA-CP, op cit. Background paper ND (June 1965) for Secretary Fowler.

18. *Michael J. Mansfield* papers, University of Montana, Mansfield Library, Missoula, MT.

19. *Census Bureau*, "U.S. Census of Population and Housing, 1960."

20. *U.S. Mint.* NARA-CP, op cit. Background paper ND (Sept. 1964) for Secretary Dillon, pp. 6–7.

21. *U.S. Mint.* NARA-CP, op cit. Letter dated April 9, 1964, to Wallace from Adams.

22. *U.S. Mint.* NARA-CP, op cit. Letter dated July 23, 1964, to A. Willis Robertson, chairman, from Dillon.

23. Although Gilroy Roberts was the engraver at this time, he had already announced his resignation effective October 8. The work was therefore assigned to his presumed successor, Frank Gasparo. He was officially confirmed as engraver on February 23, 1965.

24. *U.S. Mint.* NARA-P, entry 671, box 131, folder 1. Letter dated September 16, 1964, to Michael H. Sura, superintendent of the Philadelphia Mint, from Adams.

25. *U.S. Mint.* NARA-P, entry 671, box 131, folder 1. Letter dated September 14, 1964, to Sura from Miller. This letter gives the reverse die numbers as: 1934 D-9, 10, 21 through 40; 1935 D-1 through 5; and 1936 D-16 through 20.

26. *U.S. Mint.* NARA-P, entry 671, box 131, folder 1. Letter dated September 16, 1964, to Sura from Miller.

27. *U.S. Mint.* NARA-CP, op cit. Letter dated September 23, 1964, to Miller from Adams.

28. *U.S. Mint.* NARA-CP, op cit. Letter dated September 23, 1964, to Adams from Sura.

29. *U.S. Mint.* NARA-P, entry 671, box 131, folder 1. Letter dated September 28, 1964, to Miller from Sura.

30. *U.S. Mint.* NARA-P, entry 671, box 131, folder 1. Letter dated October 19, 1964, to Miller from Sura.

31. *U.S. Mint.* NARA-P, entry 671, box 131, folder 1. Letter dated October 28, 1964, to Miller from Sura.

32. *U.S. Mint.* NARA-CP, entry UD central files, box 42. Memorandum dated September 8, 1977, to Alan J. Goldman from Thomas G. Jurcich. This document lists dozens of experimental Martha Washington / Mt. Vernon pieces dated 1759 used to test various alloys and compositions for coins to replace standard .900 fine silver. Two dollar-size pieces are listed, one was equal parts silver and copper and the other was .800 fine silver clad on a copper/silver core with a total fineness of .500. No examples are known to exist of these experimental pieces.

33. *Hearings Before the Committee on Banking and Currency, House of Representatives*, June 4, 7, 8, 1965. Answers to questions by Rep. White to Secretary Fowler, p. 39.

34. *U.S. Mint.* NARA-CP, op cit. Memorandum dated January 13, 1965, to President Johnson from Dillon.
35. *U.S. Mint.* NARA-CP, op cit. Letter dated March 25, 1965, to Dillon from Mansfield.
36. *U.S. Mint.* NARA-CP, op cit. Letter dated April 16, 1965, to Mansfield from Fowler (via Wallace).
37. *U.S. Mint.* NARA-CP, op cit. Memorandum dated April 16, 1965, to Fowler from Wallace.
38. *U.S. Mint.* NARA-CP, op cit. Memorandum dated May 6, 1965, to Fowler from Bowman.
39. *U.S. Mint.* NARA-CP, op cit. Memorandum dated May 6, 1965, to Fowler from Wallace.
40. *Ibid.*, p. 2.
41. *U.S. Mint.* NARA-CP, op cit. Memorandum dated May 7, 1965, to Fowler from Barr. This was prepared prior to their meeting with Mansfield. Barr was later to become secretary of the Treasury for a short time, and notes with his signature quickly became popular collector's items.
42. *U.S. Mint.* NARA-CP, op cit. Letter dated May 12, 1965, to Miller from Adams.
43. *Library of Congress*, list of enrolled bills 88th Congress Second Session, September 1964.
44. *U.S. Mint.* NARA-CP, op cit. Press release dated May 15, 1965, from the Office of the White House press secretary.
45. *U.S. Mint.* NARA-P, record group 104, entry 625, box 133, folder 3 "Coinage Dies Shipped to Denver." Engravers Gasparro and Albino worked on the dollar dies.
46. *Hearings Before the Committee on Banking and Currency, House of Representatives,* June 4, 7, 8, 1965. Appendix D-1 "Mint Operations," p. 369. Philadelphia ingots were 1.5 inches x 9-3/8 inches x 5 feet and weighed 315 pounds.
47. Presumes the legal weight of a .900 fine silver dollar was 412.5 grains which equals 0.8594 troy ounces. The values are from Treasury Department records. Each coin contained 0.77343 troy ounces of pure silver.
48. *U.S. Mint.* NARA-CP, op cit. Letter dated June 17, 1965, to Adams from Miller.
49. *U.S. Mint.* NARA-P, entry 671, box 131, folder 1. Letter dated May14, 1965, to Sura from Miller.
50. *U.S. Mint.* NARA-CP, op cit. Letter dated June 17, 1965, to Adams from Miller.
51. Michael P. Lantz, letter dated November 26, 2006, to the author.
52. *U.S. Mint.* NARA-CP, op cit. Memorandum dated June 10, 1965, to Miller from William Summers, Acting Superintendent, Coining Department, pp. 1–5.
53. *U.S. Mint.* NARA-CP, op cit. File memorandum dated October 18, 1966, signed by Neisser and Frere. Memo notes destruction of two sample bags from the Denver Mint for the 1964 dollars.
54. *U.S. Mint.* NARA-CP, op cit. Memorandum dated June 10, 1965, to Miller from William Summers, Acting Superintendent, Coining Department, p. 3.
55. *U.S. Mint.* NARA-CP, op cit. *Subcommittee of the Committee on Appropriations of the House of Representatives,* May 24, 1965. Transcript of testimony by Eva Adams, director of the Mint.
56. *U.S. Mint.* NARA-CP, op cit. Memorandum dated June 15, 1965, to Howell from Adams.

57. Prior to publication of the June 4, 7–8 hearings on the Coinage Act of 1965, members of Congress were told approximately 300,000 pieces were struck. The quantity of 316,076 was first quoted in internal Mint and Treasury documents on June 15, and provided to Congress during Coinage Act of 1965 hearings. After June, the quantity internally quoted as struck varies from 316,000 to 322,000. The first published coin collector reference to quantity was in *Numismatic News* on April 24, 1973, where the figure of "300,000" was used. The first known correspondence using the 316,076 mintage was to author Ted Schwarz in a letter written on May 29, 1975.

58. *U.S. Mint.* NARA-CP, op cit. Memorandum dated May 17, 1965, to Adams from Carwile.

59. *House of Representatives Committee on Banking and Currency,* "Coinage Act of 1965" (H.R. 8746). Hearing report dated June 4, 7, 8, 1965, p. 1.

60. *Subcommittee of the Committee on Appropriations of the House of Representatives,* May 24, 1965. Transcript of testimony by Eva Adams, director for the Mint, p. 50.

61. *U.S. Mint.* NARA-P, entry 671, box 131, folder 1. Teletype copy dated May 15, 1965, 12:20 p.m. to Sura from Miller.

62. *U.S. Mint.* NARA-P, entry 671, box 131, folder 1. Teletype copy dated May 18, 1965, 2:15 p.m. to Sura from Miller.

63. *U.S. Mint.* NARA-P, entry 671, box 131, folder 1. Teletype copy dated May 24, 1965, 4:45 p.m. to Sura from Miller.

64. *U.S. Mint.* NARA-CP, op. cit. Treasury department press release dated May 24, 1965, but embargoed until May 25.

65. *U.S. Mint.* NARA-CP, op. cit. Memorandum dated May 25, 1965, from Howell to Adams.

66. *U.S. Mint.* NARA-CP, op cit. Letter dated June 17, 1965, to Adams from Miller.

67. *U.S. Mint.* NARA-CP, op cit. Affidavit dated June 11, 1965, signed by Denver Mint officers.

68. *U.S. Mint.* NARA-CP, op cit. Affidavit dated June 11, 1965, signed by Denver Mint employees.

69. *U.S. Mint.* NARA-CP, op cit. Affidavit dated June 16, 1965, signed by Larry V. Truitt and witnessed by Rolland H. Osborne from the U.S. Secret Service and Arthur W. Blake. Truitt resigned at the beginning of June.

70. *Hearings Before the Committee on Banking and Currency, House of Representatives,* June 4, 7, 8, 1965. Transcript of colloquy between Rep. Widnall and Secretary Fowler, p. 24.

71. *U.S. Mint.* NARA-CP, op cit., entry 330 (NN3-104-00-001) Central Files, box 23, folder 1. Letter dated August 3, 1965, to Adams from Miller. This does not match Summers' detailed statement; however, the August accounting likely included blanks not known to Summers when he filed his report.

72. *U.S. Mint.* NARA-CP, op cit. Letter dated August 3, 1965, to Michael H. Sura, superintendent of the Philadelphia Mint, from Adams.

73. David L. Ganz, "The 1964 Peace Dollar: the Mystery Remains," *Numismatist,* August 2004, pp. 36–40.

74. *Ibid.*

75. However, to have done so would likely have jeopardized final negotiations on the draft "Coinage Act of 1965," and President Johnson did not want to do that.

76. *U.S. Mint.* NARA-CP, entry 328-H "Miscellaneous Coinage Files," box 1, "Eisen-hower Dollar folder #1." Letter dated February 19, 1970, to Theodore from Brooks.
77. Walter Breen's assertion that Harding was given a Sandblast Proof as the first struck 1921 Peace dollar is wrong.
78. *U.S. Mint.* NARA-CP, op. cit. Letter dated June 17, 1965, to Adams from Miller.
79. The authors are not lawyers and have no credentials in any aspect of U.S. law. The statements made are the suppositions of laypersons as part of an intellectual discussion and not legal advice.
80. *U.S. Mint.* NARA-CP, op cit. Press release dated May 31, 1973, from the Bureau of the Mint.
81. *U.S. Mint.* NARA-CP, op cit. Personal memorandum dated May 1, 1973, to Thomas M. McCulloch, U.S. Secret Service, from Landis.
82. Alan Herbert, "Answer the '64 Dollar Question And You Can Be $3,000 Richer." *Numismatic News Weekly*, April 24, 1973, p. 1.
83. *Ibid.*, p. 12.
84. *U.S. Mint.* NARA-CP, op cit. Memorandum dated May 4, 1973, to Roy C. Cahoon from Landis, p. 2.
85. *Ibid.*, p. 1.
86. *U.S. Mint.* NARA-CP, op cit. Letter dated August 2, 1965, to Adams from Miller.
87. Alison Frankel, *Double Eagle—The Epic Story of the World's Most Valuable Coin.* W.W. Norton & Co., New York. 2006, pp. 219–220, 235–237.

CHAPTER 5
1. Cornelius C. Vermeule, *Numismatic Art in America.* Belknap Press of Harvard University Press, Cambridge, Massachusetts, 1971, p. 149.
2. *AdF*, AAA, op. cit. Box 2 of 6, folder 1.
3. *CFA-Peace*, NARA-DC, op. cit. Letter dated January 6, 1922, to Moore from Louis Ayres. Aitken was the only war veteran among the artists invited to compete.

CHAPTER 7
1. I am honored to have been involved with the attribution and display efforts for the SAAM medals.

CHAPTER 8
1. The term *trial strike* is used to indicate a pre-production coin made from new hubs or dies to test the ability of the dies to withstand production conditions. It is not the same as a *die trial* or *die test*, which usually consists of a single piece, often uniface. Trial strikes may be made by the thousands and then destroyed with little or no record.
2. Bowers, op. cit. pp. 2724–2725.
3. *U.S. Mint.* NARA-CP, op. cit., entry 229, box 290. Letter dated May 14, 1910, to Landis from Barber. The letter was intended to be forwarded to Director Andrew.
4. *Treasury*, NARA-CP, record group 50, entry 171W, pp. 781–814. This journal also confirms quantities reported in Mint special assay documents for deliveries 1 and 2, February 1922.
5. *CFA-Peace*, NARA-DC op. cit. February 14, 1922, telegram to Moore from Fraser.
6. Peace dollars struck at the Denver Mint in 1965 were also trial pieces, although one of them would be worth a small fortune.

7. Bowers, op. cit. p. 2769. The specific document is not mentioned. Bowers states the coin was sold to Ambrose Swasey of Cleveland, Ohio.

8. The author had examined and verbally authenticated these coins in 2010, but was unable to obtain good photos at the time. As is often the case with 1921 and 1922 pattern and experimental Peace dollars, the authentication companies' descriptions are not necessarily consistent.

9. It was incorrectly described as a "proof" in the auction catalog.

10. Before hydraulic medal presses were available, the Philadelphia Mint used a large screw press to strike medals and Proof coins. Some early Proof specimens may have been struck more than once. After hydraulic equipment was introduced, Proof coins normally received one blow from the press.

CHAPTER 9

1. *Treasurer of the United States.* NARA-CP, record group 50, entry UD-171W, vol. 1, "Standard Silver Dollars Produced under Authority of the Pittman Act, 1921–1928," pp. 781–814.

2. *Treasurer of the United States.* NARA-CP, record group 50, entry UD-171W, vol. 1 "Standard Silver Dollars Produced under Authority of the Pittman Act, 1921–1928," p. 814.

3. *Treasurer of the United States.* NARA-CP, record group 50, entry UD-171W, vol. 1 "Standard Silver Dollars Produced under Authority of the Pittman Act, 1921–1928," pp. 813–814.

BIBLIOGRAPHY

Original sources of information have been used whenever possible. These generally include official minutes and correspondence of corporations, government commissions, and the artists. Much original official correspondence appears to have been lost or destroyed. Detailed references for the origin of the Peace dollar will be found in *Renaissance of American Coinage 1916–1921*.

Adams, Eva Bertrand. Papers. University of Nevada–Reno.

Aitken, Robert Ingersol. Papers. Washington DC: Smithsonian Institution, Archives of American Art. Microfilm.

Ashbrook, William Albert. *A Line a Day for Forty Odd Years, from the diary of William A. Ashbrook*. Johnstown, Ohio. Microfilm.

Barber, Charles Edward. Papers. Colorado Springs, CO: American Numismatic Association.

Beach, Chester. Papers. Washington DC: Smithsonian Institution, Archives of American Art. Microfilm.

Benson Collection, Part I, Auction Catalog. Beverly Hills, Calif.: Goldberg Coins. 2001. http://www.goldbergcoins.com/catalogarchive/20010216/

Berridge, William A. "Some Facts Bearing on the Silver Program." *The Review of Economic Statistics* 16, no. 11 (November 15, 1934): 231–236.

Bowers, Q. David. *Commemorative Coins of the United States, A Complete Encyclopedia*. Irvine, Calif.: Bowers and Merena Galleries, 1991.

———. *Silver Dollars & Trade Dollars of the United States, A Complete Encyclopedia*. Irvine, Calif.: Bowers and Merena Galleries, 1993.

Bratter, Herbert M. "The Silver Episode." *The Journal of Political Economy* 45, no. 5 (October 1938): 609–652.

———. "The Silver Episode: II." *The Journal of Political Economy* 46, no. 6 (December 1938): 802–837.

Breen, Walter H. *Walter Breen's Complete Encyclopedia of U.S. and Colonial Coins*. New York: F.C.I. Press/Doubleday, 1988.

———. "The 1922 Type of 1921 Peace Dollar." *Numismatic Scrapbook Magazine*, July 1961. 1721–1729.

Brunk, Gregory G. *Merchant and Privately Countermarked Coins—Advertising on the World's Smallest Billboards*. Rockford, IL: World Exonumia (Rich Hartzog), 2003.

Burdette, Roger W. *Renaissance of American Coinage 1905–1908*. Great Falls, VA: Seneca Mill Press LLC, 2006.

———. *Renaissance of American Coinage 1909–1915*. Great Falls, VA: Seneca Mill Press LLC, 2007.

———. *Renaissance of American Coinage 1916–1921*. Great Falls, VA: Seneca Mill Press LLC, 2005.

Bureau of the Mint. *Annual Report of the Director of the Mint for the Fiscal Year ended June 30, 1920–1936*. Washington, DC: Government Printing Office.

Commission of Fine Arts. *Tenth Report, July 1, 1921–December 31, 1925*. Washington DC: Government Printing Office, 1926. p. 105.

Commission of Fine Arts. *Forty Years of Achievement—Commemorating the Fortieth Anniversary of the Establishment of the National Commission of Fine Arts*. Senate document no. 128. Washington DC: Government Printing Office, 1950.

Contini A. and Sons. Papers. Washington DC: Smithsonian Institution, Archives of American Art. Microfilm.

de Francisci, Anthony. Papers (1905–1965). Washington DC: Smithsonian Institution, Archives of American Art. Microfilm.

DeLorey, Thomas K. "George T. Morgan Remembered." *COINage*, September 1996.

Department of State. *Papers Relating to the Foreign Relations of the United States: 1922, Vol. 1.* Washington, DC: Government Printing Office, 1938.

Everest, Allan Seymour. *Morgenthau, the New Deal and Silver: A Story in Pressure Politics.* New York: King's Crown Press, 1950.

Fivaz, Bill and J. T. Stanton. *Cherrypicker's Guide To Rare Die Varieties of United States Coins*, volume II, 5th ed. Atlanta, Ga: Whitman Publishing LLC, 2012.

French, Daniel Chester. Papers. Washington DC: Library of Congress Manuscript Division. Microfilm.

Fraser, James Earle. Papers. Washington DC: Smithsonian Institution, Archives of American Art. Microfilm.

Fraser, James Earle and Laura Gardin. Papers. Syracuse University Library Special Collections.

Froman, Lewis A. "Bimetallism: Reconsidered in the Light of Recent Developments." *The American Economic Review* 26, no. 1 (March 1936): 53–61.

Ganz, David L. "The 1964 Peace Dollar—The Mystery Remains," *The Numismatist*, August 2004. 36–40.

Griffiths, Arthur. "A Study of the Life and Work of Harry Hayman Cochrane, The Artist." Unpublished thesis. Bates College. 1950.

Glaser, Lynn. "Anthony de Francisci, Coin Artist." *Numismatic Scrapbook Magazine*, April 1963. 998–999.

Gregory, T.E. "Twelve Months of American Dollar Policy." *Economica* 1, no. 2 (May 1934): 121–146.

Hanna, John. "Currency Control and Private Property." *Columbia Law Review* 33, no. 4 (April 1933): 617–647.

Harding, Warren G. Papers. Columbus, Ohio: Ohio Historical Society.

Hibler, Harold E. and Charles V. Kappen. *So-Called Dollars—An Illustrated Standard Catalog*, 2nd ed. Clifton, NJ: The Coin and Currency Institute, Inc., 2008.

Hoover, Irwin "Ike" Hood. Papers 1909–1933. Washington DC: Library of Congress Manuscript Division.

Jefferson Coin and Bullion. "The Peace Dollar: Idealistic and Quiet Collectible." http://www.wsrarities.com/focus/coins/news30.jhtml.

———. "Peace Dollar Model: A Modest Miss Liberty" http://www.wsrarities.com/focus/coins/news30.jhtml.

Julian, R. W. "Historical Background, Peace Dollars 1921–1964." In *Silver Dollars and Trade Dollars of the United States, A Complete Encyclopedia*, by Q. David Bowers, Irvine, Calif.: Bowers & Merena Galleries, Inc., 1993. 2693–2696.

Kohler, Sue A. *The Commission of Fine Arts: A Brief History 1910–1995*. Washington DC: The Commission of Fine Arts, National Building Museum, 1995.

Leavens, Dickson H. "The Distribution of the World's Silver." *The Review of Economic Statistics* 17, no. 6 (November 1935): 131–138.

———. "Bullion Prices and the Gold-Silver Ratio 1929–1945." *The Review of Economic Statistics* 28, no. 3 (August 1946): 160–164.

Lange, David W. "Do '26 Peace Dollars Emphasize Religious Motto?" *Numismatic News*, September 21, 1999. 20–22.

Lodge, Henry Cabot. Papers. Boston: Massachusetts Historical Society.

MacNeil, Hermon Atkins. Papers. Washington DC: Smithsonian Institution, Archives of American Art. Microfilm.

Mansfield, Michael. Papers. University of Montana–Missoula.

Marotta, Michael E., "The Peace Dollar." *The Numismatist,* June 1998. A revised version can be found at Coin Gallery Online, www.coingallery.com/cgmarotta2.htm.

"Memorandum on Silver," *American Council Institute of Pacific Relations* 2, no. 22 (November 17, 1933).

Miller, Wayne, *The Morgan and Peace Dollar Textbook.* Metairie, LA: Adam Smith Publishing, 1982.

Moore, Charles. Papers. Washington DC: Smithsonian Institution, Archives of American Art. Microfilm.

Moore, Charles. Papers (1901–1940). Ann Arbor, Mich.: University of Michigan Bentley Library.

Morey, C.R. *Sculpture Since the Centennial.* Pageant of America, Volume XII "The American Spirit in Art." Yale University Press, 1927.

Morgenthau, Henry, Jr. Papers. Hyde Park, NY: Franklin D. Roosevelt Presidential Library and Museum, National Archives and Records Administration.

Mowbrey, Harry Siddons. Papers. Washington DC: Smithsonian Institution, Archives of American Art. Microfilm.

NARA. Hyde Park, NY: Franklin D. Roosevelt Presidential Library and Museum.

NARA. Boston, Mass.: John F. Kennedy Presidential Library, Columbia Point.

NARA. Austin, Tex: Lyndon Baines Johnson Library.

National Archives and Records Administration, record groups 50, (Treasurer of the United States), 56 (Treasury Department) and 104 (Mint Bureau), College Park, Md. and Philadelphia, Penn.

National Sculpture Review. *Anthony de Francisci.* Winter 1964–1965, 6. National Sculpture Society, Inc., New York.

Neelie, Aron. "Peace Coins: Remembering The Peace Coins Of The Great War." *Finally!,* July 2001: 20.

Osborne, Katherine Gillette. Papers. Boston: Northeastern University Library Archives.

Oxman, Jeff and David Close. *The Official Guide to the Top 50 Peace Dollar Varieties.* Greensboro, N.C.: Society of Silver Dollar Collectors, 2002.

Roosevelt, Theodore, and Augustus Saint-Gaudens. *Roosevelt and Our Coin Designs: Letters Between Theodore Roosevelt and Augustus Saint-Gaudens.* Edited by Homer Saint-Gaudens. New York: Century, 1920.

Schwarz, Ted. "The Morgan and Peace Silver Dollars." *The Numismatist,* Vol. 88, November 1975; 2423. As quoted in Q. David Bowers, *Silver Dollars & Trade Dollars of the United States, A Complete Encyclopedia.*

Storer, Malcolm. *Numismatics of Massachusetts.* Lincoln, Mass.: Quarterman Publications. 1981. Reprint of 1923 edition.

Taxay, Don. *The U.S. Mint and Coinage.* New York: Arco Publishing, 1966.

Carnegie Endowment for International Peace. *The Treaties of Peace 1919–1923, Vol. II.* New York: Lawbook Exchange, 1924.

Tumulty, Joseph P. Papers. Washington, DC: Library of Congress Manuscript Division.

Van Allen, Leroy C. and A. George Mallis. *The Comprehensive Catalog and Encyclopedia of Morgan & Peace Dollars.* New York: FCI Press—ARCO, 1998.

Vermeule, Cornelius C. *Numismatic Art in America—Aesthetics of the United States Coinage,* 2nd ed. Atlanta, Ga., 2007.

Weinman, Adolph A. Papers. Washington DC: Smithsonian Institution, Archives of American Art.

Yeoman, R.S. *A Guide Book of United States Coins,* 66th ed. Atlanta, Ga., 2012.

ABOUT THE AUTHOR

Roger W. Burdette, like many coin collectors, began in the hobby by attempting to fill cent and nickel folders from pocket change. During the 1970s he specialized in coin photography, producing the images for popular advertisements and hobby books. After a hiatus of several years, he became interested in numismatic research. In nearly a decade of research he has uncovered a wide array of fresh information, including details on many previously unknown numismatic events.

Burdette is the author of three critically acclaimed numismatic books composing his *Renaissance of American Coinage* series. For his groundbreaking work he won the prestigious "Book of the Year" award from the Numismatic Literary Guild in 2006, 2007, and 2008. Digital books for collectors include *Annual Assay Commissioin: United States Mint 1800–1943* (2010) and *Silver Dollars Struck Under the Pittman Act of 1918* (2011). He has also written numerous articles for numismatic newspapers and magazines, including *Coin World, Coin Values, Coins,* and *The Numismatist.* He is a contributor to the *Guide Book of United States Coins* (the "Red Book"), the 8th, 9th, and 10th editions of J. Hewitt Judd's *United States Pattern Coins,* and the *USPatterns.com* Web site. He has contributed to other books in Whitman's Bowers Series, including those on type coins, nickel five-cent pieces, quarter dollars, silver dollars, double eagle gold coins, and others, and was a contributor to David W. Lange's *Complete Guide to Buffalo Nickels.*

In 2008 he was appointed to the Citizens Coinage Advisory Committee, a federal committee established to advise the secretary of the Treasury on the themes and designs of all U.S. coins and medals.

Roger W. Burdette lives with his daughters near Washington, D.C. He is employed by a nationally known nonprofit research-and-development corporation.

Barry Lovvorn started as a coin collector at a young age. In the early 1960s his grandfather gave him a handful of Peace dollars, and he instinctively knew the coins were special. "I have always thought the Peace dollar is the most attractive coin ever produced," he says. In early 1998 Lovvorn began his numismatic research in earnest, specializing in Peace dollars. Since then he has examined thousands of the coins, assembling a collection that has twice been honored with NGC's recognition as one of the best presentations in its registry competition.

In the *Guide Book of Peace Dollars,* Lovvorn assisted with the coin-by-coin study, interviewed past employees of the Denver Mint regarding the 1964-D issue, and contributed other substantial research.

ACKNOWLEDGMENTS

No research of this nature can be performed without the selfless assistance of archivists, research associates, curators, collection managers, and the many Peace dollar collectors who are guardians of our history. Without their dedication, patience, and understanding of the collections entrusted to their care, meaningful research would be impossible. To these I extend a sincere "Thank You!"

The efforts of the following individuals and organizations who have aided this project are also greatly appreciated:

David W. Akers
David T. Alexander
Frank Andrusiewicz
Q. David Bowers
Kenneth Bressett
Mike Byers
Broadstruck Collection
Robyn Christensen
Joseph Clossey
Jane Colvard
Beth Deisher
Richard Doty
Henry Duffy
Bill Fivaz
Kevin Flynn
Jim Halpern
Eleanor Harvey
Don Heath
Wayne Herndon
Wayne Homren
Richard Johnson
Robert W. Julian
David W. Lange
Julian Liedman
Christian Merlo

Douglas Mudd
Jeff Oxman
William B. Smith
Jeff Sam
Saul Teichman
Judith Throm
David Tripp
Leroy Van Allen
Mel Wacks
Heidi Wastweet
Fred Weinberg
American Numismatic
  Association
American Numismatic
  Society
Bowers and Merena
  Galleries, Inc.
Connecticut State
  Library
Cornell University
Georgetown University
Goldberg Coins
  & Collectibles
Harvard University
Harry W. Bass, Jr.
  Foundation

Heritage Auctions, Inc.
The Johns Hopkins
  University
Library of Congress
Massachusetts Historical
  Society
Museum of American
  History (NYC)
Numismatic Conserva-
  tion Service
Numismatic Guaranty
  Corporation of Amer-
  ica
Professional Coin Grad-
  ing Service
Saint-Gaudens National
  Historic Site, National
  Park Service
Smithsonian Institution
Smithsonian American
  Art Museum
Stack's Bowers
  Galleries
U.S. Commission of
  Fine Arts

Michael P. Lantz organized interviews with former Denver Mint employees Dean Bell and Dwight Picket. These men worked in various departments associated with the 1964-D dollars. Their recollections and comments provided valuable insight into operations at the mint in 1965.

Special thanks to David W. Lange for reviewing the manuscript and for his very helpful comments and suggestions.

Many of the images in this book were graciously provided by the American Numismatic Association, Ashbrook Center Archives, Goldberg Coins & Collectibles, Heritage Auction Galleries, Library of Congress, mikebyers.com,

NARA Collection, Numismatic Conservation Services, Numismatic Guaranty Corporation of America, Professional Coin Grading Service, Smithsonian American Art Museum, Smithsonian Institution Archives of American Art, Stack's Rare Coins, University of Nevada–Reno / Eva Bertrand Adams Papers, U.S. Commission of Fine Arts, VAMWorld.com, and Wayne Herndon Rare Coins. Some images are reproduced, with permission, from the *Cherrypickers' Guide to Rare Die Varieties*, fourth edition, volume two, by J.T. Stanton and Bill Fivaz.

The following individuals also provided Peace dollar and other images, as specified. **Frank Andrusiewicz** provided photos of a 1923-P Camp David Peace Summit counterstrike. **Randy Burgess** provided a close-up of 1922-P VAM 2A. **David J. Camire** provided close-ups of the following error coins: 1922-P cracked planchet; 1922-S edge clip / partial collar; 1923-S lamination; 1921-P broadstrike; 1921-P rim die break; undated wrong planchet. He also provided images of a 1925-P with fab-ric impression, a Peace dollar with 1993 Middle East Peace Accord counterstamp, and a 1922 high-relief pattern Proof; as well as close-ups of a1922-P, VAM 2F and a 1923-P, VAM 1A. In addition, Mr. Camire photographed a pattern Proof edge collar, the edges of 1922 high-relief and low-relief Sandblast Proofs, and a 1923-P VAM 1F, all courtesy of Numismatic Conservation Services. **Kevin S. Eikenberry** provided a photo of a Peace dollar in Redfield-hoard packaging. **Bill Fivaz** provided photos of the original bronze cast of the Peace dollar design. **Mark Goodman** photographed a 1922-P cracked planchet, 1922-P edge clip, 1922-P from end of coinage strip, and 1922-P partial collar, all courtesy of the Broadstruck Collection; he also photographed the 1922-D, VAM 4; 1922-P, VAM 4; 1923-P, VAM 3; and 1927-P, VAM 2, all coins courtesy of Ben Wengel. **Don Heath** provided a photo of a 1922-P cracked planchet. Images of the 1922-D, 1923-S, 1924-S, 1927-S, 1934-D, and 1934-S are from the collection of **Gary D. Hoop. Joseph H. Johnson III** provided images of the 1923-P. **Rob Joyce** provided close-ups of numerous varieties: 1922-P, VAMs 1A, 1F, 2C, 2E, 5A, 6, 7, 8, and 12A; 1922-D, VAMs 3, 4, and 7; 1923-P, VAMs 1B, 1C, and 1D; 1923-S, VAM 1C; 1924-P, VAMs 1A and 5A; 1925-P, VAMs 1A and 5; 1926-P, VAM 2; 1926-D, VAMs 2 and 3; 1926-S, VAMs 4, 4A, and 5; 1927-D, VAMs 2, 3, and 3A; 1927-S, VAMs 1A, 1B, 1C, 1D, 1E, 1F, and 5; 1928-P, VAM 2; 1928-S, VAMs 3, 4, and 7; 1934-D, VAMs 3, 4, and 10; 1934-D, VAM 2A; 1934-S, VAM 2; 1935-P, VAMs 1A, 1C, and 1D; 1935-S, VAMs 2, 5A, and 6. **David W. Lange** provided a photo of a Peace-dollar collecting board, as well as a close-up of the 1926-P Strong Motto variety. **David Miller** provided a photo of a Camp David Peace Summit counterstrike in original imprinted holder, along with photos of a 1922-P counterstrike memorializing the assassination of Israeli Prime Minister Yitzhak Rabin. **Pat Mullen** of Mullen Coins provided a close up of a die-break variety. **Yoichi Okamoto** photographed Treasury secretary Henry Fowler and President Lyndon B. Johnson (images courtesy of the LBJ Library). **Jeff Sam** provided photos of a 1922-P clipped planchet, photographed by Rob Shinnick. **Mel Wacks** provided photos of the Camp David Peace Accord counterstamp prototype on a Peace dollar, along with the adopted design shown on a half dollar. **Heidi Wastweet,** Wastweet Studio, provided drawings of stylus/cutter combinations for a Janvier engraving/reduction machine. **Fred Weinberg** and **Ron Karp** provided photos of a 1922-P off-center strike.

Kevin Flynn, Christian Merlo, and **Leroy Van Allen,** along with several collectors who wish to remain anonymous, also supplied images. The photograph of the Whitman Publishing / Red Book overstrike is from *A Guide Book of the Official Red Book of United States Coins.* Remaining photos were provided by the author and Barry Lovvorn.

The author is also indebted to numismatic writers and researchers of the past. They have created a foundation of knowledge upon which the present work is built, and upon which future researchers will continue to expand our understanding of America's numismatic heritage.

Note: Endnotes have generally been avoided since many of these can be found in *Renaissance of American Coinage 1916–1921,* by Roger W. Burdette. However, most of the material in chapter 4, on 1964-D Peace dollars, has never been published. As I felt it important that future researchers be able to locate original documents, I have used reference endnotes extensively in that chapter.

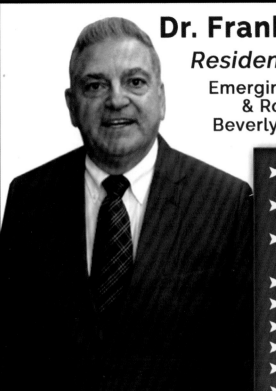

INDEX